WOMEN/MEN/MANAGEMENT

Second Edition

Ann Harriman

PRAEGER

Westport, Connecticut
London

Library of Congress Cataloging-in-Publication Data

Harriman, Ann.
    Women/men/management / Ann Harriman.—2nd ed.
      p. cm.
    Includes bibliographical references (p. –) and indexes.
    ISBN 0–275–94684–3 (alk. paper). —ISBN 0–275–94685–1
(pbk.)
    1. Sex discrimination in employment—United States. 2. Women—
Employment—United States. 3. Sexism—United States.
4. Organizational behavior. I. Title.
HD6060.5.U5H37 1996
331.4'133'0973—dc20   95–11265

British Library Cataloguing in Publication Data is available.

Library of Congress Catalog Card Number: 95–11265
ISBN: 0–275–94684–3
    0–275–94685–1 (pbk.)

First published in 1996

Praeger Publishers, 88 Post Road West, Westport, CT 06881
An imprint of Greenwood Publishing Group, Inc.

Printed in the United States of America

The paper used in this book complies with the
Permanent Paper Standard issued by the National
Information Standards Organization (Z39.48–1984).

10 9 8 7 6 5 4 3 2 1

Women/Men/Management

This book is due for return on or before the last date shown below.

Don Gresswell Ltd., London, N.21   Cat. No. 1208   DG 02242/71

*To Geri Welch and Nancy Cutler Pennebaker,
two friends whose courage, strength, and good humor in the
face of devastating events is truly awesome.*

Contents

Acknowledgments   ix

1. Point of Departure   1

2. The Social–Technical Environment   9

3. The Economic Environment   29

4. The Political Environment   45

5. About Roles and Stereotypes   69

6. Working Together   93

7. Communication   115

8. Motivation and Rewards   137

9. Leadership and Power   153

10. Performance and Perceptions of Performance   171

11. Career Choices and Career Development   191

12. A Look at the Future   213

References   227

Author Index   251

Subject Index   257

Acknowledgments

As I reread the acknowledgments from the first edition, I am struck with how much has changed and how little has changed in the intervening years. Once again I am deeply indebted to my students who, over the years, have taught me far more than they will ever realize about the realities of sex, gender, race, age, class, sexual orientation, and all the other variables that make up our diverse universe.

Had I had any idea how difficult a second edition would be, I suspect I might never have attempted it. The support and encouragement of my colleagues, my friends, and most especially my family were what made it possible.

My graduate assistant, Susan Ruiz, knew no bounds in gathering information, tracing down sources, and locating lost or missing items. Her enthusiasm, energy, and support often kept me going when I felt overwhelmed with the task.

Many faculty colleagues, both on my campus and elsewhere, have given very helpful suggestions and comments about the earlier edition, which I hope have served to make this one not only newer but better. I am especially indebted to Professors Anne Cowden and Jerry Estenson, each of whom has taught from the book, for their insights and suggestions. Mike Sparks, my department chair, has done everything in his power to see that I had the requisite time and resources, no small achievement in this era of ever shrinking budgets. Ed Del Biaggio, Executive Director of the CSUS Foundation, has been patient and long suffering. He's never complained when I pleaded "the book" as an excuse, although he must surely have wondered if it would ever be finished.

My husband and best friend, Mac (Malcolm White), has read and edited and commented on every page of every draft. His ability to spot the fallacies, challenge my assumptions, and raise the pertinent questions, has been an invaluable help. Moreover, his willingness to do *more* than an equal share of the household tasks makes my life infinitely easier than that of many professional women. And yes! I do appreciate him.

To these, and all the friends and family who have encouraged and believed, I have no words to express my gratitude. Without them it would never have happened.

1

Point of Departure

"What is the very first thing that you notice when you meet someone for the first time?" That question, a favorite of roving reporters or cocktail party guests, usually evokes answers such as "his smile," "her eyes," or "his hair." But the only true answer, of course, is "sex." Some people argue that race is more fundamental to identity than sex and therefore is the primary identifying characteristic, and that may be so. Nevertheless, most people find it essential to determine immediately the sex of another person with whom they interact. On the rare occasion when sexual identity is ambiguous or, even worse, in a case of mistaken identity, we are uncomfortable and embarrassed (Nielsen 1978).

A friend calls and says "Susie had her baby." The first question inevitably is "What did she have?" Your friend understands, of course, that your question is "Is it a boy or a girl?" For almost everything that happens to that baby from that point on will be affected by the answer to that question—the name it is given; the kinds of toys it will play with; the way it is handled, dressed, played with, and talked to; the nature of its relationships with other people; the way it will speak and be spoken to; the way it will be educated, evaluated, and entertained—all these and more will depend on whether it is male or female. And these differences will begin at the moment of birth.

While the child is still very small, adults will begin to ask it "What are you going to be when you grow up?" And here the differences between boy children and girl children become critical. A boy child will very soon understand that what he becomes will be determined by what he does, that is, by his occupation or his profession. He will answer, "I want to be an astronaut," or a fireman, or a doctor. A girl child, on the other hand, will soon come to understand that what she will be is a function of who she is. She will soon learn to answer "I want to get married" or "I want to be a mommy" (Ireson 1978). She will take her identity and her status not from her own achievements but from those of her husband and children. She probably will get married and have children; so will the little boy. The difference is that each of them will already have learned an essential element of sexual identity. Men in our society are perceived first as jobholders, second as husbands and fathers; women, no matter what their status as jobholder, will be perceived first as homemakers, second as workers.

Many books and articles have been written, are being written, and will no doubt continue to be written about the problems faced by women entering traditionally and historically male-dominated work organizations. Many others, although perhaps fewer, concern themselves with the problems that managers, presumably males, face in managing the army of new women workers entering the labor market. Why, then, do we need another book on the topic of women and men in management? In what way does this book differ from all of the others:

There are three considerations that make this book different from the others:

1. The current organizational literature, while tacitly implying that organizations are somehow gender-neutral, actually assumes a *masculine model* of work. The assumptions of masculinity are deeply imbedded in organizational processes and structures, so much so that they are nearly invisible (Acker 1990). As a result, masculine behaviors and values are considered the norm and feminine ones the deviant.

2. The current literature also assumes a *breadwinner model*. The typical worker is conceptualized as a male, with masculine skills, occupying a masculine job, carrying out his masculine duties as provider and protector of a wife and children. It fails to take adequate note of such social changes as the increased labor force participation of women, particularly married women, the decreased labor force participation of men, plural family forms, an aging work force, decreased fertility, increased education, and other social and economic changes. While these changes and trends obviously have not gone unreported, and to some extent organizations have responded to them, the majority of the literature fails to address adequately their implications or the adaptive responses that will be required.

3. The current organizational literature is rooted in the Industrial Revolution and therefore based on an "industrial model." It fails to adequately address the relationship between technology and gender, and the implications of technology change for the organization of work, the distribution of income, and the relationship between work and family.

None of this literature examines in sufficient depth the issues of sex and gender as organizational variables. Some recent studies have focused on specific characteristics or problems of female workers. Others have attempted to address the organizational problems that have arisen from the efforts of women to move into traditionally male-dominated occupations or organizations. Still others have noted the growing phenomenon of the two-paycheck or two-career family and the amount of role stress created by this change; this area is addressed mostly from the standpoint of coping strategies for the couple rather than organizational change. Almost none of the literature examines the impact or implications of masculinity on organizations; little of it examines the implications of the changing roles of both women and men. Some efforts have been made to study the problems of sexual attraction and sexual harassment in the organization, but almost no attempt has been made to address the whole issue of human sexuality and its role in organizational dynamics.

None of this literature examines in sufficient depth the interactive implications of changing sex roles and changing technology. Just as the Industrial Revolution brought about major changes in the social world that affected every sector of life, so too does the electronic revolution portend vast social change. Since jobs are a major factor in our existence, determining to a great extent our self- and public identities, major changes in the nature of jobs must result in major changes in our society and its institutions. Since contemporary organizational structures and processes are designed for efficiency, and their design rests on the assumption of a traditional nuclear family, then major changes in both technology and family life ultimately must be reflected in organizational design.

Much of the literature, as it applies to sex differences, is based on the shakiest methodological grounds. Some of the most popular and oft-quoted works are based on purely anecdotal evidence. Others are pure speculation. Still others, while attempting to meet more rigorous standards of validity and reliability, incorporate without examination assumptions about the stereotypical roles of men and women.

PURPOSE OF THE BOOK

The *masculine model* of work perceives organizational behavior as consistent with a sex-differentiated view of life. Holding a paid job is universally assumed to be central to the lives of male workers and secondary to the lives of female workers. Further, men are assumed to be the primary members of the work force while women are perceived as only secondary—a kind of "reserve army" of workers. The study of work often either excludes women altogether or treats them as a footnote. Research on male workers often is generalized to women workers, completely ignoring the possibility of sex differences; when women are included, they often are treated differently from men (Acker and Van Houten 1974; Acker 1978). In some cases, the analysis is shaped by sex-biased interpretations, for example, that men, but not women, are concerned about success on the job.

In other cases, the entire analysis of work is distorted because certain factors are defined as appropriate to either women's work or to men's work, but not to both. Stress and fatigue, for instance, may be attributed to the job itself for men's jobs, but it may be attributed to family responsibilities or the demands of dual roles for women's jobs.

This segregation of male and female roles has led to separate models for studying work, a "job model" for studying males and a "gender model" for studying females (Feldberg and Glenn 1979). The *job model* assumes that the job is central to the lives of male workers; it treats the job itself as the primary independent variable. Items like complexity, routineness, autonomy, and working conditions are used to explain performance on the job and job satisfaction, as well as off-the-job behavior, activities, and mental health for male workers.

The *gender model* assumes that the family is central to the lives of women workers; it virtually ignores the job itself and relies on personal characteristics or family situations to explain the job attitudes and behaviors of married women. Rather than looking at the tasks that women workers perform, it looks at such variables as their marital status, number and age of children, education, or husband's income, and sometimes even at the husband's attitude toward his wife working, to explain behavior and attitudes toward work. Rather than looking at differences in the organizational experiences of women and men, it looks at factors external to the organization to explain women's organization behavior (Acker and Van Houten 1974).

This bifurcated view of the work world has its historical roots in the industrial era. The Industrial Revolution brought about a separation of women's and men's roles that was virtually complete; men worked outside the home for wages while women worked in the home without pay. It was in this milieu that the study of organizations and organizational behavior had its foundations. Frederick W. Taylor's seminal work on *Scientific Management*, published in 1911, is based on his experience working with men doing hard, heavy, physical work in the mills and foundries. By the 1920s, when the Hawthorn Studies were undertaken, women were already experiencing differential status and treatment, but these differences were simply ignored (Acker and Van Houten 1974), and subsequent studies simply continued to ignore or misinterpret sex differences.

Enormous changes have taken place in recent years in both technology and women's labor force participation. An ever increasing body of research has applied the job model to the study of women workers. However, relatively little research has employed a gender model to study men workers. What evidence there is has shown repeatedly that the degree to which work is a "central life interest" varies by occupation, not by marital status, for either women or men (Dubin and Goldman 1972). Despite these well-publicized findings, the assumption persists that differences are based on sex (Feldberg and Glenn 1979).

Our purpose will be to examine these assumptions, to review the literature, and to consider to what extent the assumptions translate into practice. We will look first at the evolution of modern organizational practice to examine how these assumptions came to exist. Next we will look at contemporary practice to ask to what extent the assumptions are embedded in organizational culture and structure, that is, the extent to which they affect working relationships, opportunities, expectations, performance, appraisals, and outcomes. Finally, we will look at strategies that organizations must undertake in order to adapt to the pressures of contemporary social, technological, and political realities.

PREVIEW OF THE BOOK

In the succeeding chapters we will be looking at the very broad range of personal, social, and organizational influences that shape sexual identity and behavior, and at the way in which sexual behavior in turn affects organizational behavior.

Chapter 2 traces the evolutionary process by which contemporary sex roles emerged from the Industrial Revolution. From about the mid-nineteenth to the mid-twentieth centuries, technological change—the steam engine, the internal combustion engine, the electric motor—completely altered the process by which goods and services were produced and acquired. With technological change came social change—fundamental changes in the ways families worked and lived, changes that profoundly affected women's lives and that firmly established a clear separation between women's roles and men's roles, in both the home and the workplace.

Around the middle of the twentieth century, another technological change—electronic computers, microchips—again altered the process by which goods and services were produced and acquired. And again social change has followed technological change, in ways still evolving.

Chapters 3 and 4 look at the economic and political implications of occupational segregation, low pay, and sex discrimination in employment.

Chapter 3 examines the labor force participation rates of women and men workers, the extent to which women and men work in sex segregated occupations, and the difference in pay of those occupations. It then looks at economic theories that attempt to explain occupational segregation as well as at the way in which jobs are "priced" in the labor market.

Chapter 4 describes early attempts to improve working conditions for all workers, but especially those for women. It traces efforts of the unions to bring about reform by supporting protective legislation at the state level. It then turns to Federal efforts—statutes, executive orders, litigation—to end discrimination against women workers in both pay and working conditions.

Chapter 5 turns to social psychology, specifically to the pervasive sex roles and sex role stereotypes that sustain and perpetuate differences in behavior, in expectations, and in outcomes. Sex role stereotypes are widely held, deeply ingrained, and resistant to change. The stereotypes of women and men are nearly polar opposites. In almost every respect, women are perceived as inferior to men. The chapter concludes with a discussion of psychological androgyny and its implications for freeing both women and men from the dysfunctional aspects of sex stereotypes.

Chapter 6 focuses on relationships in the work place: male/female, male/male, and female/female; romantic, nonsexual, and adversarial. Chapters 5 and 6 together challenge the assumption of most of the literature that sex and sex roles are not significant organizational variables.

Chapters 7, 8, 9, and 10 deal with the fundamentals of organizational behavior through the lens of sex and sex roles.

Chapter 7 studies communication, both verbal and nonverbal, concentrating especially on the ways in which sex differences affect power and status within the organization.

Chapter 8 considers both rewards and motivation. Differences between women's and men's preferences for job attributes, job commitment, and job satisfaction do exist, but they are more of a function of other variables—age, education, marital status, occupation, hierarchical status—than of sex.

Differences in the degree to which women and men are motivated by the opportunity for achievement, affiliation, or power, and differences in the sources to which they attribute success or failure, all virtually disappear when other variables are considered. In fact, it is difficult to find any significant differences in either preference for rewards or motivation that do not disappear when other variables are considered.

Chapter 9 compares the way women and men exercise leadership and power. Contrary to popular belief, there are very few differences in the traits and leadership styles of women and men managers, but there are differences between women managers and women nonmanagers. Effective leadership style is more a function of the organizational situation than of the sex of the leader.

However, women, constrained by sex role stereotypes and limited by lower status, have a more difficult time than men in getting and exercising power. Power strategies that are effective for men managers may be seen as inappropriate and ineffective when used by women.

Chapter 10 covers actual performance and perceptions of self and others of performance. There are no sex differences in self-perceptions reflected by self-confidence or conformity, although women and men tend to feel confident of their abilities in different spheres of achievement. However, even when women and men have identical qualifications or perform work that is identical or objectively equal, women tend to be rated lower. The implications of that disparity are explored.

Chapter 11 compares the investment in "human capital" of women and men. Women and men differ little in the extent to which they invest their own human capital, although women do have lower expectations for the return on their investment. College-educated women expect to combine career and marriage and to earn less and advance more slowly than their male counterparts. Organizations invest less in women workers than in men, in terms of providing both opportunities for work experience and access to training and development programs and mentoring. Since the majority of men are also without mentors, Chapter 11 explores alternatives, especially the creation of intra- and interorganizational networks of advisors and friends.

Chapter 12 looks at change from three perspectives. It deals briefly with the issue of public policy and how it affects both opportunities for women workers and the needs of working families. It also deals briefly with the responsibility that individuals, both women and men, bear in achieving equity for women workers.

The major portion of the chapter looks at the need for organizational change and a plan for accomplishing it. It argues that the lack of progress for women workers is due in large part to the assumptions we have raised here—the masculine value system of organizations, the breadwinner model, and the industrial model. Efforts to improve opportunities for women often offer help and support to women in adapting to the expectations of these assumptions. Not surprisingly, these efforts often are disappointing, and they do nothing to address the problems faced by men who also fail to match the model.

What is needed instead is an extensive, organizationwide, top-down effort to change the culture of the organization to reflect the realities of modern lives. Chapter 12 discusses the need for this kind of effort and offers a plan for implementing the change. It argues that this kind of change effort is necessary not simply to achieve equal opportunity for women workers, but because it is essential to the continued success and effectiveness of organizations competing in a global economy. Anything less will perpetuate the squandering of human resources, a waste that few organizations can tolerate.

2

The Social–Technical Environment

To understand the differences in men's and women's work experiences, it is helpful to understand how we got to our present situation. To do that, we need to review the development of contemporary family patterns and contemporary organizations. As we will see, the family has changed and adapted as the demands of work have changed. In turn, the demands of work have altered with technological development. These three elements— the family, technology, and work organizations—have contributed much to the present division of labor between men and women.

The word *technology* has a great many definitions. To some it means mechanization or automation; to others it has come to be limited specifically to electronic inventions. We will be using it in its more generic sense, to mean "technique," or the whole complex of standardized means—scientific, mechanical, and organizational for achieving some predetermined result (Ellul 1964). While the history of technology, using this definition, is as old as mankind, we are particularly interested in the period from the start of the Industrial Revolution to the present postindustrial period.

THE INDUSTRIAL SOCIETY

The Industrial Revolution, which began about 1750 and continued to the beginning of the twentieth century, marked a period unequaled in history for social change. Chief among these changes was the transformation of the family from a *producing* unit to a *consuming* unit, a change that increased the segregation of roles within the family and decreased the value of the woman's work both at home and in the labor force.

The Family

The family has been the basic economic unit of society since the preindustrial, agricultural era. In rural societies, the family was typically a large, multigenerational productive enterprise. While tasks tended to be separated along sex lines, the contribution of all family members was essential to the family's well-being. Whether the family enterprise was farming or craft production, all able-bodied members worked. Based on biblical teachings, the father served as the authority figure, the head of the household (Young and Willmott 1973). However, a major priority for the family was getting and preparing food, a task that almost always fell to the women and occupied a major portion of their time. Since any cash the family earned was spent on food, women were largely responsible for handling it, which gave them a certain amount of power in the family (Tilly and Scott 1978).

Since each member of the family was involved in the production of the necessities of life, decisions about the use of time were made by the individual or by the family. A great many factors—weather, size of the family, availability of resources, demand for surplus production, family and religious customs—contributed to the allocation and scheduling of time. There was no standard work day, no overtime, no paid vacations.

With the coming of industrialization, this producing family was largely replaced by a "family wage economy." Family members now worked outside the home for wages, which were pooled and used to purchase the family's needs. In some cases, families hired themselves out as a unit, with the father bargaining for a wage rate that included himself and his children. Since transportation to work was limited, cities grew as workers moved closer to the factories. Large extended families became less common than nuclear families; living quarters were cramped, large families were less able to move about to find work, and the wage system made it nearly impossible to support aged or infirm family members. Many services that had been performed by members of the extended family came to be turned over to other institutions—schools for the young, old age homes for the elderly (Toffler 1980). Among families that remained in rural areas, both boys and girls often migrated to the cities to find work; their wages, in whole or in part, were sent home to the family, sometimes directly by the employer (Tilly and Scott 1978).

During this gradual transformation from an agricultural to a manufacturing society, labor for the mills was in short supply, and women and children were needed to fill the demand. The religious values of the time, a puritan ethic that abhorred idleness, looked with favor on their industriousness. In many cases, work that previously had been done at home, spinning and weaving, was moved to the plants (Blau 1978). Single women sometimes continued to live at home or to work in "service"; others went to live in dormitories provided by the mills until they married. In England, some unmarried women remained at home their whole lives, spinning yarn for the weavers. Because their families relied on their earnings for survival, they never were allowed to leave home to marry. They came to be known as "spinsters" (Tilly and Scott 1978).

The move from home production to work in the factory did not mean a significant social change, however. The factory girls continued to be viewed in very traditional terms. The daughters of farmers or artisans, they had always worked; the only change was in the setting. Wage work was considered a secondary occupation for them; women's real work was still raising children and running a household. Employers preferred to hire young, unmarried women, despite the high turnover. The women accepted low wages because they did not expect to stay long—and typically did not. The mill owners accepted the high turnover because the tasks were easy to learn and labor was cheap (Scott 1982).

Married women in urban working-class households were less likely than men or single women to work for wages outside the home. Food continued to be a major concern for the family; but now, instead of raising the food herself, the urban wife spent her time buying and preparing food. Fertility rates continued to be very high, and children typically remained at home until they married, so there was a great deal of work to be done. These home duties made it nearly impossible for women to work the 12-hour shifts demanded by the mills and factories, and they went out to work only if their husbands were unemployed or ill and if there were no children to send out to work. When they did work, it was often only sporadically; women formed a fairly large class of temporary and seasonal workers. Nevertheless, in the family wage system, women needed to continue to earn, and they did so by taking in boarders, by doing piecework at home, or by selling the surplus of food or clothing that they produced for their own family's use (Tilly and Scott 1978).

The change from a rural, producing economy to a family wage economy brought about greater differentiation between male and female roles. Although the wife's activities continued to be vital to the welfare of the family, it was the husband's wages (and to a lesser extent the children's wages) that provided for the necessities of life. The interdependency of the farm family was replaced by a different and less equal interdependency in the city.

As the industrial era continued, the occupational mix of the work force gradually changed. The number of factory and mill jobs available to women, as well as the number of jobs in domestic service, began to decline, but jobs in the "tertiary sector" of the economy, the services sector, began to increase. Office work had always been a male-dominated occupation; young men did clerical work as part of a general apprenticeship in business, often in preparation for advancement. In the mid-1800s, the main technology of the office was pen and paper, a time-consuming and monotonous method. Gradually, as the volume of paperwork increased, clerical tasks were separated from administrative work and from the opportunity for advancement. Copy work was given out to women—usually married women or widows supplementing the household income—to be done at home. They were paid by the word, and of course the pay was low (Scott 1982).

Technology, specifically the telephone, the telegraph, and the typewriter, had a significant impact on the performance of office work and on women's employment. Typewriters, called "writing machines," started becoming available by about 1850, and by 1900 they were widely available at affordable prices (Giuliano 1982). Typing, filing, and stenography, that is, the management of information, became components of full-time occupations. Secretaries frequently were called "female typewriters." Ambitious young men moved into sales, advertising, or administrative positions; women moved into and soon dominated almost completely the new clerical occupations (Scott 1982).

Office work differed from factory work in that it was cleaner and safer. Like nursing and teaching, which also came to be female-dominated fields, it was considered respectable for middle-class women. But, like factory work, office work kept women in a labor market separate from that of men and perpetuated cultural stereotypes of women's capabilities. The jobs of secretary and telephone operator quickly replaced factory work as the typical female occupation. Like factory jobs, these jobs were designated as employment for single women, and many employers enforced age limits of between 18 and 25. Women often were required to leave their jobs when they married (Scott 1982). The separation of home and work for women was increased, and women's need for education increased slightly also, but in no way were either women's wages or women's integration into the male labor force enhanced. Wherever women worked, they earned less than men; whatever occupations women entered, men left (Tilly and Scott 1978).

By the turn of the century life began to change again. Men's wages had risen sufficiently that the family no longer needed to concern itself with survival alone. A greater variety of consumer goods became available, along with increased income to purchase them. The target income for families tended to rise, and, while family life did not change dramatically, the separation of male and female roles became even more distinct. Both infant mortality and fertility rates fell, and child labor laws and compulsory education kept children out of the work force. Adult children continued to live at home until they married, continuing to contribute their wages to the family income but usually reserving some money for their own use (Tilly and Scott 1978).

Contrary to popular belief, increased prosperity and the development of labor-saving technologies did not lighten the domestic work load of women (Goode 1971). To be sure, they made housework less onerous. Technological changes were slower in coming to the household than to the factory, but some improvements were available as early as the nineteenth century. Items like soap, candles, textiles, and clothing, which once were made in the home, now could be purchased. Stoves replaced the open hearth for cooking and heating. Later, gas and electricity became available for heating, cooking, and lighting; indoor plumbing and the washing machine certainly reduced the back-breaking burdens of the housewife. Still later, vacuum cleaners, refrigerators, dishwashers, freezers, and convenience foods saved time and made the work easier (Rothschild 1983).

Although this array of appliances and conveniences dramatically changed the housewife's job, they did not necessarily make it easier. New tasks took on significance as old ones were replaced; shopping, servicing household equipment, and travel to do household errands all took time. Urban children required more supervision than farm children; city smoke and grime required more laundry and housecleaning (Vanek 1978).

Further, attitudes about the housewife's job were changing. Along with the availability of household appliances came a rise in the standards of household cleanliness. Around the turn of the century, advocates of the "domestic science movement" were interested in raising housework to the status of a profession and in educating women to do it well (Vanek 1978). Lillian Gilbreath, a pioneer in industrial engineering, conducted research into the improvement of housework (Trescott 1983) and the application of the principles of *Scientific Management* to the home. The American Home Economics Association successfully lobbied government for money to educate women in principles of health, sanitation, and nutrition. Women's magazines gave advice on how to keep husbands happy, children polite, and the house clean (Vanek 1978). Women were urged to keep their homes not only clean but attractively decorated; meals were expected to be not only nutritious but creative and artistic as well. A new emphasis on child rearing required mothers to be experts in the psychological, physical, and educational development of their children (Scott 1982).

Household technology to some extent reversed the trend away from the production of goods and services. For one thing, at the same time that labor-saving devices were becoming more available, household help was becoming less available. Women who had relied on domestic servants now found themselves pushing the vacuum cleaner or cooking the meals (Vanek 1978). For another, appliances like the washing machine, the iron, and the home freezer reduced the urban housewife's reliance on services provided outside the home. When women produced these goods and services themselves, the work was removed from the family wage economy. Women did not receive wages for their productive activity, therefore, as far as society was concerned, they did not work.

The home sewing machine also made it possible for women to produce goods in the home. As in preindustrial times, women again could make clothing at home instead of purchasing it ready-made. But the sewing machine soon became an instrument for exploiting women as well. Factories had, of course, used sewing machines for many years (sometimes owned by the women workers, who were forced to buy them from their employers

with weekly deductions from their wages). When lightweight machines suitable for home sewing became available, many machines were sold along
with a contract with a clothing manufacturer. The woman could pay for
her machine and earn additional money by doing piecework for pay in her
home. For middle-income women, such employment was a supplement to
the family income and provided a few hours a day of profitable employment during hours that were convenient to her. But for many poor women
who were seeking to earn a living, the low rates made long hours a necessity
and turned many urban homes into mini-sweatshops (Scott 1982).

Industrial technology, then, took some tasks that had been performed in
the home and moved them to the factories; it created factory jobs for young
women until they married. Technology also split clerical work from administrative work and created office jobs for young, unmarried women.
Technology made the work of married women in the home less unpleasant
and physically demanding but no less time-consuming. In so doing it increased the occupational segregation and the division of labor between the
sexes. It did nothing to increase the earnings of female-dominated occupations or the job opportunities for married women.

By the early twentieth century the split between production and consumption was nearly complete. Single women worked for wages until they
married or perhaps until their first child was born; married women toiled
in the home, preparing food, bearing and raising children, and managing
the home. If they did paid work, it was likely to be only temporarily, it
was likely to be in a sex-segregated occupation, it often entailed piecework
done at home, and it was very likely to be low paid. White women rarely
worked for wages outside the home unless there was some serious family
problem, and a strong sentiment against women intruding into the labor
force discouraged them from doing so. Black women, mostly in the south,
and immigrant women in the northeast, however, were much more likely
to be in the paid labor force (Blau 1978). A woman's role became increasingly one of caretaker and her work unpaid and devalued (Baxandall, Gordon, and Reverby 1976). Women's roles came to be associated with
consumption and men's with production. Their role segregation was nearly
complete, and while there continued to be a great deal of interdependency,
there was less and less equality.

The Work Organization

The invention of the steam engine, perhaps more than any other single
breakthrough, changed the way in which work was performed the world
over. Machines in all productive processes, mines, mills, steelworks, or
woodworking, could and did work harder, faster, and more reliably than
men. Factories grew up around the engine. For the first time it was possible,
even essential, to have many hundreds of people working in one place

purely because it was more productive to do so (Jenkins and Sherman 1979).

The urgent need for capital and for economies of scale demanded that small owner-managed businesses give way to ever larger and more complex entities, and the modern corporation was born. Industrialization and the growth of large corporations in turn introduced several "rules" or "principles" of organization: standardization—of both work and workers; specialization—division of labor and professionalism; synchronization—concern with the use of time and with punctuality; concentration—of capital, of resources, and of workers; maximization—of profits, of growth, and of size; and centralization—of political and economic power (Toffler 1980).

To maximize profit returns on their capital investments, plants had to operate 24 hours a day. Because the workers' tasks were highly interdependent, synchronized schedules of 12-hour shifts were a necessity. Unlike the preindustrial era, workers no longer were able to decide for themselves the allocation of time to work or leisure, nor were they able to decide their own working schedules. Workers now were required to work long shifts, night or day, at times prescribed by their employers. Even leisure time was standardized and synchronized; vacations and holidays, paid or not, were taken when and in the amount determined by the employer or by the union contract. Toffler (1980) argues that mass education had a "covert curriculum" consisting of three courses—one in punctuality, one in obedience, and one in doing rote, repetitive work—the three subjects most needed by workers on the modern assembly line.

These changes were not without their protesters. Two major opponents in England were the Luddites and the Chartists. The Luddites were named after Ned Lud, who led his fellow workers in destroying "frames," the knitting machines employers had begun to install in the workshops of the textile industry (Leontief 1982). Lud and his followers believed that the machines would create widespread unemployment. But they mainly were concerned that traditional skills would not be needed and that, while jobs might be available, they would be less attractive and require less expertise. The Chartists, a more radical group, focused more on working conditions. Luddism was a short-lived but bitter movement: Chartism lasted somewhat longer, but it too lost momentum and died in the mid-1800s (Jenkins and Sherman 1979).

The protest movements were futile: workers had no choice but to conform to management's terms. They no longer were able to produce for themselves the requirement for their existence and were dependent on the corporation for their livelihood. Finding or keeping work often required the family to be mobile. Workers were able to meet these demands because of the division of labor in the family. The worker could work whenever and wherever he was needed *because* he had a homemaker wife who pre-

pared his food, raised his children, managed his household, and, if necessary, supervised a move.

Over time, partly as a result of advancing technology, conditions improved. The development of the automobile transformed the transportation
industry, and mass production brought price reductions. Both public transportation and private cars became available. Mass production methods
made work even more intense and repetitious and the environment more
hostile, but mass transit made it possible for people to live further distances
from the factory and eased the crowded housing conditions. The electric
motor, smaller and more efficient than the steam engine and capable of
enormous adaptation, made possible new manufacturing technologies and
created an enormous number of jobs. It also became the basis for most of
the "labor-saving" household appliances. The de-skilling of jobs and the
decline of crafts continued, however (Jenkins and Sherman 1979).

As jobs became more and more routinized, standardization was extended
to wages as well as to hours and to performance. With impetus from the
labor movement, standardized hourly wages became the accepted practice.
In preindustrial times, labor was rewarded on the basis of its *output*, that
is, farm produce or craft products were used or exchanged according to
their relative value. In the industrial system, labor was rewarded for its
input, that is, the worker was paid for the time he spent on the job rather
than the quality or quantity of production. Since the family wages had to
support the whole family, hourly wages were set at a rate that was consistent with the worker's family responsibilities.

In the early twentieth century, the labor movement began to bargain for
"in-kind" services as well as wages, later to be dubbed "fringe" benefits.
The amount and kind of these benefits were based not only upon the needs
of the worker, the breadwinner, but also upon the needs of his dependent
family as well. Clearly, health insurance was a great advantage to the
worker, particularly in the days that preceded workmen's compensation,
disability insurance, Social Security, vested pension plans, or unemployment insurance. But health insurance for the worker alone did not protect
him from financial ruin if a member of his family suffered catastrophic
illness; high wages alone did not protect the worker's family in the event
of his death or disability. Since wives typically did not work for wages, and
in fact were encouraged to remain out of the paid labor force, social protections for workers and their families came to be the responsibility of the
employer.

Thus a *breadwinner model* evolved. In the social and economic times
that accompanied the growth of large work organizations, this kind of
symbiotic relationship between job and family served both satisfactorily, if
not well. The family was utterly dependent on the breadwinner for his
earnings; he, in turn, was equally dependent on his employer. On the other
hand, the corporation was dependent on the worker for his labor, while

he, in turn, was dependent on his wife to maintain the home and raise the children while he worked. The system required both in order to function (Goode 1971).

This breadwinner model was the one that existed at the midpoint of the twentieth century and to a large extent persists today. The important question is, to what extent is it functional today, given the changes that have occurred in family life, in women's participation in the paid work force, and in technology? Are contemporary organizational processes that are built on this breadwinner model the most appropriate for the organization? For the family?

THE POSTINDUSTRIAL SOCIETY

The beginning of the end of the Industrial Revolution came in the middle of the 1950s, when two events occurred. The balance of the American work force shifted from manufacturing goods to delivering services, and the first commercial computer became available. One event made this country the first "postindustrial" nation; the other allowed the computer (the twentieth-century steam engine) to become more than just an instrument of science, but a tool of the booming service industry (Hallblade and Mathews 1980).

The shift from a manufacturing to a service society has the potential for social changes as great as those associated with the coming of mechanization. What these impacts will be, either for workers or for work organizations, we can only begin to perceive. In the time since the end of World War II, enormous change, both technological and social, has already taken place.

Changes in the Family

At the end of the nineteenth century, American newspapers and magazines were full of speculation about the crisis of marriage and the family. From the 1900s down to the 1930s, discussion of the decline of the family became increasingly intense. Four developments gave rise to a steadily growing alarm: the *rising divorce rate*, the *falling birth rate* among "the better sort of people," the *changing position of women*, and the so-called *revolution in morals* (Lasch 1980).

The French have an axiom that translates roughly as, "The more things change, the more they stay the same." Certainly these four developments could be said to be the cause of as much alarm at the end of the twentieth century as they did a century earlier. Divorce rates are at an all-time high; birth rates are falling among middle-class couples and rising among poor teenagers; the entry of married women into the labor force is having a dramatic effect on the lives of both women and men; and the sexual revolution has certainly affected the whole fabric of society.

Yet, despite these obvious changes, it is as true today as it was a century ago that the American family is alive and well. The most significant difference between then and now is that, rather than one modal class breadwinner family, there now exists a plurality of family and household forms.

Divorce Rates. The bad news (perhaps) is that families have undergone enormous changes, and certainly the rate of dissolution is at an all-time high. However, the good news is that, despite these changes, the majority of people continue to live in families.

Divorce rates rose unevenly higher for most of the period from 1915 to 1975, then leveled off in the mid-1970s at a high rate. In 1990, about 9 percent of the population over age twenty-five were currently divorced, up from an estimated 2.6 percent in 1950 (Wetzel 1990). About two out of every three (66 percent) of all first marriages survive, and a fairly high percentage of divorcees enter into a second marriage, of which about 44 percent end in divorce.

Families also are getting smaller and more diverse in form. In 1950, 88 percent of all family households were made up of married couples; of the remaining 12 percent, 9 percent were maintained by a single woman and 2.7 percent by a single man. In 1990, by contrast, only 79 percent of families were married couples; the number of families maintained by women had risen to 16.5 percent and the number headed by men to 4.3 percent. The number of married couple households with children present had declined from 44.2 percent in 1960 to 27 percent in 1988, and the number of all households with children had fallen from almost one-half in 1960 to just over one-third in 1989 (Wetzel 1990).

The last several decades also have seen an increase in the number of nontraditional family forms and nonfamily households. The former may include cohabiting (unmarried) couples, "blended" or reconstituted families that involve stepparenting, gay and lesbian couples—with or without children—, never-married single parents, and voluntarily childless couples. The latter include many people living alone; some of these are young adults who postpone marriage and live separately from their parents, others are older widowed or divorced individuals living separately from their children.

So, in fact, divorce rates are up, but they have not increased since the mid-1970s. Nineteen out of twenty adults marry at least once in their lifetime, and the great majority of people, young and old, expect to marry and to live in a family setting (Levitan and Belous 1981). What is significant for our purposes, and for American managers, is not that divorce is shattering the American family, but that myriad family forms now exist. The typical family form of the industrial era, the breadwinner husband with a homemaker wife and several children, is now a distinct minority.

Birth Rates. Another phenomena apparently troubling society at the end of the nineteenth century was the declining birth rate, particularly among middle-class and upper middle-class couples. In 1897, Theodore Roosevelt worried about "the diminution of the birth rate among the highest classes"; fears abounded that the highest races soon would be outnumbered by their inferiors, who were thought to reproduce with total disregard for their ability to provide for the rising generation (Lasch 1980).

The birth rate has fluctuated enormously in the last century. It was high in the 1920s, dropped very low during the depression of the 1930s and the war years of the 1940s, rose to an all-time high during the 1950s and early 1960s—the "baby boom" years. By the early 1970s, the total fertility rate had fallen below the replacement level and has remained there ever since (Wetzel 1990).

The falling birth rate reflects the decision of couples to postpone childbirth and to limit the number of children that they bear, rather than of large numbers of couples opting for childlessness. The reasons for the decline are numerous. Rates dropped rather propitiously during the early 1960s, a time associated with the increased availability, efficacy, and safety of birth control methods, especially the birth control pill. The 1973 Supreme Court decision to permit legal abortion also may have had an effect (Scanzoni and Scanzoni 1981). Other explanations include the changing roles of women, including the increased participation of married women in the paid labor force, the increased cost of childrearing, changing values, longer years spent in education for both women and men, and the somewhat later age at which young people are entering first marriages.

At the same time, however, a dramatic increase has occurred in the number of children born to unmarried women. According to a recent Federal report, in 1960, slightly more than 5 percent of all births were to unmarried women; by 1992, that figure had risen to almost 25 percent. Between 1982 and 1992, the proportion of white women giving birth outside of marriage increased from 10 to 17 percent; for Hispanic women, the proportion increased from 16 to 27 percent; and for black women, the increase was from 49 to 75 percent. Further, the report indicates that this increase is not limited to undereducated women. The number of single mothers who had attended at least one year of college increased from 5.5 percent in 1982 to 11.3 percent in 1992; the proportion of women in managerial or professional jobs who had out-of-wedlock births increased from 3.1 percent in 1982 to 8.2 percent in 1992 (*San Francisco Chronicle* 1993).

The social implications of these changes are many and varied. Less obvious, but no less real, are the managerial implications. The contemporary family, unlike the family of a century, or even half a century ago, presents multiple and diverse demands on its breadwinners and the organizations that employ them. A simple, universal model of work no longer meets the needs of these families.

Changing Roles. In order to understand the significance of changes in family roles to postindustrial society, it is important to understand how those roles impacted the development of industrial society.

Today, as compared with the industrial era, couples marry later, women bear their children later, they bear fewer children, and they live longer. They are better educated than their grandmothers; in fact, they are as well educated as their male counterparts. They, like their grandmothers, tend to start work when they are single, but few can afford the luxury of choosing to stop work when they marry or when their first child is born. Even those without a financial need often choose to combine marriage, childrearing, and paid work. Consequently, unlike their grandmothers, a relatively small portion of their lives is devoted to bearing and raising children and a very significant share is spent in the labor market.

Like their grandmothers, however, they continue to maintain the major responsibility for childrearing and household maintenance. Almost regardless of education level, occupation, income, or age, in married couples with children where both parents work full time, the woman does significantly more of the household duties. On the average, women spend 15 hours a week more than their husbands on housework and child care—a figure that adds up to an extra month of 24-hour days each year, an extra year of 24-hour days each dozen years (Hochschild 1989).

This extra burden of family responsibility might be less onerous if work hours were growing shorter. In fact, they are growing longer. The long days and weeks required during the industrial era did gradually grow shorter over time, up until the 1930s. Since then, however, they have not only not gotten any shorter, in fact, over the last two decades, they have grown longer. Modern families, and women in particular, now work longer and harder than in any other time in history (Schor 1991).

The Revolution in Morals. The "sexual revolution," cause of much consternation in the 1960s and 1970s, is of course not really a revolution at all but instead a rather abrupt change in sexual attitudes and behavior. The current period of change is, in many ways, a repeat of a similar period of change occurring early in the twentieth century. What one means by the term, of course, is open to debate. For many people, apparently, a sexual revolution connotes an increase in female (but not male) nonmarital sex (Scanzoni and Scanzoni 1981). For others, it means an increased acceptance of a wide repertory of sexual behaviors. For still others, it means increased acceptance of and openness toward a variety of sexual lifestyles.

Unquestionably changes have occurred in sexual mores in recent years. During two time periods, one beginning around 1915 and the other around 1965, rather sharp increases occurred in female sexual behavior. Prior to that time, Protestant values and Victorian prudery had assigned to women the necessity of remaining virginal until marriage and faithful to their mates after marriage. Although these moral expectations also applied to men, a double standard always prevailed. Somewhere in the early part of this century, probably starting about 1915, the number of women who had experienced premarital sex doubled in one decade. From that point until the mid-1960s, the number increased at a gradual but steady rate. Then, once again, a sharp increase occurred in the number of women having sex before marriage, in the number of women pregnant at the time of marriage, and the number of women having extramarital affairs. During this time, the age of first coitus grew lower and the extent of noncoital sexual activity among adolescents increased (Scanzoni and Scanzoni 1981).

Although these two periods of change occurred fifty years apart, they occurred in very similar social contexts. Both the first and second sexual revolutions coincided with unpopular wars; World War I in the earlier period, Vietnam in the second. Each was concurrent with an active women's movement. The first period marked the culmination of nearly seventy years of effort to win the vote, an effort that was resisted vigorously on the grounds that it would have a negative effect on women's virtue and purity. The second period coincides with the rebirth of the women's movement, after nearly forty years of hiatus, and the effort to enact the Equal Rights Amendment. The first feminist movement involved itself in other issues as well as suffrage, notably the effort to win the right to disseminate and use birth control. The second movement's rebirth was coincident with the availability of the birth control pill and the IUD (intrauterine device). Each period was marked by a high level of hedonism: the roaring '20s and the rebellious '60s (Tannahill 1980).

The significance of a sexual revolution is not a breakdown of moral values or a rise in permissiveness but its association with larger social issues. When women demand increased autonomy, increased equality, and decreased paternalism, they also demand and exercise the right to greater sexual freedom. These changes do not spell a threat to the family. They do, however, underline for management the fact that women are seeking and demanding autonomy and equality in both their personal and work lives.

As we approach the end of the twentieth century, the loss of "traditional values" that so concerned our forefathers a century ago continues to be a cause for concern: the breakdown of the family, a declining birth rate, a revolution in morals, and the changing roles of women. Yet enormous change has occurred. From the standpoint of the postindustrial society, these changes add up to a very different social world. Fears of the breakdown of the family, while persistent, appear to have been greatly exaggerated. Families have not disappeared, but the definition of what constitutes a family has broadened. Changes in sexual mores and in women's roles have led to very different expectations of women's participation in and rewards from paid employment.

A number of questions are raised by these social phenomena. What effects will social change have on work organizations? How will technology affect the work organizations? How will it affect the family?

Changes in Work Organizations

There are two possible scenarios for the future. One is optimistic: Technology will continue to replace hard, dirty, unpleasant jobs with robots while creating increasing numbers of high-skilled, technical jobs. Productivity increases will increase our standard of living while at the same time reducing the number of hours of work required. Older workers will be offered inducements such as shorter hours to persuade them to remain in the work force; couples with children will be offered extended parental leaves, employer-sponsored day care, educational tuition, and other inducements to produce children while continuing employment.

The other scenario is pessimistic: Technology will eliminate many jobs and deskill many more. Only those with the highest technical knowledge and skills will be able to find satisfactory employment. Others will work at increasingly low-paid, low-skilled jobs, and many will be unable to find any paid work at all. Wealth will tend to be increasingly concentrated in the hands of elites. Rather than using jobs to raise their socioeconomic status, lower class families will find themselves slipping ever deeper into poverty, and increasingly will rely on transfer payments for survival. Women will continue to work in sex-segregated jobs that are low-paid and low-skilled, and will continue to bear an unequal share of the household labor.

Unfortunately, the latter scenario is the one that appears to be emerging. The computer, and more particularly the transistor and the microchip, have dramatically changed the way we work and the kind of work that we do. The immeasurable speed, miniature size, and daunting capacity of the microchip are almost inconceivable to most of us. The number of uses to which they can be, and have already been, put seems to be infinite, and we are constantly reminded that electronic technology is still in its infancy. Electronic technology has dramatically changed nearly every occupation or profession; in medicine, in law, in education, in finance, in design, and in manufacturing the use of computers has revolutionized the way work is performed. Telecommunications have revolutionized office work; in three generations we have seen clerical work go from copying documents at home, to using typewriters and copy machines in the office, to the use of word processors, E-mail, modems, voice mail and facsimile machines anywhere there is a telephone connection. The innovations have changed the way we work and have increased productivity enormously; without them, our whole system of commerce would be impossible.

Increases in productivity also have brought their share of problems. The major concern, for our purposes, is the same one that was raised by critics of the Industrial Revolution—the displacement of labor. Two questions are raised: Does technology eliminate jobs? And does it deskill jobs? The conventional wisdom has always argued that automation creates more jobs than it eliminates, and to a great extent that was true of the industrial era. Successive waves of technological innovations brought with them "a spectacular growth of both employment and real wages" (Leontief 1982). The conventional wisdom also has argued that the new jobs are more highly skilled than the old ones, but in this case the Luddites were right. Industrialization did, in fact, lead to the deskilling of many jobs and the decline of crafts (Jenkins and Sherman 1979).

Machines in the industrial era displaced human muscle, but machines in the postindustrial era increasingly replace the human nervous system in both the production and service industries. The relationship between man and machine is being transformed. Human labor always has been a principal factor in production, but electronic technology has so increased productivity as to make traditional definitions meaningless. Some types of labor are being replaced faster than others. Agriculture has been transformed so that it is now more highly mechanized than manufacturing. Despite resistance from labor unions, the mining, manufacturing, and construction industries have become highly mechanized and employment is down dramatically. On the other hand, the number of white collar workers has increased dramatically (Ginzberg 1982). But technology appears to have checked the growth in this sector as well (Wheale 1984). Usually, less skilled workers are replaced first and the more skilled ones later, but there are exceptions to this rule (Leontief 1982).

Despite many efforts to reverse the trend—through training and retraining programs, investment credits, or reduced working hours—unemployment levels have continued to rise in the last four decades. In 1945, the irreducible level of unemployment was considered to be 2 percent; by the 1960s, that figure had risen to 4 percent; in the 1990s, it is closer to 9 percent. While not all of this increase can be attributed to technological unemployment, neither can its existence be ignored (Leontief 1982). Considerable evidence supports the view that, as computers become more and more sophisticated, the trend to technological unemployment will increase.

Technological change has impacted women's jobs differently from men's jobs, and, contrary to most expectations, technological displacement appears to have had a disproportionate effect on women workers. The experience of AT&T demonstrates part of the reason for the differential impact of technological displacement. In 1971, the company undertook an aggressive effort to implement an Affirmative Action plan, which came about as a result of an EEOC (Equal Employment Opportunity Commission) finding that women and minorities were clustered at the lowest levels of employment. The plan included moving both men and women into nontraditional jobs. However, the plan coincided with a period of rapid technological change in which many skilled male-dominated jobs were eliminated. The net result was that, while both men and women were affected, both the technological displacement and the affirmative action effort benefited men more than women (Hacker 1979).

A parallel concern about technology is that it will not only eliminate many jobs but will make the remaining ones increasingly repetitious. Some experts have predicted that computer technology will result in greater decentralization, structural complexity, and autonomy for administrators and higher levels of skill and responsibility for workers (Blau and Jusenius 1976). But the preponderance of the evidence suggests that both administrative and operating jobs will become more routine and repetitive. Also, women again seem to be disproportionately affected by this deskilling of jobs.

Studies of office automation in the insurance industry, which is a fairly typical service industry, between 1961 and 1980 found the following:

- The introduction of new technology was labor-saving, and some occupations were eliminated altogether.

- The continued expansion of clerical activity more than offset savings in labor, so that the clerical force grew slightly overall; however, there was a sizable reduction in the number of traditional clerical jobs.

- The new technology has been used not only to reduce the number of jobs, but also to reorganize the work; occupations are narrower, more specialized, and more standardized.

- The expansion of computer-related occupations has increased the total number of jobs and created some new, higher paid occupations. But the workers displaced by automation do not appear to benefit; the new jobs are on a technical level and largely held by males. Women from traditional clerical jobs are unlikely to be moving up into these jobs. Rather, a new layer of largely male workers, recruited from a different labor pool, has been inserted into the office. The women in the traditionally female clerical categories are likely to find not only higher unemployment but also the deskilling of their jobs and reduced opportunities for advancement (Feldberg and Glenn 1983).

Further, the reorganization of work brought about by automation may also involve changes in worker autonomy. For instance, with computerization, a great deal of information can be centralized in one place, be available simultaneously to many employees, and be constantly updated or revised. This centralization allows low-level clerical jobs (usually held by women) to be redesigned to cover a broader scope of information. But it also allows closer supervision. Monitoring systems can keep track of the work done by each clerk, and automatic call distributors can allocate incoming phone calls and record the number of calls answered or lost. A tally can be kept of each clerk's errors. Each part of the job must be handled according to specified procedures and within a specific time frame. Although the clerk has access to more information and appears to be performing a wider range of duties, in fact she is required to have less knowledge of procedures and has less opportunity to use her judgment about modifying those procedures (Feldberg and Glenn 1983).

Technological advances since the mid-1950s, the beginning of the post-industrial era, have already dramatically reshaped the social world we live in. We have come to accept as commonplace achievements and innovations that were outlandish fantasies just a short time ago. We have come to accept change at an unprecedented rate. In spite of the wonders of technology, however, in medicine, in telecommunications, in business, and in our homes, we need to be aware of some of its broader impacts. Technology has caused displacement. Many occupations have been eliminated altogether, and in others growth has slowed. Those eliminated are often, but not always, the least skilled. Further, technology has resulted in many jobs becoming more routine and repetitious, which in turn makes them susceptible to further automation. Other jobs that appear to have been enriched have, in fact, become less autonomous. New, more technical jobs are often created, but they rarely go to the displaced worker.

This disparity of impact may have as much to do with organizational structure as with the nature of technology. Compared to women, men often have better access to computing equipment, have fewer co-workers in the same room with them, are able to be more flexible in their working hours, and perceive themselves as having higher levels of control over their work environment. With the exception of word processing technologies, men tend to use computing equipment more frequently than women, receive more frequent training in computer use, and experience more autonomy in the performance of their jobs (Iacono 1989).

The work organization at mid-century relied on a breadwinner model, a model that made sense given the technology and the family structure of the times. That model is clearly not viable for the new century. Socio-technological change requires structural change—a new model of work that is more diverse and more responsive to both the needs of the organization and the needs of the workers.

SUMMARY

Prior to the invention of the steam engine, self-contained extended families in a rural society worked together to create the goods and services necessary for survival. Each member of the family, young or old, contributed according to his or her ability. Work and leisure schedules were determined by desire or necessity, not by a clock. Getting and preparing food were major concerns, and they primarily were the responsibility of women, as, of course, was the bearing and raising of children.

The Industrial Revolution brought about enormous social change. The development of the factory system enhanced the division of labor within the family and the occupational segregation of women and men in the work

force. Because of the rigorous demands on men workers, families relied on
the services of a full-time homemaker wife. Because of the economic conditions, the size of the family, and the life expectancy, most women spent
all of their adult lives in childbearing and childrearing. Even when labor-
saving devices became available that made women's work less onerous, the
amount of time women spent on housework and child care did not decrease; instead, standards and expectations increased. The household division of labor was thoroughly established: Man was the breadwinner;
woman was the helpmate.

From the beginning of the factory system young women typically worked
until they married. After marriage, they seldom worked for wages outside
the home except in cases of emergency, but they often earned extra money
by taking in boarders or by doing piecework—sewing or copying—at
home. In fact, some homes became mini-sweatshops.

Men, the breadwinners, became the mainstay of the industrial system.
As wages and benefits were improved over time, partly through the efforts
of the labor movement, they were expanded to provide not only for the
worker himself but for his wife and children as well. Women were episodic
members of the work force. They worked in only a small number of occupations; their pay was low and their benefits minimal.

In the postindustrial era, much has changed and much has stayed the
same. Most people live in families, but the definition of family has changed
greatly. Families are smaller, divorce and remarriage are more frequent,
and many are responsible for elderly parents as well as children. The birth
rate is very low, and the portion of the life span spent in childrearing is
much smaller. Women are more independent, both financially and sexually,
than ever before.

The majority of women work more or less continuously throughout their
lives, and women have come to expect equal opportunity and equal treatment in the work place. As women share the breadwinner role with their
husbands, increasingly they look to their husbands to share their homemaker roles. Still, women work longer hours than ever before and continue
to carry the major burden of getting and preparing food, and bearing and
raising children. While modern technology permits greater flexibility in the
scheduling of time, most work schedules are governed by the clock rather
than by the demands of the work or the preference of the worker.

The modern corporation, built upon the breadwinner model, has lost its
breadwinner. It now faces an everincreasing variety of employees attempting to balance personal or family life with job expectations. In order to
survive, it must consider demands for equal opportunity within the organization without regard to sex or marital status (or race, religion, national
origin, age, disability, or sexual preference). It also must adopt rules and

compensation packages that consider the needs of two-paycheck families, with or without children, single-parent families, single individuals, or any of the other forms of family or household. No longer will a "one size fits all" approach be suitable for this highly diverse work force.

3

The Economic Environment

The "woman problem" in organizations is one that is always susceptible to argument, some of it vehement. In recent years, conflict and confusion created by Affirmative Action and Equal Employment Opportunity programs have exacerbated the perception of the problem. Inevitably, a book such as this will cause someone—usually, but not always, a white male—to protest that problems no longer exist *for* women, only problems *about* women. Women, they will argue, now are at least the organizational equals of men, and, in fact, the men are the victims of something ambiguously referred to as "reverse discrimination."

Before we begin our discussion of sex roles and organizational roles, then, we need to consider these charges. We will do so by examining some data on the actual experience of women and men in the labor force and the trends in that experience over the last two or three decades. These data will show that, despite the changes that have occurred, women and men still tend to work in different occupations and women still earn less.

Next we will attempt to understand the causes of these persistent inequities. Economic theories, specifically *neoclassical* theories, such as the *Human Capital* theory or the *Overcrowding* theory, base their arguments on supply and demand. *Segmented labor market theories* argue that women are relegated by employers to secondary jobs with low pay and little opportunity to acquire firm-specific skills, that is, that the differences are a result of discrimination. These theories all assume that low wages are inherently a function of occupational segregation, that women earn less because they work in lower paying occupations. The comparable-worth approach, on the other hand, argues that female-dominated jobs are paid less, not because they require less skill or ability, but simply because of long-standing, systemic devaluing of work performed by women. We will look at each of these in turn.

LABOR FORCE EXPERIENCES

Whether or not an individual becomes and remains a member of the work force, what job she or he will hold, and how much the job will pay— all of these are affected to some extent by gender.

Labor Force Participation

It is hard to imagine that anyone could be unaware of the increased role of women in the work force in recent years. On the other hand, few are aware of the extent to which men's labor force participation has declined. In 1960, 37.3 percent of adult women were in the workplace; by 1989, that number had risen to 69 percent. In 1960, 83.3 percent of adult males were in the work force; by 1987, that number had shrunk to 78 percent (Schor 1991). By 1990, 45 percent of the labor force consisted of women. One-half of all black workers, 45 percent of all white workers, and 40 percent of all Hispanic workers were women.

The average 16-year-old male today can expect to spend 39 years in the labor force, and a typical female of that age can expect 30 years of labor force involvement (U.S. Department of Labor 1990a).

The Increase in Women's Labor Force Participation. Since 1979, women workers have accounted for 62 percent of the increase in the size of the labor force. The largest increase in women's participation has come in the middle years of life—between ages 24 and 54—a period when women in the past tended to leave the work force to raise families. Factors that contribute to women's increased labor force activity include:

• declines in fertility rates—labor force participation is inversely related to fertility; the fewer children a woman has, the more likely that she will be in the labor force.

• increased higher education—for both women and men, the higher the level of education, the higher the probability that they will be in the labor force.

• abating job discrimination against women and changing attitudes towards women's role in society.

• increased employment in the service sector—the shift from a manufacturing to a service economy means that a substantial proportion of new job creation has been in occupations traditionally open to women.

• the increased availability of part-time work—both voluntary and involuntary part-time employment has grown steadily over the last two decades; some—but only a small portion—of this growth has been in more or less permanent jobs with good pay, skill requirements, and advancement opportunities (Tilly 1991).

• the increase in the number of single-person and single-parent households.

- the decline in wages of men workers, which makes women's participation necessary.

These developments do not, however, paint a rosy outlook for women workers. The last four items combine to explain, in part, the continued low earnings of women workers. Although many service sector jobs are high-income professional and managerial positions, as are some part-time jobs, a much greater number are in low-paying and unstable sales, service, and clerical occupations—frequently in small and relatively unstable organizations. These firms tend to hire a large proportion of part-time workers for a variety of reasons—greater flexibility in scheduling, lower compensation costs, or technological change that makes workers more productive in shorter shifts (Tilly 1991). The economic hardships created by this kind of employment, in turn, make it essential that other family members enter the labor market to supplement family income (Nord 1969). The prevalence of this type of employment helps to explain why such a large proportion of single-parent families live below the poverty level.

The Decrease in Men's Labor Force Participation. Since 1960, and especially since 1974, labor force participation of males under age 64 has declined sharply (Rosenfeld and Brown 1979). The decrease has occurred at both the beginning and end of their work lives. Men tend to stay in school longer, thus entering the labor market later (although the majority combine work and school), and many are leaving it earlier, mostly because of poor health but also because of better Social Security benefits and pensions (Levitan and Gallo 1990). Some withdrawals are voluntary, but most of these men would continue to work if jobs were available.

The reasons for involuntary withdrawal from the labor force include:

- poor health—nearly one-half of the men retiring between the ages of 55 and 69 do so because of poor health.
- unemployment—retirement is a more honorable estate than unemployment, and some workers retire as a way of dealing with long-term chronic unemployment. Older workers with low skill levels who are laid off find it especially difficult to find new employment; but, in the recent wave of corporate mergers and downsizing, even many managers and professional workers have been unable to find jobs comparable to those they left.
- education level—men with low educational achievement find it more difficult to find work as they grow older.
- pressures to take early leave.
- plant closings, corporate restructuring, and age bias (Schor 1991).

The primary reason for increased voluntary retirement is financial. The decision to retire voluntarily is often also influenced by such factors as a secure pension, the absence of dependents, the desire for leisure, increases in Social Security benefits, and the conditions on the job, for example, boring or monotonous tasks (Rosenfeld and Brown 1979).

Family Membership and Labor Market Participation. Married men are no longer the mainstay of the labor market. In 1955, husbands constituted 52 percent of the labor force. By 1977, that figure had shrunk to 41 percent, and by 1982 it was down to only 35 percent. At the same time, the percentage of the labor force made up of wives was on the increase; by 1982, they made up almost 25 percent. In 1982, more than 70 percent of the labor force lived in married-couple families (Klein 1983), and one-half of all married couples were in multiearner families (Waldman 1983). Another 10 percent of the work force lived in families maintained by women on their own, most of which were single-earner families (Klein 1983).

Married men are no longer the mainstay of the family, either. In 1988, 56 percent of all wives and 81 percent of all husbands were in the labor force, and these rates varied very little even for families with children. Fifty-seven percent of mothers with children under age 6 and 71 percent of mothers with children under 18 were in the labor force. Among divorced women, 71 percent of those with children under 6 and 85 percent of those with children under 18 were working (O'Neill 1991).

Unemployment. Until very recently, women have had higher rates than men for both cyclical and secular unemployment. That is, unemployment rates have been chronically higher for women than for men, and women workers have been harder hit by recessions than men workers. However, during the last two recessions, while women were hard hit, men suffered even greater job loss. The differences have to do with where the job loss occurred. In the recession of the early 1980s, women lost a substantial number of jobs because of cutbacks in Government employment. In the recession of the early 1990s, women suffered the biggest loss of private sector jobs in twenty years, as cutbacks occurred in the service-producing industries. However, in both periods, the number of unemployed men expanded by one and one-half to three times the increase in the number of unemployed women, the majority in the hard-hit goods-producing industries (Goodman, Antczak, and Freeman 1993).

Occupational Segregation

Despite over thirty years of active efforts to integrate the work place, women still tend to work in female-designated occupations. They account for only 8 percent of the engineers, 12 percent of the law enforcement officers, 19 percent of sales representatives (other than retail clerks), 8 percent of electrical and electronic repairers, and less than 4 percent of mechanics. On the other hand, they make up very large shares of the lower paying professional and technical jobs—93 percent of the registered nurses, 71 percent of the teachers below the college level, 92 percent of the bookkeepers and accounting clerks, and 67 percent of the social workers (U.S. Department of Labor 1990b).

Despite the growth in women's labor force participation during recent years, the degree of occupational segregation has declined only slightly. In 1989, about one-third of all women workers were clustered in the six most prevalent female occupations (U.S. Department of Labor 1990b). As with unemployment trends, the changes that have taken place appear to be more related to the loss of male-intensive jobs than to a breakdown of segregation. However we examine the data, we cannot avoid the certainty that workers tend to be concentrated in sex-segregated occupations, and that those occupations designated as "women's work" are paid less.

Differences in Earnings

From the time when workers left the farm to enter the industrial world of hourly wages, women workers always have been paid less than men workers. Up until thirty years ago, women who did the same work as men in the same factory or mill were paid less than their male co-workers. The *Equal Pay Act of 1963* made it illegal for employers to pay women less than men for doing work that was "the same or substantially the same and performed under similar working conditions," so long as the difference was based purely on sex (see Chapter 4 for a discussion of the EPA). However, since for the most part women did not work side by side with men, but were concentrated in female-dominated occupations, women have continued to earn less than men.

In the last decade, the gap has diminished some. In 1980, the median weekly pay of full-time women workers averaged just under 60 percent of the pay of full-time men workers; by 1992, the gap had shrunk to 70 percent. The figures, of course, vary by age, race, and education. White women averaged 69 percent of white men's earnings, African-American women 62 percent, and Latino women 54 percent. Women with bachelor's degrees averaged about 5 percent more than men with a high school diploma (Mollison 1993). The gap is narrowest for young workers and gets steadily larger with age. In 1988, the ratio of female to male hourly wages for 25–29-year-olds was 83 percent and for 55–59-year-olds it was 59 percent (O'Neill 1991).

Despite the improvement, however, women still earn less, even in heavily female-dominated occupations. For registered nurses, where women hold 93 percent of the jobs, women's earnings average only 90 percent of men's. For teachers, the ratio is 85 percent, for social workers, 85 percent; for bookkeepers and accounting clerks, 84 percent (U.S. Department of Labor 1990b).

And yet even these figures fail to tell the whole story, since they depend on median *weekly* earnings, and women are more likely than men to have their hours cut or to be laid off. If we compare median *annual* earnings, rather than median weekly earnings, the ratio of women to all workers is closer to 66 percent (Horrigan and Markey 1990).

Nevertheless, the gap is narrowing, partly a reflection of true growth. Women have increased their labor force participation as well as their education level, which have resulted in increased earnings. But part of the explanation also lies in the fact that men's wages have been declining, or at least not rising as quickly (Marshall 1993).

Thus we can see that the nature of the work force and of the family have changed dramatically. While the majority of workers continue to live in married-couple families, men's labor force participation has fallen, the percentage of the labor force made up of husbands has fallen, the number of married men working at multiple jobs has decreased, and the number and percentage of single-earner families has fallen. During the same time, the proportion of the labor force made up of women has risen, the number of wives and mothers in the labor force has risen, the number of married women working at two jobs has risen, and the number of women working full time and maintaining their own families has risen. Unemployment and underemployment for men have risen higher and faster than rates for women, but the rates continue to be very high for married women with young children and especially for single women maintaining their own families.

Clearly, despite the gains women have made, they still tend to work in female-dominated occupations and to earn considerably less than men. Economic theory attempts to explain this phenomenon through the dynamics of the market; others assert that the differences simply reflect sex (and race) bias in the way wages are determined.

ECONOMIC THEORY

Economists have long struggled with the constant and unrelenting reality of sexual inequality in the labor market. Some economic theories try to explain this inequality. We turn our attention to two categories of these—neoclassical and institutional.

Neoclassical Theory

Neoclassical theories are concerned with the market—with supply and demand. The primary analytical category is the individual, who is assumed to exercise freedom of choice and to behave rationally to maximize his/her utility. But maximization of welfare is subject to constraints, mainly income and prices, which also are the main determinants of individual behavior. The neoclassicists assume individuals to be identical, "timeless, classless, raceless, and cultureless" creatures (Amsden 1980). Individual preferences and social, cultural, or ideological influences are referred to as *tastes*; they are beyond the interest or concern of the neoclassicist, who assumes them to be trivial and idiosyncratic.

Among neoclassicists, two major theoretical propositions are used to explain sexual inequality in the work place—one is the Human Capital approach, the other is the Overcrowding approach.

Human Capital Theory. This approach is concerned with the allocation of time and also with the division of labor within the family. An individual "invests" in his/her human capital through time spent in education or on-the-job training; employers invest in their employees' human capital by providing on-the-job training. A worker's productivity is a function of his/her human capital, and earnings are a function of productivity. But women and men choose to allocate their time differently, men in paid work and women in family duties and responsibilities. Women's lower earnings, then, are not ascribed to injustice, but to their lower acquisition of human capital. Women earn less because their labor market participation is discontinuous, that is, they leave the labor market during periods of childbearing and childrearing, because they spend fewer years in the market, and because during periods of discontinuity their skills tend to depreciate. Further, women anticipate these discontinuities in employment and avoid jobs that contain skill training or learning components, since they perceive little return for such investment. In this model, women's lower earnings are a result of their choice not to invest in their human capital (Mincer and Polachek 1974).

Women's occupational segregation also is explained by human capital theorists as a matter of choice. The argument goes as follows. Wages on the job rise continuously over the life cycle as experience mounts. Dropping out of the labor force through intermittent participation has adverse effects on earnings potential. Aside from the period of no earnings, reentry earning levels are lower than what they would have been if the individual had worked continuously. This loss of earnings that can be attributed to periods of work intermittency is referred to as *atrophy*. But atrophy occurs in different occupations at different rates and hence influences occupational choice. In other words, the woman who anticipates that her labor force participation will be interrupted by childbearing and childrearing will choose those occupations where the least atrophy occurs and avoid those where the most occurs. Therefore, women with the greatest "home time" are least likely to enter managerial and professional occupations. A Human Capital theory advocate asserts that, "If women were to have a full commitment to the labor force, the number of women professionals would increase by 35 percent, the number of women in managerial professions would more than double, and women in menial occupations would decrease by more than 25 percent" (Polachek 1981).

Overcrowding Theory. This approach also is based on supply-and-demand analysis. It argues that women (and blacks) are restricted to a limited number of menial occupations because of "demand factors," that is, demand exists for these workers in menial occupations and not in prestigious ones. Employers will hire women and blacks in prestigious occupations only on the condition that they will work for less money than the employer would have to pay white males. The result is that those in restricted occupations receive lower wages and those in nonrestricted occupations receive higher ones (Bergmann 1974).

That neoclassical theories come in for substantial criticism should come as no surprise. Proponents of Human Capital theory present empirical data which show that as much as one-half of the differences in wages between women and men can be explained by differences in their work-experience histories (Mincer and Polachek 1974), but critics put the figure at closer to one-fourth (Sandell and Shapiro 1978). In either case, a good deal of the difference is left unexplained (Rosenfeld 1979).

But regardless of these discrepancies, the theory does not resolve the chicken and egg question, that is, the extent to which low levels of human capital are the cause or the effect of labor force instability. Low wages due to discrimination may discourage women from investing in human capital, and low investments in human capital perpetuate women's lower earnings (Amsden 1980).

Another criticism of Human Capital theory is that it relies heavily on "tastes." For example, it argues that, as a result of the division of labor within the family, women *choose* those occupations that are lowest paid. But it ignores the fact that both male and female occupations require varying amounts and types of skills. Some female and some male occupations require lengthy general training; some require lengthy firm-specific training. Some male and some female occupations require few skills and do not provide a potential for productivity increases through experience. Some male and some female occupations experience atrophy of skills during periods of absence from the labor market. Reliance on women's role in the family might explain a greater tendency to find women in low skilled jobs but not in the other types of jobs. Finally, the model assumes that women choose female-dominated occupations, knowing that they pay less, as a matter of personal preference. It does not explain why only women have "tastes" for these lower paying jobs or why such a large proportion of women should exhibit such tastes (Blau and Jusenius 1976).

The Overcrowding hypothesis also has come in for criticism on the grounds that it is insufficient and may be a better explanation of the consequences of segregation than of its causes. It, too, relies on tastes. It argues that workers are perfectly substitutable for each other and that employer tastes prevent integration, that is, that employers have a taste for discrimination against women and will hire them only when the wage difference between female and male labor is large enough to compensate for the problems they will incur by hiring women. But it does not explain why so many employers would have these tastes or why they should be so strong (Blau and Jusenius 1976). Because of these shortcomings, critics of neoclassical theory turn to institutional approaches to try to explain the dual phenomena of occupational segregation and differential earnings.

Institutional Theories

This body of literature is sometimes referred to as the Segmented Labor Market (SLM) theory. It argues that the problem of wage inequality is due to occupational differences between women and men of equal qualifications. Discriminatory hiring practices, not tastes, crowd women into sex-typed jobs, which in turn exerts downward pressure on their pay. The problem, then, is really one of job discrimination, not wage discrimination (Amsden 1980).

The explanation for this job discrimination lies in a concept of dual labor markets, a primary market and a secondary market. Jobs in the primary market possess such characteristics as high wages, good working conditions, employment stability, chances of advancement, equity, and due process in the administration of work rules. Jobs in the secondary market tend to have low wages and fringe benefits, poor working conditions, high turnover, little chance of advancement, and often arbitrary and capricious supervision (Rosenfeld 1979). Since jobs in the primary market require the development of job-specific skills, employers want to screen out those who are likely to be unreliable or intermittent workers (Doeringer 1967). If employers believe that women (or blacks) are on the average less qualified, less reliable, or less stable than men and whites, and if the cost of obtaining information about individual applicants is excessive, they will discriminate against blacks and women by assigning them only to the secondary market. Sex or skin color becomes a proxy for relevant data not sampled and the employer engages in "statistical discrimination" (Phelps 1980).

Another Segmented Labor Market theory defines typologies of sectors of the economy based on the development of the capitalist system. In this analysis, one sector is defined by large centralized (monopoly) capital, that is, a small number of large firms that wield virtual monopoly power in their environment. The second sector is defined by decentralized capital, that is, many small firms in a highly competitive economy. The nature of these capital sectors is such that jobs in the monopoly sector tend to have characteristics similar to those in the primary labor market, while those in the competitive or periphery sector tend to be like those in the secondary market (Rosenfeld 1979). These sometimes are referred to as "structured" and "unstructured" labor markets (Rubery 1978).

A refinement of the dual labor market theory posits an "internal labor market" theory (Blau and Jusenius 1976). In this model, the job structure of a firm can be divided into two categories of occupations on the basis of how they are filled. First are those job categories that are filled from sources external to the firm through the recruitment of new workers. Such jobs are generally restricted to lower level positions. Second are those categories that are filled from internal sources through the promotion and upgrading of presently employed workers. Access to this second type usually occurs through advancement up well-defined promotion ladders. The process by which workers move up these career ladders is through the acquisition, either formally or informally, of added knowledge or skills that are mostly specific or unique to the firm.

According to this model, competitive market forces operate principally at the entry level. Those jobs that are filled from within typically require firm-specific skills. These skills are acquired through the performance of some jobs and not others, hence some jobs are preparation for promotion up the organizational ladder and some are not, which tends to work against the development of a purely competitive market. Instead, an internal labor market is developed, that is, an administrative system that both allocates labor and determines wage rates within the firm.

Labor is allocated through the administrative system that determines the job categories within which both horizontal and vertical mobility will take place. As a result, advancement opportunities open to workers generally are determined by the entry-level job to which they originally were assigned. Clearly, not all workers in a given entry-level job will be promoted to higher level ones, but promotional opportunities are limited to workers in those specific occupations.

Wages are determined by the job evaluation plans or other administrative arrangements that establish base pay rates for each occupational category and specify wage relationships among occupations. Custom and administrative arrangements typically work to maintain relationships among occupations; merit and seniority typically determine pay differentials within occupations. The internal labor market, then, specifies a relatively rigid set of wage relationships and promotional possibilities, each of which primarily is defined by job categories.

Two elements of this internal labor market model are relevant in explaining both occupational segregation and the male/female wage differential. First, because of its reliance on merit and seniority, the internal market tends to treat workers as groups, rather than individuals; hence, the greater the homogeneity of the group, the greater the efficiency of the process. And sex is an obvious basis for differentiation. Second, there is a vital link between job segregation and wage differentiation. The organization has the greatest latitude to differentiate among individuals or groups at the entry level. It has narrower but still broad discretion in allocating workers among job categories filled from internal sources, where it must select individuals only from appropriate promotion ladders. It has the least discretion in wage differentiation among individuals within the same job category. By assigning women to those entry-level jobs that have the least promotional potential, and by paying these jobs at the lowest rate, the organization is able to differentiate between women and men employees and to maintain its internal relationships. Hence, "wage rates might almost be considered the monetary (or value) dimension of the job structure" (Blau and Jusenius 1976).

The internal labor market model relates to dual market theory in that the jobs in the internal labor market share characteristics with jobs in the primary market: entry is restricted to relatively few lower level jobs; promotion ladders are long; and worker stability is encouraged by high wages, opportunities for advancement, good working conditions, and provisions for job security. At the other extreme, the secondary market is more like a set of "unstructured markets": It offers numerous ports of entry and short or nonexistent promotion ladders, while discouraging worker stability by low wages, little opportunity for advancement, poor working conditions, and little job security. Since a long-term relationship between a worker and a firm is important to jobs in the primary sector, employers tend to select new workers whom they perceive as having the potential for job stability. Thus, both pure discrimination and statistical discrimination tend to keep women from primary sector jobs, even if they possess the relevant qualifications.

Like neoclassical theory, institutional theories also have come in for their share of criticism. Some truth attaches to the assumption of the labor market that women are less stable workers than men. The question is whether this is a cause or an effect of occupational segregation. Neoclassical theory argues that it is a cause, that because of individual women's family obligations, they choose or are chosen for those occupations where the negative effects of intermittent labor force participation are least. Their low pay is the price they pay for childbearing and childrearing. Institutional theory, particularly internal labor market theory, argues that it is both a cause and an effect. Women are treated as a class, not as individuals, and the class is perceived as being unstable in its labor market participation. As a result of this statistical discrimination, women are segregated into jobs in the secondary sector. And because jobs in this sector offer little or no reward for stability, its occupants tend to be unstable workers. Critics argue that the theory, while useful, does not go far enough, that in fact we must go outside of economics for an explanation of discrimination (Arrow 1976).

JOB WORTH

Segregating women and men into separate occupations might create no problem at all if only those jobs typically held by women paid as much as those traditionally held by men. If clerical work, nursing, teaching, or social work were as well paid as the skilled crafts or technical positions, then women could continue to work in these occupations without being denied economic equity. Why are they not? One hypothesis is that female-dominated jobs are paid less than male-dominated ones requiring equivalent levels of human capital *because* they are held by women. The disparity is the result of a long-standing devaluation of women's work, going back to the time when men went out from the home to work for wages and women remained in the home to produce goods and services without pay.

There is some evidence to support this charge. The Department of Labor's *Dictionary of Occupational Titles* (*DOT*) rates the complexity of 30,000 job titles: it is the world's most comprehensive and widely used compensation reference. The *DOT*, one study found, rated health and child care professionals, including nurses, on the same level of complexity as dog pound attendants. The work that women do caring for children and adults, sick or well, was considered less complex and less valuable than the work men do caring for dogs. In Denver, registered nurses were paid less than tree trimmers in the parks; in California public schools, librarians and teaching assistants were paid less than custodians and groundskeepers. These obvious disparities arise even in the presence of long-established job evaluation systems, which appear on their face to be gender-neutral.

The basis for the concept of job evaluation was developed nearly one hundred years ago by Frederick W. Taylor as part of the Scientific Management movement. Taylor argued that jobs should be designed for the utmost efficiency, workers should be trained to do a job exactly as it had been designed, and evaluation and compensation should be based upon the relative difficulty of the job, entirely separate from the personal characteristics or abilities of the job holder. Most job evaluation methods in use today were developed in the 1930s and 1940s for use in determining the value of manufacturing jobs typically filled by men.

Job evaluation determines the relative complexity of jobs within an occupational group. To determine pay, a wage survey determines the amount paid for equivalent jobs within the labor market. Usually, each occupational category is treated separately. Clerical jobs, for instance, are evaluated as a class. Once the relative complexity of the jobs has been established, pay is determined by surveying the market to find what similar clerical jobs are being paid. If women's jobs are underpaid because they are filled by women, that is, if the market is inherently biased against female-dominated occupations, then using the labor market data simply perpetuates long-standing, institutionalized discrimination.

One way to test for discrimination is to make comparisons within the firm across occupational boundaries, to compare such female-dominated occupations as clerical workers with male-dominated ones such as craft workers or laborers. Studies that have used this approach have consistently demonstrated a significant gap between female-dominated and male-dominated jobs determined by the firm to be comparable (Doherty and Harriman 1981).

The most difficult aspect of job evaluation is always in achieving objectivity. No system can be completely objective. The critical questions are what compensable factors are included and how they are weighted, and that always comes down to a subjective decision. The four methods of job evaluation, in order of objectivity, are ranking, classification, point plans, and factor comparison plans.

- *Ranking* is the simplest and also the most subjective.
- *Classification*, used by many public employers, uses only one compensable factor, skill. Since many variations of skill are possible, that too is highly subjective.
- The *point plan*, originally developed by the consulting firm of Hay and Associates, is the one used most frequently. It identifies several compensable factors—such as skill, knowledge, ability, and working conditions—that are of value to the organization, and then assigns a complex system of weights and points. The point system has gained popularity because it has a semblance of objectivity.
- The *factor comparison plan*, the most objective and least used, involves the comparison of key jobs to determine which ones contain greater amounts of compensable factors. But even this system requires subjective judgments, and, more particularly, it assumes that the current wage for the key jobs is the correct one (Berg 1976).

These job evaluation methods were not designed to measure the comparable worth of male- and female-dominated jobs; they were designed to determine the comparable worth of jobs within occupational families. While apparently value-neutral, they are inevitably subjective and often can be shown to be biased in favor of male-dominated occupations. The bias takes a number of forms, for example:

- The prerequisites, tasks and work context associated with women's jobs are less visible. Compare, for instance, fire fighters and flight attendants in relation to their perceived responsibilities for handling crises. The skills of firefighters in handling emergencies are perceived as central to the job. The flight attendant, whose position was originally created by Federal Aviation Administration regulations requiring trained staff to work with passengers in case of emergency, is perceived as a waitress in the sky. In each position, only a small amount of time is spent dealing with emergencies, but for the firefighter it is perceived as central and for the flight attendant it is invisible.
- The prerequisites, tasks, and work context associated with women's work are included in the evaluation framework but are not valued at equivalent levels of complexity as those that favor males' occupations. The factor of "responsibility," for instance, is considered more complex, and therefore is given a higher rating, when the position is responsible for financial assets than when it is responsible for human life. And jobs with responsibility for financial assets are more likely

to be held by men, while those responsible for human life are more likely to be held by women.

- The weights assigned to factors differentially associated with men's job classes are substantially higher than the weights assigned to factors differentially associated with women's classes. For instance, a job requirement for managerial or technical knowledge will receive a significantly higher rating than a requirement for human relations skills (Steinberg 1990).

Beginning in the mid-1970s, women employees in many organizations, often supported by their unions, began to seek and get job evaluation studies that were less biased and that cut across occupational boundaries. The National Academy of Sciences (NAS), at the request of the Equal Employment Opportunity Commission (EEOC), studied the issues involved in measuring the comparability of jobs. A review of twenty-five years of studies based on the Human Capital model found that these studies were able to explain only a portion of the earnings gap. The remaining—unexplained—gap often is attributed to discrimination. Occupational classification offers a better explanation of pay disparity than any particular compensable factor. The study concluded that "discrimination is likely operating in the labor market with significant effects on women's earnings and the pay rates of women's jobs" (Hartmann and Treiman 1983).

The NAS researchers also reviewed the operation of labor markets, focusing on the institutional model. They concluded that most firms exhibit job segregation by sex, and that much of that segregation is the result of the placement of newly hired individuals. To some extent placement is determined by supply, but even so, much of the earnings differential was the result of differential placements when individuals first enter. Men and women with equal qualifications are assigned to different entry-level jobs with differing implications for their futures (Hartmann and Treiman 1983).

The researchers concluded that substantial discrimination exists in the labor market and that "the wage rates of jobs held traditionally by women are depressed relative to what they would be if women had equal opportunity in the labor market."

SUMMARY

The labor market has undergone enormous changes in the last two decades. The number of women in the labor market has increased dramatically, with the greatest change among women in the middle years. The majority of married women, including married women with children, are in the work force. During the same period, the percentage of men in the work force has declined, and the changes for men occur at the beginning and ending of their careers. Men often stay in school, and hence out of the labor market, longer, but the great majority of the decline has come from older men who leave the labor market either voluntarily, through early retirement, or involuntarily because of poor health.

The composition of the labor force also has changed; the proportion of jobs in male-intensive industries has declined, and the proportion in the clerical and service sectors has increased. Nevertheless, a high degree of occupational segregation still persists, and women still earn on the average only about 70 percent of what men earn.

Economic theories that attempt to explain occupational segregation and the lower wages of women fall into two categories. The neoclassical theories, and specifically the Human Capital theories, explain the differences on the basis of choice, that is, women put greater value on their family roles than on their work roles and therefore choose occupations that require a lower investment in human capital. Segmented labor market theories, on the other hand, assume that occupational segregation and pay disparity occur as a result of discrimination against women.

Comparable worth models extend the segmented or internal labor market theories and focus on the evaluation of disparate jobs within the individual firm. They agree that differential job placement perpetuates job segregation, and they argue that those jobs to which women are relegated are underpaid because of long-standing bias in the market. They assume that the comparable worth of jobs should be determined in relationship to dissimilar occupational classifications within the firm, rather than to similar occupations in the labor market.

In Chapter 4, we turn to political and legal remedies for job segregation and pay inequity.

4

The Political Environment

From the onset of the Industrial Revolution, workers struggled against business owners for better working conditions. They were joined in their struggle by labor leaders and various reform movements. The struggle was waged on two fronts, through collective bargaining and through legislation. Legislation, in turn, depended for its effectiveness on both the regulatory agencies that administer it and the courts that interpret it.

In the nineteenth and early twentieth centuries, the two basic approaches came to be divided, at least to some extent, by sex. In a very general sense, men came to achieve their employment gains through participation in the labor movement, women through legislation. Early legislation aimed at protecting women and children from exploitive employers had the effect, if not the intent, of increasing the discrimination against women. More recent legislation has been aimed at protecting women (and minorities) from discrimination.

It would be impossible to understand the contemporary political/legal environment without some knowledge of these historical origins. We will start with a review of state "protective legislation" and then turn to an overview of the major pieces of federal civil rights legislation. We will review the role of the government and of the courts in interpreting and applying the legislation to the elimination of sex discrimination, including sexual harassment and comparable worth.

PROTECTIVE LEGISLATION

The industrial movement that began in the early nineteenth century gradually took over many of the tasks that women had traditionally performed in the home. As this occurred, more and more women left the home to work as weavers, spinners, seamstresses, laundresses, and waitresses. While working conditions for all workers during this period were deplorable, they were much worse for women than for men. Women worked longer hours, their work rules were stricter, and their work places were more unsafe and unhealthy than those of men. Aside from the long hours, factory women were subjected to incredible noise, heat, and air pollution. Tuberculosis was common and incurable.

Further, as the nineteenth century progressed, the disparity increased. The labor movement began as early as 1825 to agitate for a 10-hour day for men workers, and eventually a 10-hour, six-day week became commonplace in most occupations. The major exception was factory work, which still had the most women workers. Women often worked 11 to 13 hours a day, sometimes seven days a week, while men in some occupations worked only 50 hours or less a week (Baer 1978).

Public attention was focused on these appalling conditions when, in 1911, a fire at the Triangle Shirtwaist Company in New York City burned at least 143 women workers to death. Triangle was an exceptionally anti-union company that had been the target of a prolonged strike just two years earlier. It was notorious for its terrible working conditions. When fire broke out in the loft of the factory, the women workers were unable to escape because the company had locked the doors to the stairs from the outside to keep employees from stealing or escaping. There were no fire extinguishers; the only fire escape would have taken three hours to clear everyone from the building. Most of the women died within twenty minutes, their bodies never identified. They were buried in numbered coffins (Baxandall, Gordon, and Reverdy 1976).

The reasons why differences arose between women workers and men workers in hours and working conditions, and why they persisted, are too complex to examine in detail here. However, two questions are significant. One is why change was sought through legislation rather than collective bargaining; the other is why legislation was sought, and enacted, to protect women and children and not adult men.

Legislation or Negotiation

The gains that were made in the working conditions of men came about mostly through unionization and collective bargaining. The unions began in the early nineteenth century to pressure for reduction in hours and for improved working conditions. Strong unions in heavily organized industries were successful in achieving these goals. Where they lacked the strength to accomplish their goals collectively, they often turned to legislation to accomplish reform. For example, as early as 1842, employees in Massachusetts petitioned the state legislature for a law imposing explicit, enforceable limits on their work week. After nearly two decades of effort, the workers finally settled in 1867 for a bill that set maximum working hours only for women and children. The legislature was willing to adopt this measure to protect women's (but not men's) health; the male workers were willing to accept it because they believed that the restrictions would be applied to all workers. Hence the workers were accused of having decided to "fight the battle from behind the women's petticoats" (Ratner 1980).

With few exceptions, the unions rarely sought universal hours legislation thereafter. Many states enacted laws limiting the number of hours that women could work, prohibiting their work during certain hours (typically at night), restricting them from certain occupations that were considered hazardous, barring them from places where liquor was served, prohibiting or limiting work during pregnancy, and requiring pay equal to that of men.

Legislators were unwilling to enact protective legislation for men, but would adopt it for women because of what was perceived as the state's legitimate interest in the woman's role in childbearing and childrearing. Proponents argued that, because women on the whole were weaker than men, and because only women were capable of bearing children, working conditions that were tolerable for men were dangerous for women and therefore should be prohibited. Further, since a woman's primary duties were assumed to be in her home, the state took an interest in "easing the burden of motherhood," not by reducing her share of the home duties but by ensuring that she was not overtaxed in the work place. In 1908, the Supreme Court turned back a challenge to Oregon's protective legislation by agreeing that the state had a legitimate interest in women's reproductive health, and that precedent was not overturned until after the passage of the *Civil Rights Act of 1964* (Baer 1978).

Women and Men in the Labor Movement

From the beginning of the labor movement, women were far less active than men, for several reasons. The industries they worked in had the worst conditions and were also the least amenable to change. Women were not perceived by labor leaders to be permanent members of the labor force, and indeed women workers tended to perceive themselves as temporary workers. Since they expected to leave the labor force when they married, they had less incentive to work for change. Further, since participation in a union was illegal and highly risky, as well as time-consuming, workers with the most to gain also had the most to lose. Thus women workers, who needed the most from labor organizations, were the least organized.

Pressure for legislation to protect women and children workers came not only from male union leaders but also from the growing army of social reformers and the few women who were labor leaders and organizers. The reformers supported sex-specific legislation because they were genuinely concerned about the plight of women workers, and unions accepted it in hopes that its protections would be extended to male workers.

But the male-led unions have been accused of having another reason for pursuing protective legislation for women, a less benevolent and purely economic one. Male workers viewed women as a threat to their jobs, and since women were paid lower wages, the threat was exacerbated. Their response was to exclude women, rather than to organize them. Excluding them would assure that they would continue to be available to perform the appropriate tasks at home (Hartmann 1976). The union movement, its critics charge, deliberately sought protective legislation as a means of excluding women from some occupations and reducing their participation in others. Statutes that restricted the number of hours that women could work, or that proscribed their participation in specified occupations, made women on the whole less desirable employees than men. Statutes that required equal pay for equal work greatly reduced an employer's incentive to hire women if men workers were available. The net result was to reduce the competition from women for the best-paid, most sought-after jobs (Berch 1982). While there is some evidence that the unions were more concerned with men workers than with women, there is little support for the contention that these motives were either widespread or effective (Ratner 1980).

So, to answer the questions raised above in a greatly oversimplified way, we can say that legislation was pursued over negotiation because it was more effective in areas and in industries that were not heavily unionized. The legislation that was enacted was sex-specific because lawmakers could be persuaded that the state had a legitimate interest in protecting women's childbearing abilities but not in protecting men's overall health, and the labor movement accepted the compromise. The charge has been made, but not satisfactorily proven, that the unions were more interested in keeping women out of the labor force than in protecting their rights in it.

From 1867 until 1964, states continued to enact sex-specific legislation limiting the hours and working conditions of women workers. These laws were repeatedly challenged in the courts and just as repeatedly upheld as legal and constitutional (Baer 1978). During the 1930s, the U.S. Congress adopted the *Fair Labor Standards Act of 1938*, which extended uniform hours protection to all workers. Most of the protective laws were suspended during World War II because of a national "manpower" shortage. At the same time, the War Manpower Commission issued guidelines providing for equal pay and prohibiting sex discrimination. But when the war ended, the legislation was reimposed. From then until the late 1960s, sex-specific legislation that restricted women from certain occupations remained on the books in many states, despite all court challenges to its constitutionality and political efforts to amend or appeal it.

It was in this context that the U.S. Congress took up the issue of discrimination against women in the early 1960s, first with the *Equal Pay Act of 1963* and later with the *Civil Rights Act of 1964*.

FEDERAL LEGISLATION

Questions of civil rights, both for women and for people of color, are as old as the Constitution itself. We will concern ourselves here with the body of legislation that has been enacted by the Congress during the last half of the twentieth century.

The *Equal Pay Act of 1963*

The *Equal Pay Act of 1963* can hardly be said to be a major departure from the paternalistic posture of protective legislation. An amendment to the *Fair Labor Standards Act of 1938*, it was carefully drawn as a limited, narrow assurance of pay equity. Although the Kennedy Administration had proposed a broader bill, the Congress was willing to adopt only the narrowest of statutes. The act forbids:

paying wages to employees . . . at a rate less than the rate at which (the employer) pays wages to employees of the opposite sex . . . for equal work on jobs the performance of which requires equal skill, effort, and responsibility, and which are performed under similar working conditions (29 U.S. 206 [d][1]).

The legislative history of the bill shows clearly that the Congress understood that women and men seldom work at jobs that meet this equal work standard, that is, that are the same or substantially the same and are performed under similar working conditions. It is quite clear also that they did not intend for this bill to assure equal pay between jobs that were comparable but markedly dissimilar. Further, lest there be any doubts, the lawmakers provided employers with four affirmative defenses against charges of sex discrimination in pay. Differences in pay are not in violation of the act if they are based on a seniority system, a merit system, a system that measures earnings by quantity or quality of production, or a differential based on *any factor other than sex*. Responsibility for enforcement of the Act was placed with the Wage and Hour Division of the U.S. Department of Labor, which was permitted to issue "interpretive bulletins" but not binding regulations. The Department of Labor could bring suit for back wages and injunctions, but only the Department of Justice could file criminal actions in the case of willful violation (Bureau of National Affairs 1963).

In 1979, enforcement of the Equal Pay Act was transferred to the Equal Employment Opportunity Commission (EEOC), which issued new and more restrictive guidelines to employers (Greenlaw and Kohl 1982). A number of court cases have established that jobs need not be identical, only substantially equal, in order to be compared. Job descriptions or classifications are irrelevant in showing that work is unequal unless they accurately reflect the actual content of the job. Thus, despite its narrow scope, the Equal Pay Act has been successful in reducing pay disparities based on sex alone or on artificial or superficial job differences that serve as thinly veiled justifications for sex discrimination (Doherty and Harriman 1981).

The *Civil Rights Act of 1964*

The *Civil Rights Act of 1964*, while a much broader based bill, was designed primarily to address the problem of race discrimination. An extremely controversial bill, it was passed in the wake of the assassination of President John Kennedy, but not without the strongest possible protests of representatives from the southern states. Title VII of the bill covers employment discrimination; in its original form, it covered discrimination on the basis of race, color, religion, and national origin.

When the bill reached the floor of the Congress, after having proceeded painstakingly through the committee process, a number of amendments were proposed by its opponents, in the hope that by confusing and weakening it they could ultimately defeat it. Among the amendments was one proposed by Congressman Howard Smith of Virginia to add "sex" as a protected category, setting off what came to be known as "ladies day" in the Congress (EEOC 1964).

On February 12, 1964 (Bird 1968) Mr. Smith assured the Congress that:

I am very serious about this amendment . . . I do not think it can do any harm to this legislation; maybe it can do some good. I think it will do some good for the minority sex . . . I think we all recognize and it is an indisputable fact that all throughout industry women are discriminated against in that just generally speaking they do not get as high compensation for their work as the majority sex. . . . That is about all I have to say about it except, to get off of this subject for just a moment to show you how some of the ladies feel about discrimination against them, I want to read you an extract from a letter I received the other day. This lady has a real grievance on behalf of the minority sex.

He then went on, amid great laughter, to read a letter from a woman in New York asking for an amendment to correct the present imbalance that exists between the number of males and females in the country, "a grave injustice to womankind" that "shuts off the right of every female to have a husband of her own."

I read that letter just to illustrate that women have some real grievances and some real rights to be protected. I am serious about this thing. I just hope that the committee will accept it. Now, what harm can you do to this bill that was so perfect yesterday and is so imperfect today—what harm will this do to the condition of the bill?

Congressman Emanuel Cellar from New York, chair of the House Judiciary committee, rose to read a letter from the Women's Bureau of the Department of Labor (signed by a man), asking that the amendment be withdrawn so that it could submit a separate bill. But first he felt compelled to argue that women were not in the minority in his home. ". . . the reason we have been living in such harmony for almost half a decade is that I usually have the last two words, and those words are 'yes dear'." However, he went on to argue quite seriously that the bill would cause social upheaval by requiring total equality.

Would male citizens be justified in insisting that women share with them the burdens of compulsory military service? What would become of traditional family relationships? What about alimony? Who would have the obligation of supporting whom? Would fathers rank equally with mothers in the right to custody of children? What would become of the crimes of rape and statutory rape? . . . Would the many State and local provisions regulating working conditions and hours of employment for women be struck down? You know the biological differences between the sexes. In many states we have laws favorable to women. Are you going to strike those laws down?

But the frivolous nature of the debate continued. The men repeatedly pointed out that they, not the women, were the minority sex, and several Congressmen referred to themselves as "second-class citizens." Mr. Cellar offered such wisdom as:

Lives there a man with hide so tough
Who says "Two sexes are not enough?"

Congresswoman Martha Griffiths of Michigan led the serious debate in favor of the amendment. Arguing that, "if there had been any necessity to have pointed out that women were a second-class sex, the laughter would have proved it," she went on to present a cogent example to demonstrate that, if the bill passed without including sex in its coverage, it would provide less coverage for black women than for black men and that "white women will be last at the hiring gate."

Ms. Griffiths was joined by several other Congresswomen in serious support of the bill. Facetious support came from many southern Congressmen, some of whom had been among the most vigorous opponents of the Equal Pay Act the previous year. Some sincere opposition was raised by proponents of the Act who feared that the amendment would "clutter up the bill" and be used later to destroy it; they too were joined by the Act's opponents. Despite the antics of its opponents, the amendment was adopted on the floor by a vote of 168 to 133. Title VII of the Civil Rights

Act of 1964 was passed into law providing protection for women as well as minorities against discrimination in employment.

Unlike the bill itself, the issue of sex discrimination never received serious consideration or debate in any committee of the Congress. So hastily and so poorly drawn was the amendment that two days later the House again took up the matter, to add the word "sex" in several places where it had been accidentally omitted (to make the bill consistent throughout) and "to make the requirement for no discrimination on the basis of sex subject to a bona fide occupational qualification exception" (EEOC 1964). This lack of careful consideration has raised doubts in the enforcement agencies and in the courts as to the serious intent of Congress to prohibit sex discrimination and has made it difficult for women to find remedies to sex discrimination under Title VII.

Title VII, with the 1972 amendments added to extend coverage and strengthen enforcement, makes it unlawful for employers, labor unions, joint apprenticeship committees, or employment agencies covered by the Act to discriminate in the areas of hiring, firing, or terms of employment. Subsequent amendments have added older workers, the disabled, and Vietnam era veterans to the list of protected classes. It prohibits employers from limiting, segregating, or classifying employees or applicants in protected groups in any way that would deprive an individual of employment opportunities. It prohibits discrimination as it relates to wages, fringe benefits, assignments or promotions, use of facilities, or training. For the first time, Title VII gave women a legal basis for insisting that they be allowed to compete with men for jobs and promotions, as well as that they be paid the same as men once such jobs and promotions are secured (Doherty and Harriman 1981).

Executive Orders

A third body of federal regulation on discrimination in employment is found in a series of Executive Orders (orders issued by the President of the United States). Executive Order #11246, issued in 1964 and subsequently amended several times, prohibits employment discrimination on the basis of race, color, religion, national origin, age, or sex by employers with federal contracts and by contractors working on federally assisted construction projects. In other words, "any person" who contracts with a federal agency to furnish supplies or services or for the use of real or personal property. It may also apply to labor unions and employment agencies. Responsibility for the administration of the order lies with the Office of Federal Contract Compliance and Programs (OFCCP) within the Department of Labor (Pemberton 1975).

A paradox created by the major difference between Title VII and the Executive Orders lies in the issue of "affirmative action." Title VII requires employers to be color- and sex-blind; it states specifically that no employer is required "to grant preferential treatment to any individual or group on account of any imbalance which may exist." The Executive Orders, on the other hand, have required the use of affirmative action, a term that has been interpreted by the compliance agencies and the courts to mean active, affirmative plans to overcome the effects of past discrimination, often by pursuing numerical "goals and timetables" (Block and Walker 1982). Affirmative actions include not only widespread and extensive recruitment efforts to reach qualified minorities and women, but also special training programs, identification of career ladders, creation of subprofessional job classifications as "bridging classes," and the reevaluation of minimum job qualifications to recognize alternative education and experience categories. Opportunities must be expanded, not only for qualified but also for "qualifiable" candidates. In other words, Title VII requires that employers not grant preferential treatment; the Executive Orders require that they do.

Not surprisingly, these programs have caused an enormous amount of controversy. Critics tend to lump both affirmative action and equal opportunity programs together and to be highly critical of both. Their criticisms cover several grounds—that the programs force employers to lower qualifications in order to find women or minorities to fill *de facto* quotas, that they discriminate against white males, that they are costly to business, that they are unsuccessful in achieving their goals, and that discrimination has been eliminated, making the programs unnecessary. *Forbes* magazine charges that "throughout American business, newly entrenched affirmative action bureaucrats are enforcing discrimination by race and sex—in favor of the "protected classes" . . . —as decreed by Washington." They conclude that "bean counting has replaced merit in America" (Brimelow and Spencer 1993).

Despite these criticisms, and despite the weaker enforcement during the Reagan and Bush Administrations, equal opportunity law today is stronger than ever. When the Supreme Court handed down several decisions during the 1980s that made it more difficult for victims of discrimination to bring their cases to court, the Congress overrode those decisions in the Civil Rights Act of 1991, and President Bush reluctantly signed it into law.

The courts, with few exceptions, also have upheld the right of employers to give preferential treatment to members of protected groups to achieve sex and race parity. Allan Bakke, a white male twice denied admission to the medical school at the University of California, Davis, sued the Regents of the University on the grounds that students admitted under a special admissions program for disadvantaged students had lower grades and test scores than he. While the U.S. Supreme Court ordered his admission to the school, it also upheld the right of schools to devise special admissions programs so long as they did not constitute numerical quotas. A year later the Court upheld the right of Kaiser Aluminum and Chemical Company to use a voluntary quota system to reserve 50 percent of the positions in its training program for blacks, who made up only 2 percent of their employees and 39 percent of the local labor force (Block and Walker 1982). Since then, the courts have heard many challenges to affirmative action and, while narrowing the scope of the plans considerably, so far have upheld the principal on which they are based.

However, critics and supporters of affirmative action programs do agree on one thing, that they have had only a minor effect on achieving equity in the work place. Both agree that some progress has been made in reducing the disparity between white and minority earnings, and both agree that the progress is more likely attributable to economic growth, to civil rights protests (Feagin and Feagin 1978), or to geographic mobility (Sowell 1982) than to affirmative action programs. Supporters argue that programs have been less than successful because too few resources have been devoted to the effort; critics believe that the very concept of compensation for past discrimination is ill-conceived and unworkable (Glazer 1975; Gross 1978). Opponents include many members of the protected groups themselves, who often find that such programs perpetuate the demeaning paternalism inherent in protective legislation. All would agree that, at best, affirmative actions are and should be a temporary path to the ideal of equality of opportunity for all workers. The goal is not, and should not be, statistical parity. The goal is equality of opportunity.

TITLE VII AND SEX DISCRIMINATION

Given the circumstances under which Title VII was adopted, its success in achieving an end to discrimination lay not in the law as written but in the ability of the government and the courts to enforce it. It did not get off to a promising start. Before the 1972 amendments, the EEOC's primary role was a conciliatory one. It could bring charges, but only individuals or the Attorney General could initiate complaints or bring suit. The Attorney General rarely acted, and most individual victims were hesitant to do so. Further, the first director of EEOC publicly stated in 1966 that the sex provision was a "fluke" that had been "conceived out of wedlock," remarks that drew criticism from Representative Martha Griffiths on the floor of the House (Baer 1978).

To these problems were added weak management, an ineffective organizational structure, and inadequate staff or budget. The organization has been plagued from its inception with personnel problems and poor performance, even after the 1972 amendments added the power to bring suit against private employers. The situation improved during the Carter administration, but the conservative administrations of Presidents Reagan and Bush made little effort to improve implementation or extend the protections of the law.

Defining Discrimination

Despite its weaknesses, the EEOC was able to develop policy guidelines that often were used by the courts in settling important and controversial cases, particularly in race discrimination cases. For example, neither Title VII nor the Executive Orders gives a formal definition of discrimination. When the issue was brought to the Court in the landmark *Griggs v. Duke Power* case (401 U.S. 424 [1971]), the EEOC guidelines served as the basis for the Court's precedent setting ruling. In that case, the justices adopted the EEOC view that even employment practices that appear to be neutral on their face in terms of equal *treatment* and even in terms of *intent* could be discriminatory if they had disparate *effects* on members of protected groups. The only defense available to the employer would be to prove beyond doubt that the questionable practice was necessary for the operation of the business and was in fact related to job performance (Abramson 1979).

Sex as a Bona Fide Occupational Qualification (BFOQ). Title VII provides that, even if sex discrimination is proved, an employer has the defense of showing that sex is a bona fide occupational qualification (BFOQ). The interpretation of this provision was crucial to the effectiveness of the act; anything but a very narrow definition would essentially nullify the act as far as women were concerned. The EEOC guidelines argued that sex is not a BFOQ when the employer relies on assumptions of comparative behavior of women and men, stereotyped characterizations of the sexes, or preferences of customers, coworkers, employees, or clients. The issue came to court in the case of a male seeking a job as a flight attendant. The airline argued that being a woman was a BFOQ for flight attendants on the basis of psychologists' testimony that anxious passengers would be more reassured by feminine attendants. The EEOC's guideline prevailed. The court ruled that the airline was required to safely transport passengers and freight by air, but not to serve food and drink or to "comfort" passengers. These optional services, should the airline decide to offer them, could be provided equally well by male or female cabin attendants. Customer preference did not constitute a BFOQ (*Dias v. Pan American World Airways*, 442 F. 2d 385 [5th Cir. 1971]). It often has been said that the decision is so narrow that the only jobs in which sex can be considered a BFOQ is a sperm donor for males and a wet nurse for females. In other cases, the Court has upheld this view defining as illegal the refusal to hire women, but not men, who are parents of preschool-age children, or to require women to quit their jobs when they marry (Gilbreath 1977).

Protective Legislation as a Bona Fide Occupational Qualification. Another potential stumbling block for Title VII was the question of whether protective legislation could be used as a BFOQ defense, a question that ultimately spelled out the fate of such legislation. The Act itself is silent, saying only that:

nothing in this title shall be deemed to exempt or relieve any person from any liability, duty, penalty, or punishment provided by any present or future law of any State or political subdivision of a State, other than any such law which purports to require or permit the doing of any act which would be an unlawful employment practice under the title.

Very well! What does that mean? Are protective laws legal or illegal? Are they a BFOQ? In the debate over amending Title VII to include sex, opponents argued that it would, in fact, eliminate such protective statutes. Congresswoman Griffiths responded: . . .

Some protective legislation was to safeguard the health of women, but it should have safeguarded the health of men also. Most of the so-called protective legislation has really been to protect men's rights in better paying jobs (EEOC 1964).

She was joined by Congresswoman Katherine St. George of New York, who concluded an impassioned appeal for passage saying:

We do not want special privileges. We do not need special privileges. We outlast you—we outlive you—we nag you to death. So why should we want special privileges?

Nevertheless, the EEOC took a cautious stand toward overriding protective legislation. In its first guideline, issued in 1966, it indicated its belief that the law was not intended to disrupt state protective laws and that these laws were a basis for the application of the BFOQ defense. Within a year it revised its position, declaring that it would make no determination in cases where conflicts existed between Title VII and state protective legislation except in cases where the clear effect of the law was discriminatory. In these cases their only action would be to notify claimants of their right to sue. Still a third guideline, issued in 1968, reaffirmed the belief of the commission that Congress did not intend to overturn these laws but stated its own belief that some of the laws were no longer relevant because of changing technology and the expanding role of women workers in the economy. It announced that it would consider these laws as a basis for BFOQ defense but would not accept a law whose effect was clearly discriminatory rather than protective (Baer 1978).

The matter was finally resolved when the court ruled that, if a job required lifting or other strenuous work, a woman must be given a chance to demonstrate her qualifications for the job. It went on to conclude that state laws did not create a BFOQ, that the earlier EEOC guidelines were not controlling, and that the laws were void under Title VII (*Rosenfeld v. Southern Pacific Company*, 293 F. Supp. 1219).

In a similar case, the court went a step further, shifting the burden of proof that sex is a BFOQ to the employer. It enunciated the rule that an employer must have "a factual reason for believing that all or substantially all women would be unable to perform safely and efficiently the duties of the job involved." In this case, the court asserted, the employer had assumed on the basis of stereotyped characterizations that few or no women could meet the weight-lifting requirement and that all men could. In the matter of protecting women from risks, the court held that:

Title VII rejects just this type of romantic paternalism as unduly Victorian and instead vests the individual woman with the power to decide whether or not to take on unromantic risks. Men have always had the right to determine whether the incremental increase in remuneration for strenuous, dangerous, obnoxious, boring or unromantic tasks is worth the candle. The promise of Title VII is that women are now to be on an equal footing. We cannot conclude that by including the bona fide occupational qualification exception Congress intended to renege on that promise (*Weeks v. Southern Bell*, 277 F. Supp. 117 [S.D. Ga. 1976]).

In the ensuing years many cases, mostly class actions, were brought to court challenging hours and weight restrictions and job prohibitions. The courts struck down most sex-specific laws, and state legislators struck down the remaining ones. What statutes remain on the books are no longer enforced (Ratner 1980).

Pregnancy, Reproductive Hazards, and Title VII

One issue in which the court's view departed from that of the EEOC was the problem of how to deal with the pregnant employee. The paradox here is apparent. Protective legislation has been consistently upheld since 1908, when the court held that the state had a legitimate interest in protecting women from injury during pregnancy. Yet the Supreme Court resorted to fairly tortuous reasoning to find that employers did not violate Title VII protections by denying sick leave, disability insurance, or health insurance coverage to female employees to cover disabilities resulting from normal pregnancies.

The Court did rule that maternity leave policies that mandated extended periods of absence violated the due process clause of the 14th Amendment (Baer 1978). However, it found no sex discrimination in California's disability insurance plan, which excluded pregnancy disabilities from its coverage but did cover such sex- and race-singular disabilities as hemophilia, prostate operations, circumcisions, and sickle cell anemia. It reasoned that:

there is no risk from which men are protected and women are not. Likewise, there is no risk from which women are protected and men are not (*Geguldig v. Aiello*, 417 U.S. 484 [1974]).

It repeated this language and extended the line of reasoning to a company health insurance program that covered sports-related injuries, injuries incurred while committing a crime, prostate surgery, circumcision, and hair transplants but excluded pregnancy. In that case (*General Electric Company v. Gilbert*, 429 U.S. 125 [1976]) the majority based its decision on the logic that the only possible sex discrimination occurs when men and women are treated differently with respect to a shared situation or characteristic (Abramson 1979). Since men cannot be pregnant, the Court was saying, it is not discrimination against women to deny them health benefits for pregnancy disabilities. The plan does not discriminate against women; it simply removes one condition, pregnancy, from the list of covered conditions.

The Court continued this verbal hairsplitting in two more cases. In one case, women were required to take unpaid maternity leave during which they lost all accumulated seniority, even though seniority rights were retained for all other types of disability leaves. The Court rejected the loss of seniority but upheld the validity of the required unpaid leave, on the astonishing grounds that payment would constitute a benefit that men cannot and do not receive (*Nashville Gas v. Satty*, 98 S. Ct. 347 [1977]). That logic was extended even further in a case challenging a retirement plan that required women to make larger contributions than men. In overturning the plan, the Court distinguished between it and the disability plan upheld in the Gilbert case. The disability plan, the decision argued, distinguished between two classes of people: pregnant and nonpregnant. While all pregnant people were female, nonpregnant ones were both male and female, so no discrimination existed. However, the pension plan was discriminatory since all women were required to pay higher pension contributions than men (*City of Los Angeles v. Manhart*, 46 L.W. 4347 [1978]).

Clearly, some escape from this quagmire was needed. The justices had argued in Gilbert that the problem was that Congress had failed to explain its intent in outlawing discrimination on the basis of sex. Lacking evidence of Congressional intent, the Court was reluctant to draw any inferences on its own. In addition, the Gilbert decision triggered considerable response from the media and from women's organizations such as the National Organization for Women (NOW) (Huckle 1981). Despite considerable political opposition, Congress responded with the Pregnancy Discrimination Act of 1978, which technically was an amendment to the Civil Rights Act of 1964.

The Pregnancy Discrimination Act broadened the definition of sex discrimination to encompass pregnancy, childbirth, or related medical conditions. Discrimination on the basis of these factors in hiring, promotion, suspension, discharge, or in any other term or condition of employment is defined as an unfair labor practice and is prohibited. An employer cannot:

- require women to take leave set arbitrarily at a certain time in their pregnancy;
- fail to grant full reinstatement rights to women on leave for pregnancy-related reasons, including credit for previous service and accrued retirement benefits as well as accumulated seniority;
- fail to pay for disability or sick leave for pregnancy, childbirth, or related medical conditions in the same manner as it pays for other employee disability or sick benefits;
- refuse to hire or promote a woman because she is or could become pregnant;
- ask pre-employment questions about a woman's childbearing status (Trotter, Zacur, and Gatewood 1982a; Trotter, Zacur and Gatewood 1982b);
- require women to provide medical evidence of infertility in order to work at jobs that present "reproductive hazards," such as exposure to lead (*UAW et al. v. Johnson Controls, Inc.*, 499 U.S. 113, L. Ed. 2d 158, 111 S. Ct. 1196 [1991]).

The history of Title VII has shown that the courts, and to a lesser extent the EEOC, have been reluctant to expand the definition of discrimination and the coverage of the Act to apply to women in the same way they have for minorities. Where the EEOC has issued strong and clear guidelines, the courts have tended to follow their leadership. But in the absence of a strong message from the EEOC, and given the unusual circumstances in which sex came to be covered in the Act at all, the courts have proceeded cautiously, indeed. The issue of pregnancy discrimination and reproductive hazards seems at last to have been resolved by Congress and the courts. Two other sex-related issues have caused both the courts and the EEOC enormous problems. One is the issue of sexual harassment as a form of sexual discrimination. The other, comparable worth, remains a politically and economically disturbing conundrum.

Sexual Harassment and Title VII

Phyllis Schlafly, testifying at hearings of the Senate Labor and Human Resources Committee, said:

[sexual harassment on the job is not a problem for] the virtuous woman except in the rarest of cases. When a woman walks across the room, she speaks with a universal body language that most men intuitively understand. Men rarely ask sexual favors of women from whom the certain answer is "no."

A great many working women would take exception to Ms. Schlafly's "blame-the-victim" statement. No matter how you define sexual harassment, it is a widespread problem. The extent of the problem, and the differences in perception, were dramatically portrayed in the fall of 1991 when the whole country sat transfixed before their televisions to watch the Senate confirmation of Clarence Thomas to become a justice of the U.S. Supreme Court. Anita Hill, a Yale educated attorney, accused Thomas of making sexually explicit remarks to her and pressuring her for dates while he was chair of the EEOC. Members of the Senate Judiciary Committee, all men, and much of the country, seemed unable to believe that a man in his position would act that way or that a woman in her position would tolerate it. Yet many women watching at home recognized the pattern of behavior that Hill was describing; they could not know whether her accusations were true, but they knew that women often experience similar treatment.

The Thomas–Hill hearings focused attention on this long-standing problem as no other event ever had. But for a number of years while the courts had been considering the issue, the EEOC had issued guidelines to employers, and legislative bodies at the state and Federal levels had enacted legislation. What all of these efforts add up to is that sexual harassment is now a form of illegal sexual discrimination for which both individuals and employers can be held responsible.

Neither the Civil Rights Act of 1964 nor the 1972 amendments made any mention of sexual harassment; they merely proscribed sexual discrimination. It was only after a series of lower court cases that sexual harassment came to be considered an illegal form of sex discrimination. Although the lower courts began in the 1970s to come to this position, it was not until 1986 that the Supreme Court ruled on the issue, and not until the Civil Rights Act of 1991 that Congress passed legislation.

The Early Court Cases. Two women who rejected the sexual advances of their supervisor eventually resigned rather than face the continued abuse. The court rejected their claim of sex discrimination under Title VII, taking the position that harassment committed by the supervisor was the act of the supervisor only and bore no relationship to the employer. Since the supervisor's conduct was not the result of a company policy, the court concluded that the corporation had more to lose than to gain by the conduct and therefore should not be held liable. The court said:

[The supervisor's] conduct appears to be nothing more than a personal proclivity, peculiarity, or mannerism. By his alleged sexual advance, [he] was satisfying a personal urge (*Come v. Bausch and Lomb*, 490 F. Supp. 161, DC AZ [1975]).

In a similar case, a supervisor made a sexual approach to a woman employee while the two were discussing possible job advancement for her. After she rejected the supervisor's sexual "suggestions," which were accompanied by force, he harassed her in the form of disciplinary layoffs and threats of demotion. Fifteen months after the original incident, the victim was terminated. The district court's response was that this was not sex discrimination, merely discrimination due to sexual activities. The decision said, in part:

Title VII is not intended to provide a federal tort remedy for what amounts to physical attack motivated by sexual desire on the part of a supervisor and which happens to occur in a corporate corridor rather than in a back alley (*Tomkins v. Public Service Electric and Gas Co.*, 422 F. Supp. 553, DC NJ [1976]).

The courts continued to hold that employers were not liable for sexual harassment under Title VII unless they had a policy permitting it, which of course no employer did. The courts also seemed to worry that, if they found for the plaintiffs, they would be opening the doors to a flood of cases, a concern that suggests that they recognized how pervasive is the problem (Seymour 1979).

However, Tomkins was overturned on appeal, and the tide began to turn. The Appeals Court ruled that the lower court had tolerated the supervisor's sexual demands and this created a prerequisite for continuation of, or advancement in, or advancement in, her job. From that point on, in a series of cases in the late 1970s, the courts ruled that Title VII is violated when acceptance of sexual advances by a supervisor is made a condition of job retention or when a supervisor takes retaliatory actions because a female employee refuses sexual advances (Sawyer and Whatley 1980).

EEOC Guidelines. As the direction of the courts became clear, the EEOC issued guidelines spelling out the definition of and responsibility for sexual harassment. The guidelines assert that unwelcome sexual advances, requests for sexual favors, and other verbal or physical conduct of a sexual nature constitute sexual harassment when:

1. submission to such conduct is made either explicitly or implicitly a term or condition of an individual's employment;
2. submission to or rejection of such conduct by an individual is used as the basis for employment decisions affecting such individual; or
3. such conduct has the purpose or effect of unreasonably interfering with an individual's work performance or creating an intimidating, hostile, or offensive working environment.

The EEOC guidelines lay out the employer's responsibility:

• An employer is responsible for its acts and those of its agents and supervisory employees with respect to sexual harassment regardless of whether the specific acts complained of were authorized or even forbidden by the employer and regardless of whether the employer knows or should have known of their occurrence.

- With respect to conduct between follow employees, an employer is responsible for acts of sexual harassment in the work place where the employer (or its agents or supervisory employees) knows or should have known of the conduct, unless it can show that it took immediate and appropriate action.

- An employee also may be responsible for the acts of nonemployees, with respect to sexual harassment of employees in the work place, where the employer (or its agents or supervisory employees) knows or should have known of the conduct and fails to take immediate and appropriate corrective action.

- Prevention is the best tool for the elimination of sexual harassment. An employer should take all steps necessary to prevent sexual harassment from occurring, such as affirmatively raising the subject, expressing strong disapproval, developing appropriate sanctions, informing employees of their right to raise and how to raise the issue of harassment under Title VII, and developing methods to sensitize all concerned (*Federal Register* 1980).

The guidelines recognize two types of sexual harassment—*quid pro quo* and *hostile environment. Quid pro quo* ("this for that") harassment occurs when the victim is asked for some form of sexual favor in exchange for some job benefit or, conversely, threatened with retaliation for refusing. These situations are relatively clear cut—although not always easy to prove; they occur whenever an employee is pressured for sexual favors and is at risk for refusing.

Hostile environment harassment occurs when sexual conduct that is unwelcome or unwanted is so pervasive or persistent that it interferes with the victim's physical or mental health or with her (or his) ability to perform on the job. The hostile environment can be created by repeated sexual jokes, comments, or noises; by the display of sexually explicit materials; and by gestures or stares (Friedman, Boumil, and Taylor 1992).

It is this form of harassment that causes so much difficulty and misunderstanding. To be considered illegal harassment, conduct must meet the following criteria:

1. It must be *unwelcome* or *unwanted*, not just involuntary. Employees may participate in sexual behavior because they fear the repercussions or retaliation if they refuse. Thus, their actions may be voluntary but nevertheless unwanted.

2. The conduct was sexual in nature.

3. A pattern of persistent or repeated harassment existed that a reasonable person would find offensive (Wagner 1992).

U.S. Supreme Court Decisions. In 1986 the first sexual harassment case reached the Supreme Court. In *Meritor Savings Bank v. Vinson*, the plaintiff, Michelle Vinson, sued her employer alleging hostile environment sexual harassment. Vinson had been hired by the bank as a teller-trainee and was promoted several times on the basis of merit. After four years she was terminated for excessive use of sick leave. A year later she filed suit, charging that her supervisor, Sidney Taylor, had followed her into the ladies room, fondled her in front of co-workers, and raped her several times. She admitted that she had had sex with Taylor forty to fifty times. Vinson did not use the bank's internal reporting process because she feared reprisals, and instead took her claim to the EEOC. Despite the bank's defenses that the relationship was ongoing and voluntary, and that they could not take remedial action because they had not been notified, the Supreme Court found in favor of Vinson (*Meritor Savings Bank v. Vinson*, 106 S. Ct. 2399 [1986]).

In 1993, the Court again took up the issue, this time in *Harris v. Forklift Systems Inc.* Teresa Harris had worked for the company as a manager for over two years, during which she and other women workers were repeatedly subjected to offensive remarks and sexual innuendoes by the company president, Charles Hardy. Hardy, she charged, repeatedly asked his female employees to retrieve coins from his front pants pocket, or to retrieve objects he had thrown on the ground in front of them while he made derogatory remarks. He remarked to Harris, in the presence of other employees, "What do you know," "You're only a dumb ass woman," and "We need a man as rental manager." He once stated, in front of other employees and a client, that he and Harris should "go to the Holiday Inn to negotiate [Harris'] raise." After Ms. Harris complained to Hardy, he apologized and promised to stop, but a month later he suggested publicly that she had promised a customer sexual favors to secure an account. Ms. Harris resigned and filed suit for sexual harassment.

The district court dismissed the case on the grounds that, although Hardy's behavior was offensive, it was not severe enough to interfere with her work performance or to affect her psychological well-being. The Supreme Court, in a unanimous decision, reversed the lower court and sent the case back for rehearing. The opinion advised that, in assessing a hostile environment claim, the "totality of the circumstances" must be examined, including the "frequency of the discriminatory conduct, its severity, whether it is physically threatening or humiliating, or a mere offensive utterance, and whether it reasonably interferes with an employee's work performance" (*Harris v. Forklift Systems Inc.*, 92–1168 [Nov., 1993].

These two cases support the EEOC guidelines and clarify three important elements of hostile environment sexual harassment cases:

1. *Psychological well-being.* Conduct is illegal if it creates an environment that reasonably would be perceived as hostile or abusive. It need not be psychologically abusive or so severe that it completely destroys the victim's emotional and psychological stability.

2. *Interference with work performance.* The victim need not demonstrate "tangible effects" from the conduct, such as diminished performance, only that the conduct made it more difficult to do the job.

3. *Reasonable person standard.* While the Court rejected the more stringent "reasonable woman" standard that some lower courts had applied, it agreed that the conduct must be viewed from the perspective of the victim and not "stereotyped notions of acceptable behavior."

Civil Rights Act of 1991. In spite of these Court decisions, Title VII still did not provide compensatory or punitive damages; so victims had to rely on state statutes or civil suits, an action usually taken after they had left the job. The final step in providing relief occurred with the passage of the Civil Rights Act of 1991, which permits both compensatory and punitive damages up to certain specified limits. Compensatory damages can include back pay, front pay, expenses for medical treatment of pain and suffering, and attorney's fees. Punitive damages are available only for cases of intentional discrimination; the amount depends on the size of the employer's work force, up to a maximum of $300,000 for employers of more than 500 workers (Wagner 1992). These limits, however, do not preclude victims from bringing a separate civil suit, and the Act provides the right to a jury trial.

Sexual harassment is physically and emotionally destructive to its victims. It is a wasteful, disruptive, and costly misuse of employers' resources. It is illegal, and many employers have taken steps to eliminate it from their work places. Yet it continues to occur wherever women work. Victims are entitled to both compensatory and punitive damages and jury trials, and those who have suffered through the agonizing process of litigation and won their cases have often received very substantial awards. But by the time a case comes to the Court, both parties have lost. Management must take all steps to prevent sexual harassment, not just on humanitarian grounds, nor even on legal grounds, but on the grounds of sound management practice.

Comparable Worth and Title VII

Since the passage of the Equal Pay Act of 1963 and the Civil Rights Act of 1964, and the issuance of the Executive Orders, efforts by government and by women's advocates to achieve equity have moved ahead along two fronts: one has been the effort to achieve equal pay for equal work; and the other has been to attempt to reduce occupational segregation, specifically by attempting to move women into male-dominated occupations. The first effort has been fairly successful; the second has been much less so.

A third approach has been to address pay inequities in female-dominated occupations, that is, discrimination based on the "comparable worth" of jobs. As we saw in Chapter 3, recent research has attempted to establish to what extent the pay disparity between women and men workers is the result of differences in the characteristics of the jobs or the characteristics of the individuals holding them, and to what extent it is the result of sex discrimination. The results of these studies seem to confirm beyond reasonable doubt that at least some of the wage disparity is a result of discrimination.

Attempts to address the problem through the Courts or through legislation have failed. As long ago as World War II, the War Labor Board required employers to pay women the same as men for jobs that were comparable, based on traditional job evaluation methods (Harriman and Horrigan 1984). The board found that some employers, after conducting job evaluation studies, reduced the wage rate from one-fifth to one-third if it was being performed by women (Newman 1976). But when the war ended the board was dismantled, many women left the labor force, and employers reverted to the familiar pattern of paying women less than men.

The Kennedy Administration proposed a comparable worth bill to the Congress in 1962; Congress rejected it in favor of the equal pay standard of the Equal Pay Act of 1963. For the next fifteen years, comparable worth was virtually ignored. Neither the women's movement nor the EEOC nor the unions pursued it. Then, in the late 1970s, the situation was reversed. The EEOC took up the issue and began to bring comparable worth suits to court. The labor movement began to use it as an organizing issue, and in 1981 the AFL-CIO unanimously endorsed a comparable worth resolution at its national convention (Hartmann and Treiman 1983). Unions, especially those representing public sector employees, have bargained both for comparable worth studies and for salary adjustments to remedy the inequities found in the studies. Women's groups, very late to come to political lobbying, began to lobby for comparable worth legislation at every level of government. A number of state and local governments adopted comparable worth statutes, the Federal congress held hearings, but no legislation was enacted (Harriman and Horrigan 1984).

Comparable Worth and the Courts. The courts have been extremely reluctant to become involved in declaring comparable worth to be a form of illegal discrimination (Harriman and Horrigan 1984). Part of the difficulty goes back again to the cavalier way in which the Congress came to include women in Title VII. In the absence of hearings or testimony to the contrary, the courts have continued to assume that it was not the intent of Congress to wage battle over sex-based wage discrimination. Further, language included in Title VII clouded the issue. The pertinent amendment reads:

It shall be an unlawful employment practice under this title for any employer to differentiate upon the basis of sex in determining the amount of wages or compensation paid or to be paid to employees of such employer if such differentiation is authorized by the provision of [*The Equal Pay Act of 1963*] (29 U.S. 206[d] [42 U.S.C. 2000e-2h]).

This language, introduced and adopted almost without discussion, could be interpreted in two ways, and for years the courts dealt with resolving that question alone. The language could mean either that (1) the amendment limits Title VII to the equal work standard of the Equal Pay Act, or (2) an employer could raise the same affirmative defenses for unequal pay, that is, a merit system, seniority system, incentive system, or anything other than sex.

Under the first interpretation, comparable worth cases could not be brought to the Court at all. Even if employers deliberately and knowingly paid lower wages for jobs in female-dominated classes, since such practice would not be illegal under the Equal Pay Act, it would not be illegal under Title VII. Under the second interpretation, cases could be brought to the Court under Title VII, and employers could use any of the four affirmative defenses to justify the unequal pay.

The issue was resolved in 1981 when the Supreme Court adopted the interpretation that the amendment merely permits employers to raise one of the affirmative defenses (*County of Washington v. Gunther*, 452 U.S. 161 [1981]). This case, originally filed in 1974, was brought by female jail matrons in Oregon whose work was similar to that performed by male jail guards. The employer evaluated the female jobs at 95 percent of the worth of the male jobs, but the women were paid only 70 percent of the evaluated worth of their jobs while the men were paid 100 percent of the evaluated worth of theirs. The Court agreed that sex-based compensation cases under Title VII were not limited to the equal pay standard. The justices expressed their unwillingness to deprive victims of discrimination of a remedy but also stressed they were not endorsing the controversial issue of comparable worth.

All that the Gunther decision accomplished was to settle the procedural issue. The Court sent the case back to the district court to be heard on its merits. After eight years, the plaintiffs had won the fight to bring their case to the Court. By that time, the case was moot; the parties entered into a consent decree and Alberta Gunther and her codefendants each received $3250 in back pay (Harriman 1983).

The Gunther case appeared to open the courtroom doors to women who work in female-dominated occupations, and a number of suits were filed. The one that received the most attention was brought by the American Federation of State, County and Municipal Employees (AFSCME) against the state of Washington (Remick 1983). AFSCME argued that the state had intentionally discriminated against women by ignoring its own job evaluation studies. The district judge agreed and awarded back pay to 1974, when the first comparable worth study was conducted, an award that could have run as high as half a billion dollars. The decision was overturned on appeal, however, and the appellate courts have rejected all subsequent comparable worth claims. The Reagan Administration strongly opposed the concept, the Chair of the U.S. Civil Rights Commission called it "the looniest idea since Looney Tunes," and Clarence Thomas in his role as head of the EEOC persuaded the commission to reject the program under Title VII. For the time being, the legal question of comparable worth was dead, at least in the United States (Weiler 1991).

The Future of Comparable Worth. The issue has not gone away. At least a dozen states, and many more local governments, have implemented pay equity programs, often as a result of negotiations with public sector unions. These agreements are sometimes but not always reflected in legislation or Executive Orders. The outcome has not been the disaster that comparable worth opponents predicted. The pay equity adjustments have produced sizable gains for incumbents in these jobs. They have not, as predicted, done violence to the payroll budget of the employer, nor have they caused difficulty in recruiting and retaining male employees in male-dominated jobs (Weiler 1991).

As we saw earlier, the historical relationship between women and the unions has not been a particularly rewarding one for either. The unions have tended to represent men and send women to government for relief, an approach women were willing to take. But in recent years, just as the government and the courts have backed away from the issue, the labor movement has greatly increased its interest in organizing women workers. Blue collar employment in the smoke stack industries, the traditional stronghold of the labor movement, is declining rapidly and union membership is at an all-time low. Unions must move in to white collar and public sector occupations in order to survive, and in fact the greatest increases in union membership in the last two decades have been in these heavily female-dominated organizations.

Comparable worth offers a powerful organizing issue for the unions; it speaks directly to the economic concerns of enormous numbers of working women. Those unions seeking to organize and represent women— AFSCME, the American Nurses Association, and others representing clerical and service employees—have been the most actively involved (Harriman and Horrigan 1984).

SUMMARY

Ever since the Industrial Revolution, workers have fought for better pay, shorter hours, safer and healthier working conditions, and greater job security. Much of the pressure for these changes came from the labor movement, which was primarily a men's movement. Women had the greatest need but also the least to contribute to the union movement. Reform was pursued through two avenues, at the bargaining table and through legislation. However, when protective legislation was adopted by many states, it covered only women workers. Over time, the welfare of men workers came more and more to be the concern of the unions, and the responsibility for women workers fell to the state. Whatever the intentions of the reformers, the result was to increase the occupational segregation of women and to decrease their earnings.

During the 1960s, several pieces of federal legislation were enacted that addressed, directly or indirectly, the issue of sex discrimination, including sexual harassment. The Equal Pay Act of 1963 bans unequal pay for equal work, unless the difference is based on a nondiscriminatory merit system, a seniority system, an incentive system, or anything other than sex. Title VII of the Civil Rights Act of 1964, and its 1972 and 1991 amendments, prohibits discrimination in all employment practices on the basis of race, religion, national origin, or sex. Executive Orders extend the coverage of these bills to Federal employees and Federal contractors. This legislation is supplemented by many state regulations.

Despite the reluctance of the courts to interpret the law broadly where women are concerned, this body of legislation has been used to strike down protective legislation. It also has been used to achieve equal pay for equal work, to reduce employment discrimination against women, and to prohibit the sexual harassment of women in the work place. When the courts refused to extend protection of the law to pregnant women, Congress enacted the Pregnancy Discrimination Act of 1978.

Much has changed in the political and economic environment of the work place since the beginning of the Industrial Revolution. However, as we stand on the brink of an electronic revolution, much still remains the same. Women and men no longer work 12-hour days, they rarely work under unsafe or unhealthy working conditions, and they are more protected against financial disaster either from illness or injury or economic fluctuations. Those changes have come about through a combination of legislation and negotiation. But women still earn less than men, and they continue to work in segregated occupations. The major change seems to be that the majority of women now work continuously throughout their lives, they perceive themselves as permanent members of the labor force (even if others fail to perceive them that way), they perceive themselves as victims of sex-based wage discrimination, and they are willing and able to pursue change through the same avenues that have been effective for men—through legislation, through litigation, and through collective bargaining.

5

About Roles and Stereotypes

The one thing that we can say with confidence about women and men is that they seem to be quite different from each other. Women and men lead lives that are different but complementary in many ways. Some of these differences are biologically determined; only men can father children, and only women can bear and nurse them. When we speak of these differences, the terms we use are *male* and *female*. Most differences, however, are a function of social custom or device; we call these *role* differences and use the terms *masculine* and *feminine*. In this chapter we will be looking at the evidence of sexual differences, at some explanations for those differences, and at the notion of psychological androgyny, an alternative way of conceptualizing sexual identity.

NATURE AND NURTURE

There are obvious physical differences and less obvious trait differences between women and men. These differences frequently are seen as being true sex differences, although research tells us that many—perhaps most—of the nonphysical differences are learned, not innate.

Sex Differences: Female or Male

Males on the average are taller, heavier, more muscular, and more aggressive than females and also are more susceptible to illness. After adolescence, males excel in quantitative and visual spatial ability. Females have always been widely believed to excel in verbal ability and verbal creativity, but recent studies suggest the differences are so small as to be meaningless (Hyde and Linn 1988). Also, very little difference has been found for abilities such as intelligence, creativity, or cognitive style. On personality characteristics such as love, sociability, nurturance, dependency, empathy, or emotionality, areas in which males and females are perceived to differ significantly, there is very little evidence that real differences exist (Maccoby and Jacklin 1974).

It is fair to say, then, that actual sex differences have been greatly exaggerated. However, circumstances that are perceived as real are real in their consequences. So long as these perceptions exist, differences in experience are sure to follow. It is also important to bear in mind when we talk of sex differences that we are talking about statistical rather than individual differences. Differences that occur between males and females are distributed over normal and overlapping curves. While men on the average may be stronger or more aggressive than women on the average, an individual woman may be stronger or more aggressive than a good percentage of the male population, or the reverse.

Gender Differences: Feminine or Masculine

Because our world is infinitely complex, we simplify our understanding by grouping physical and social phenomena into categories. For this reason natural scientists divide the physical world into genera, phyla, etc. Social scientists study human behavior in the forms of roles, role sets, and stereotypes. In studying sexual behavior, social scientists look for "sex roles" and "sex-role stereotypes." A *role* is the expected and actual behaviors or characteristics that are associated with a particular social "status" in our society (Duberman 1975). A *stereotype* is the set of traits or characteristics that are attributed to all individuals who occupy a particular role. Stereotyping occurs when the observed traits or behaviors of some members of a role group are attributed to all members of the group by the larger society. A stereotype exists when a broad cross section of the population agrees that certain traits or behaviors are commonly associated with a particular role.

Statuses can be either "ascribed" or "achieved." We acquire *achieved* statuses through individual effort or ability. One achieves the status of an engineer or a social worker, the status of husband or father, or the status of friend through individual behavior. *Ascribed* statuses, on the other hand, are assigned at birth and include such characteristics as race, age, and gender, as well as son or daughter, sister or brother. They normally cannot be changed.

To every status, whether achieved or ascribed, certain roles become attached, and in the case of gender these come to be known as *sex roles*. Roles are learned over a lifetime through the process known as *socialization*. Most children learn their sex roles through the process of *role-taking*, that is, through observation and control within the family. What is considered an appropriate sex role will vary from culture to culture, religion to religion, region to region, class to class, and family to family. Also, people will vary in the extent to which they conform to or deviate from the norms of the sex role assigned to them. Hence, gender roles, as opposed to gender statuses, are learned and therefore can be *un*learned or *re*learned. One cannot change one's sex, but one can change one's sex role (Duberman 1975).

For example, one might occupy the status of "manager" in our society, an achieved status. That status carries with it certain rights, obligations, and prestige, along with certain expectations of behavior, all of which constitute the role of manager. Managers are expected to plan, organize, direct, control, and staff the organization over which they have managerial responsibility. Managers also are expected to be knowledgeable about the organization, the industry, and the environment of the firm, and to have some skill and ability in managing human resources. Managers are further expected to have certain traits—to be rational, equitable, and decisive. All of these are part of the managerial role. When we encounter a person whose job title is manager, then, we make certain assumptions about that person—that she or he carries all the job activities and the job privileges of a manager. We assign to that person all the personal characteristics that we associate with the role of manager. We see the manager not as an individual but as a manager. That is the effect of stereotyping.

Stereotypes usually have some basis in reality, and they serve a useful purpose in helping us to understand the social world in which we live. The difficulty is that, partly because they are rooted in reality, they are very difficult to change. Human nature being what it is, we tend to dislike ambiguity. When we observe someone behaving in a way that is different from what we associate with their stereotyped group, for example, we observe a manager who makes inconsistent or emotional decisions, we experience something called *cognitive dissonance*: two notions which we believe to be true are in opposition to each other (Festinger 1957). If our stereotype is accurate, this person who is a manager also must be rational. But our information contradicts this knowledge. We can observe that this person has the title of manager, and we also can observe that his or her behavior is quite irrational. Something is clearly wrong. Either our stereotyped belief or our observation must be in error. Do we change our stereotype of managers? Or do we disbelieve our senses? Probably neither. Instead, we may conclude that this particular person is not a typical manager. S/he is, we say, a *deviant*: s/he deviates from the stereotypical behavior of people of the class of manager. Thus we are able to maintain both our stereotyped belief and the accuracy of our perceptions.

Roles and stereotypes have enormous power to shape our behavior. The learning of roles, and particularly sex roles, starts almost at the moment of birth. We dress infant boys and girls in different clothes. Boys' outfits are likely to be brightly colored and decorated with airplanes or sports symbols; girls' are more likely to be pastel colors and decorated with hearts and flowers. Boys' crib toys resemble footballs, toy trucks, building blocks; girls' more likely cuddly dolls or animals. We even describe newborn infants differently. Boys are "strong," "hefty," "handsome"; and girls are "dainty," "sweet," and "pretty." Boys at these earliest stages are being taught to be active and self-reliant; girls are learning to be passive, dependent, and nurturing. The stories that are read to them are likely to perpetuate this stereotype, the boys acting independent roles, the girls more passive ones (Kortenhaus and Demarest 1993).

A girl who deviates from these norms and adopts masculine behaviors during early childhood will likely receive approval; a tomboy is cute, and friends and family will all assume that when she reaches puberty and takes an interest in boys, she will assume her "natural" role. But a boy who adopts feminine roles will have a much harder time; it will not be assumed that he will change at puberty. Each is exhibiting deviant behavior, but being a tomboy is cute and being a sissy is not. Boys and girls who behave according to the norms for their sex appropriate roles will be seen as acting "naturally."

The importance of all of this is that sex roles and sex stereotypes have a significant effect on how we behave, on how we view ourselves, and on how our behavior is perceived by others. It is essential, then, to understand the nature of masculine and feminine sex roles and sex stereotypes in contemporary society.

A list of the traits associated with gender stereotypes leads to two conclusions (Broverman et al. 1972) (see Table 5.1). First, the number of desirable traits associated with masculinity is more than double the number of desirable traits considered feminine. Second, the feminine traits considered desirable are not ones that would be considered important or valuable in most professions or occupations. Thus men are seen as being aggressive, independent, unemotional, objective, dominant, active, competitive, logical, worldly, skilled in business, adventurous, self-confident, and ambitious—all traits that are related to the concept of competence. Women, on the other hand, stereotypically are seen as being exactly the opposite of men on all of these dimensions. Desirable traits for a woman are being talkative, gentle, tactful, religious, quiet, empathetic, aesthetic, and expressive—traits associated with passivity.

Gender, Race, and Social Class

Social scientists who measure gender stereotypes find that they are both consistent and persistent, that is, they are widely held and are relatively resistant to change. Research thus far has given little consideration to the relationship between gender and race or social class (Reid and Comas-Diaz 1990), perhaps because these are sensitive issues (Scarr 1988). What evi-

Table 5.1
Male-valued and Female-valued Stereotypic Items

Competency Cluster: Masculine Pole Is Preferred

Masculine Pole	*Feminine Pole*
Very aggressive	Not at all aggressive
Very independent	Not at all independent
Not at all subjective	Very subjective
Not at all easily influenced	Very easily influenced
Very dominant	Very submissive
Very competitive	Not at all competitive
Very logical	Very illogical
Very worldly	Very home oriented
Feelings not easily hurt	Feelings easily hurt
Very direct	Very sneaky
Very adventurous	Not at all adventurous
Can make decisions easily	Has difficulty making decisions
Very self-confident	Not at all self-confident
Very ambitious	Not at all ambitious
Never Cries	Cries Easily

Warmth-Expressiveness Cluster: Feminine Pole Is Preferred

Feminine Pole	*Masculine Pole*
Very talkative	Not at all talkative
Very tactful	Not at all tactful
Very gentle	Very blunt
Very aware of feelings of others	Not at all aware of feelings of others
Very religious	Not at all religious
Very gentle	Very rough
Very quiet	Very loud
Very interested in own appearance	Not at all interested in own appearance
Very neat in habits	Very sloppy in habits
Very strong need for security	Very little need for security
Enjoys art and literature	Does not enjoy art and literature
Easily expresses tender feelings	Does not express tender feelings easily

Source: Inge Broverman, Susan Vogel, Donald Broverman, Frank Clarkson, and Paul Rosenkrantz. Sex role stereotypes: A current appraisal. *Journal of Social Issues* 28 (1972): 59–78.

dence does exist suggests that both race and social class have significant effects on stereotypes of women (Landrine 1985; Smith and Steward 1983) and that these stereotypes are held by a wide spectrum of people, regardless of age, region, race, gender, marital status, education level, or social class.

Stereotypes do vary with social class. In the *upper class*—about 1 percent of the population—women tend to acquire the status of their husbands. Girls are expected to marry men of their own class, and great emphasis is put on feminine grace and beauty. Husband and wife roles are clearly separated. The woman's role is that of hostess and companion; she may participate in community activities as a means of finding self-expression but almost never works at a job or career. The man earns or manages the family's wealth. Both women and men tend to adopt feminine norms in interpersonal behavior, that is, there is an absence of overt aggression.

The *upper middle class*—about 9 percent of the population—includes the upwardly mobile career executive and his alter-ego, the executive wife. The wife is devoted to her husband's career and enhances it in a number of important ways. The wife may hold a professional position, or she may be a full-time homemaker. In either case, she will be involved in the traditional role of wife and mother.

Upper middle-class wives are the ones most subject to role conflict. These women increasingly find their traditional roles changing and being redefined. They want recognition as wives and mothers, but they want something more besides. This something more may take the form of a career or of participation in social, community, or creative interests. The traditional behaviors of the feminine role are considered mandatory; the role conflict arises when the "something more" becomes mandatory as well.

In the *lower middle class*—about 40 percent of the population—most women are in the labor force, and their wages are often what lifts the family's income into the middle class. Lower middle-class husbands are skilled, semiskilled, and lower white collar workers; lower middle-class wives might be clerical workers, school teachers, or civil service workers. The husband is clearly the head of the household; the wife's job, if she has one, may be an extension of her housewife role. She may be "helping out." However, husband and wife share many joint activities. Unlike the executive husband in the upper and upper middle classes, the husband has sufficient time to take an active part in family life.

The *working class*—also about 40 percent of the population—is the most difficult to describe because of the social changes that are taking place. Many workers, especially those who are unionized, have high earnings and are experiencing both social and geographical mobility, including moving to the suburbs; others, however, have seen their earnings drop as unemployment or underemployment replace high-paid manufacturing jobs.

Still, by dividing the class into two subgroups, we can make some generalizations.

The traditional working-class family closely follows the breadwinner model. Gender roles are clearly segregated, and both sexes subscribe to an "ideology of patriarchy" and male dominance. But the husband/father's actual power in the family is often circumscribed by his lack of success in the labor force and by a lack of involvement in family affairs. The father sees his role as strictly limited to that of economic provider; sharing in domestic chores or having his wife work outside the home are threats to his masculinity, a view shared by the wife. It may be she who really runs the family—managing the household finances, bearing and rearing the children, and maintaining the household—much like the homemaker wife of the industrial period. She may do all this, and hold a job, while carefully maintaining the fiction that the husband is the head of the house (Hacker 1975).

Gender roles are learned early and well in this traditional working-class family. For girls, marriage is the chief objective, although most know that they will work at mundane jobs after marriage. There is little expectation that they will go to college. Courtship and romance are highly valued, and sex often is used as an inducement to marriage. Working-class boys and girls are kept segregated in school and social activities, and each sex tends to hold highly stereotyped views of the other, which often results in difficulty in communication.

A nontraditional version of the working-class family is emerging, particularly where the husband and wife have graduated from high school or have moved to the suburbs. The increased education seems to provide not only greater earning power and self-esteem, but also greater ability to reason and to communicate. The move to the suburbs seems to break traditional ethnic traditions. In this version of the working-class marriage, the balance of power is more evenly weighted. There is more sharing of responsibility and a deeper emotional involvement. Wives are more likely to work outside the home, and husbands and wives tend to share home improvement projects or plans for the children's future made possible by extra income. For the working-class male, however, the modern marriage is a mixed blessing. More and more is being demanded of him, emotionally and sexually, than ever before. He is often being asked to redefine himself, a difficult task for the best of us, and one for which he has little guidance and few models.

The *lower class* is made up of people who live at or near the poverty level throughout their lives. Families are often unstable. If the father works, it may be at low-skilled, low-paid jobs, which are often seasonal or intermittent. Sex roles are highly segregated. Husbands do not participate in household chores; fathers often rely on physical coercion to exert power.

Both women and men adopt masculine behaviors in interpersonal behavior, acting out their anger and aggression.

Young people growing up in urban slums hold little hope of getting ahead by their own efforts. They live in the here and now, searching for excitement and pleasure, sometimes involved in crimes, gangs, drugs, or other destructive activities. They see their only hope of a better life in luck, in crime, or perhaps in athletics, but not in education or hard work. They have children at a younger age and have more children than middle-class families.

Race and ethnic differences in sex-role behavior are also evident. In Latin America and in Mediterranean and Middle Eastern societies, sex roles are rigidly enforced, and men and women have very little social interaction (Safilios-Rothschild 1977). Traditional values, which are deeply embedded in religious beliefs, tend to persist in these cultures, although the extent to which they are found currently depends in part, as it does in the United States, on socio-economic status. Socialist countries such as Sweden, China, and the former Soviet Union have adopted national policies of equality between the sexes, but even there old traditional values die hard (Yorburg 1974). In cultures where men and women are kept segregated, where sex roles are rigidly enforced, and where women are considered greatly inferior to men, the only possible relationship between women and men is a sexual one. Women learn from an early age to attract male attention by flirting, teasing, and dressing up. Men learn to look to women only for sex and to compete with other men for the most desirable women. In our country, groups that derive ethnically from traditional cultures tend to repeat the patterns. That is, men and women have little social interaction, their relationships are mainly sexual, and the double standard is rigidly adhered to (Safilios-Rothschild 1977).

Regardless of social class, regardless of race or ethnic background, males and females are shaped by society, to a greater or lesser extent, into some kind of sex roles. These roles in turn have enormous influence on both their personal and working lives. As a result of the socializing influences, they will have vastly different life experiences.

THE FEMININE EXPERIENCE

Chapter 2 traced the process by which male and female roles changed in the last century as a result of technological and economic changes. We can go back much farther and find three images of women's work that have predominated throughout western history, from the golden age of Greece and Rome, through the Middle Ages, and through the history of Judeo–Christian religious teachings. They are woman as inferior, woman as evil, and woman as love object (Hunter 1976).

In ancient Rome, women had achieved a kind of women's liberation.

They were more independent than women had ever been in any point in history and enjoyed access to education, property, and divorce. This development prompted some writers to viciously ridicule all women who attempted to move out of an inferior position. So successful were these attacks that succeeding generations of historians have blamed the liberation of women for the breakdown of the family, for an increase in hedonism and debauchery, and ultimately for the decline and fall of the Roman Empire.

The image of woman as evil pervades the course of history. Early Greek mythology blamed evil on Pandora, and early biblical writings blamed it on Eve. Jesus and Paul did not label women as evil *per se*, but through their teachings sex came to be associated with sin and celibacy with the highest form of Christianity. The natural extension of that linkage was that woman came by her very nature to be viewed as the source of evil, the temptress. From there it was a relatively short step to burning women at the stake as witches.

Despite the threat of evil and temptation that women presented, the tradition of woman as love object also goes back a very long way. It is found in the early Hebrew literature, particularly in the beautiful love poem, *Song of Solomon.* The Christian church maintained throughout the medieval period its disapproval of sex and love, but in the secular world the notion of chivalry glorified women and attributed to them qualities that improved the nature of men. The feminine role was always a passive one. Women were to be beautiful; they were to inspire men to acts of *derring do* and creativity. But if they succumbed to the blandishments of their adoring knights, they lost their virginal qualities and again became associated with evil and sin. They were put on a pedestal, a rather precarious position in which to live (Hunter 1976).

Women in the Victorian era, that is, at the time when the middle classes were beginning to emerge from the working classes, found themselves placed in this role of purity and passivity. The rationale for withholding the vote from women was the fear that exposure to the rough and tumble world of politics would shock their sensibilities, or even worse, corrupt their morals (Tannahill 1980).

These historical images can be found in contemporary views of womankind. Contemporary stereotypes can be broken into several categories, including housewife, "bunny" (seductress), club woman, career woman, and athlete (Clifton, McGrath, and Wick 1976). The two traditional roles, housewife and seductress, produce very distinct stereotypes among both women and men. The housewife stereotype conforms very closely to the traditional sex role and to the image of woman as love object. Housewives are seen as faithful, gentle, kind, sensitive, sympathetic, dependent, cooperative, emotional, tender, conservative, casual, calm, generous, agreeable, secure, and loyal.

The seductress stereotype is also distinct and strongly held. It describes women as glamorous, good-looking, pleasure-loving, romantic, excitable, passionate, frivolous, and sensual. Housewives and "bunnies" are seen as having almost no attributes in common: housewives are not romantic, passionate, and sensual; and bunnies are not gentle, kind, sensitive and tender.

A third stereotype is suggested by three other categories: club woman, career woman, and athlete. None of these is seen as a distinct stereotype, but they share a number of common elements. All three of these roles, which are relatively independent of men, are ascribed as having strongly masculine traits: active, aggressive, hardworking, alert, confident, ambitious, competitive, persistent, and independent. These traits are associated with competence and are the most highly valued. But unfortunately they are traits valued only in men, not in women. Women who display these traits sometimes are described as argumentative and boastful, and are perceived as having lost their femininity (Clifton, McGrath, and Wick 1976).

So, in the nature of stereotypes, despite the rapidly changing roles of women, they continue to be seen either as evil or as a love object, but in either case as inferior. Stereotypes of women can be differentiated from a single category (female) or from a variety of categories. Feminine roles can be distinguished by social class. But the fact remains, that women who adopt traditional feminine roles are seen as normal, healthy women; women who adopt nontraditional roles may be seen as competent, but they also are seen as unfeminine. Women still face the conflict of being seen as feminine and therefore second-class adults, or seen as competent but unfeminine (Broverman et al. 1970). What a choice!

THE MASCULINE EXPERIENCE

Despite the lack of significant differences between women and men in any but biological terms, the ideology of male dominance and male superiority persists. Until fairly recently, relatively little serious evaluation of masculine roles and stereotypes took place. As in the study of organizations, the assumption was made that male is normal, and most research on women has studied how they differ from men. Only recently has there been more extensive study of the life experiences of men. While the literature is sometimes controversial, sometimes superficial, and often rooted in ungrounded assumptions, one thing seems clear—the masculine role is as limiting to men as the feminine role is to women (Pleck 1976).

The masculine role can be divided into two subsets, labeled *instrumental* and *expressive*. The *instrumental* role includes the expectations that males will be physically active and adept, and that they will achieve success in the work place. The *expressive* role includes the expectation that they will suppress all expression of emotionality—that they will be "cool." Little boys, like little girls, learn their sex roles early, and they learn them well.

Boys learn very early the importance of being good at sports, of being dominant, and of "acting like a man." They learn very early the negative outcomes that go with acting like a girl, of being a sissy. They may not always understand what it is that they are to do, but they know well what it is they are not to do. They are *not* to let anyone overpower them, they are not to be afraid, they are not to cry, they are not to do anything that girls do.

The Instrumental Role

The instrumental aspects of the masculine role include being physically and mentally strong and providing for one's family. Patriarchy has always been a part of the social system: the Industrial Revolution made the bread-winner's domination over the family complete. But it also had two significant negative effects on masculinity: it reduced the amount of physical labor that jobs required, and it reduced the amount of time that young boys spent in the company of men (Bly 1990). The social response to these changes was a marked increase in institutions that permitted boys to learn masculine behaviors and men to validate their masculinity. The institutions most effective for these purposes were sports, war, and boys clubs, notably the Boy Scouts.

The values of the Protestant Work Ethic regard hard work and providing for one's family as synonymous with masculinity. The American tradition of rugged individualism was and is highly regarded. Yet with industrialization the actual work that men did was increasingly less physically demanding, and their pay and benefits were increasingly standardized. Men came to feel that their masculinity was being diminished. At the same time, young boys were increasingly in the company of women, both because of the fathers' nonparticipation in family activities and because of the increasing number of female school teachers. It is no small coincidence that Teddy Roosevelt and his Rough Riders became instant national folk heroes. Roosevelt represented everything that was valued in the name of masculinity and much that ordinary men saw themselves as losing (Dubbert 1979). Since roles historically are passed down from one generation to the next, the concern that masculine values and behaviors were not being properly preserved was of no small consequence. Out of this concern came a greatly increased emphasis on the teaching of instrumental roles and an increased avoidance of expressive roles.

A number of organizations sprang up that presented opportunities to express one's manhood and to teach manly virtues to the younger generation. The Young Men's Christian Association (YMCA) and especially the Boy Scouts met these requirements. The Boy Scouts were founded in South Africa and appeared in the U.S. in 1910. Within a decade it became the largest male youth organization in the history of this country. It turned the idle street gang into the active Scout patrol. It would turn "sissies, hot house plants, little Lord Fauntleroy types, puny, dull or bookish lads, and dreamers" into boys who were "full of life and energy, full of ideas, filled with ideals and with heroes." The American scouting movement added to the Scout oath the condition "To keep myself physically strong, mentally awake, and morally straight," and added the tenth law "A Scout Is Brave" (Hantover 1978).

The Scout movement attracted adult males as well as young boys. Scouting offered men the dual opportunity to teach young men the manliness and virility that had occurred naturally in earlier times and to express their own manliness, which was now seen to be eroding. Young, college-educated men in white collar occupations, perhaps the ones experiencing the greatest threat to their masculine identity, were eager to validate their manhood by taking the role of scoutmaster. The same concern for the separation of young men from their fathers and other older men persists today; it is the major premise of the popular book *Iron John* (Bly 1990). Surely no one could have anticipated that the Boy Scouts would be embroiled in a controversy over whether homosexual boys should be allowed to be scouts or homosexual adults allowed to be leaders.

Participation in sports also took on new meaning around the turn of the century. It is not clear how this came about, but it probably had its roots in Victorian Christian morality, which maintained that a moral person was a good steward of mind and body. For whatever reason, a sports craze swept the country. The YMCA, which had been active in this country since before the Civil War, promoted gymnastic and athletic programs to "protect against the allurement of objectionable places of resort" (Dubbert 1979, p. 165). President Theodore Roosevelt endlessly extolled the virtues of such sports as running, rowing, football and baseball, boxing and wrestling, shooting, riding, and mountain climbing. Schools were encouraged to offer physical education and sports programs, and a link was perceived between having a healthy, active body, a good mind, and a good character. Team sports began to be popular, amid some criticism. They encouraged *spectatorism* rather than participation, and they failed to offer the display of prowess and virility that individual sports required. Nevertheless, football and baseball games drew huge crowds and created a new breed of heroes. Even in the colleges, physical and athletic ability often took precedence over intellectual prowess in the validation of masculinity.

Sports activity, like the Boy Scouts, was attractive to men because it gave them a safe retreat from feminine influence. The sports arena became a sort of modern equivalent of the men's hut found in primitive societies. There fathers and sons could share an interest and participation in sports, and, free from the mother's interference, the boys would learn the manly virtues. The world of letters and fine arts was left to women; the world of sports was the exclusive domain of men. The rougher the game, the more manliness it represented, and football became a national obsession. Colleges were rated as much for their football teams as for their academic programs. Indeed, academic and intellectual pursuits were seen to make a man soft and weak. If a man must indulge in activities of the mind, then it was essential that he counterbalance that behavior with bruising physical activity to restore his mind and body to health.

When World War I began, it was widely assumed that a generation of youth raised on sports, athletics, and particularly football would be moral and physical giants, ready to march bravely into war to serve their country. The results were disappointing. Over one-third of the three million men drafted into the armed services in 1917 were found to be unfit for service. The public reaction, however, was not to reject the notion that sports participation would build men, but to resolve to do the job better. Roosevelt and others chafed at the reluctance of President Wilson to enter the war. Military training and service were enormously popular ideas; they would build *men* out of *boys*. They would bring out the best in men (Dubbert 1979). War was romanticized, glorified, idealized; it represented the quintessential display of manhood.

In the years after World War I, sports continued to be enormously popular, although increasingly men took on the role of spectator rather than participant. Team sports drew huge audiences, which legitimized the spectator role (Gagnon 1976). Boxing also became enormously popular, and men like Jack Dempsey and Gene Tunney became household words. Tunney, however, failed to achieve hero stature because he was considered unmanly. He did feminine (expressive) things like reading poetry and talking about Shakespeare. Baseball hero Babe Ruth, a poor boy who made good by his own Herculean effort, was more the stuff of national worship (Dubbert 1979). Schools continued to emphasize athletic programs, and boys continued to feel the need to participate in team sports. The majority of men, however, now validated their masculinity vicariously; instead of active participation, they watched while others performed.

Throughout the depression years, many men (and women) found themselves once again living in poverty. Men's role as breadwinner was again threatened. National sports heroes helped to ease the burden of frustration and restore shattered self-esteem. And when World War II broke out young men were given an opportunity to develop their character and test their masculinity; once again old men could demonstrate their toughness by sending young men into battle. Football and war, then, became the two arenas for the validation of masculinity.

When the sons of the World War I doughboys marched off to war in 1942, the romanticized vision of war was very much intact. Good boys, normal boys, were eager to get into the war and into action. Military service was (and is) widely accepted as the *sine qua non* of masculine achievement, even though war, like work, has become highly automated (Gagnon

1976). The closer one came to actual battle, the more masculine one became. Hence the foot soldier, the marine, the Green Berets in Vietnam were seen as having more courage and aggressiveness than their officers (Stouffer 1949). Those who were unable to serve for reasons of health or age were pitied; those who avoided military service were vilified.

Thus, enormous emphasis is put on winning—in sports, in war, in business, and in politics. Boys are trained from an early age in organized sports activities like Little League and Pop Warner football. These organizations often are criticized for the pressure they put on young boys to perform and to win, but parents continue to encourage (or push) their sons to participate (Fasteau 1974). For high school boys, the importance of participation in sports is exceptionally high, particularly considering that few will regularly engage in sports as adults. Nevertheless, studies of high school students show that even the most average student athlete holds higher prestige than the most gifted intellectual student (Coleman 1961).

Participation in high school or college athletics, like military service, is a badge of masculinity that men continue to wear throughout their lives (Messner 1987). Political candidates who can claim war duty or college football duty have a significant advantage at the polling place. Every president from Harry Truman to George Bush had served in the military: none failed to campaign on his war record. Bill Clinton's opposition to the Vietnam War and his lack of military service were used against him during and after the election campaign. President Bush had once seemed unbeatable for reelection in the wave of popular support surrounding the Persian Gulf War. Unlike the Vietnam War, which the United States lost and which continues to be a divisive issue, the soldiers who fought in Desert Storm came home to a hero's welcome.

The conventional wisdom holds that sports builds masculine character, that it teaches boys how to compete and win in the rough and tumble world, and that it teaches them how to work with other people as part of a team. Indeed it is often argued that women are disadvantaged in their managerial careers because they lack the character-building experiences of team sports and military service (Harragan 1978). It could be as easily argued that successful athletes come to the game with physical talent and mental toughness in hand, and that the intense intrateam competition for playing time is more likely to induce individualism than team work. And what of the boys—the majority—who are not talented enough to make the team?

If very few men and boys actually play football, and if in fact it fails to build character, why does it remain a national obsession? Folklorist Alan Dundes argues that football, like the Boy Scouts, fraternities, and other exclusively male organizations, is a form of ritualized homosexual behavior. The equipment worn greatly exaggerates the male physique, enlarged head and shoulders, narrowed waist, genitals emphasized by a metal codpiece. So garbed, players are allowed to touch, pat, and hug each other in ways that are otherwise denied to men. By examining "football folk speech," Dundes concludes that football is analogous to what he calls *male verbal dueling*. Verbal dueling is the modern machismo version of physical dueling in more primitive cultures, where males who outmaneuvered or overpowered their adversaries further humiliated them by making them act like females, for instance, by forcing them to assume a supine position. Verbal dueling, like football, almost always takes place in the presence of others, and often includes explicit and symbolic language suggesting that the adversary is like a woman, hence not a man. Football involves such activities as "penetrating" the adversary's "end zone," "scoring," "spiking," "popping" an opposing player, or "making a pass" to a "tight end" or a "split end." Football players who fail to live up to their team's expectation are accused of being female; they are called "sissy," "pussy," or "cunt." Dundes concludes that on the football field

sexual acts carried out in thinly disguised symbolic form by, and directed towards, males and males only, would seem to constitute ritual homosexuality. American football is an adolescent masculinity initiation ritual in which the winner gets into the loser's end zone more times than the loser gets into his (Dundes 1978).

The popularity of football, indeed of all team sports, may be explained in its metaphorical relationship to war. Why, for instance, is the national anthem sung at the beginning of most sports contests if not to symbolize the warlike aspects of the tournament? The national anthem is probably heard more frequently at the start of major league baseball games than in any other time or place. Indeed the words "play ball" have, for all practical purposes, been permanently added to the concluding notes. Some children may not be aware that the words are not properly a part of the anthem.

What is the link between masculinity and money? To what extent does the provider role embody masculinity? Again, very little is known, except that the links are strong ones. Psychiatrists, for example, report that both men and women equate moneymaking with masculinity. For some men, the relationship is so strong that the loss of a job or a drop in income produces impotence. Even a relationship to a woman who earns a substantial income can be threatening to some men's libido. This reaction is not, of course, totally without foundation. Just as the man has learned to believe that his masculinity is related to his ability to earn money, so many women have learned that their future lies in marrying a man with a high earning capacity. Hence, for her as well as for him, the size of the paycheck becomes a measure of his masculinity (Gould 1976). How frequently does this occur? What mitigating variables apply? What demographic variables are significant? Very little is known beyond the fact that the relationship exists.

As work has become less physically demanding, the role of the business

executive has become a metaphor for masculine power and competitiveness. Like sports, business success as an expression of masculinity has its
roots in religion, but it goes back farther than the Victorian age. Weber
(1930) has argued that the phenomenal growth of capitalism would have
been impossible without Protestantism. Certainly Luther, and more particularly John Calvin, made sacred the right and obligation of men to work
hard, save their money, and "get ahead." The nineteenth-century robber
barons, entrepreneurs like John D. Rockefeller, Andrew Carnegie, Thomas
Edison, and Henry Ford, were the very embodiment of the Protestant Work
Ethic and were the heroes of their day. These men all came from poor
families, had little education, worked hard, were devout churchgoers, and
came to command huge enterprises and fortunes through their own industry. They were hailed for their capitalistic spirit, which was equivalent to
the rugged individualism of the frontiersman. They were the captains of
industry. Although they are often criticized as exploiters of both workers
and the environment, there remains an enormous respect, almost awe, for
their independence and their accomplishments. In our time, these values are
personified by men such as Donald Trump, Bill Gates, or perhaps H. Ross
Perot.

Today, the vast majority of business men are not entrepreneurs but hired
managers in modern conglomerates. And the hired manager has suffered a
lot of criticism over the years. From Sinclair Lewis' (1922) *Babbitt* to William Whyte's (1956) *The Organization Man*, contemporary writers have
decried the loss of integrity and the loss of individualism in the corporate
manager. As America's domination of the world's economy has shrunk, her
business leaders have taken the blame. They are frequently depicted as too
stupid, too short-sighted, or, worse, too weak and ineffectual to stand up
to Asian or European competitors. Michael Crichton's highly acclaimed
book *Rising Sun* (1992), for example, characterizes American business and
government leaders as "impotent" against the "assault" of Japanese business. The problem is not that business leadership no longer offers a test of
manhood, it is that American leaders are failing the test.

The Expressive Role

The expressive role of masculinity should more properly be labeled the
masculine *in*expressive roles. Bruce Feirstein (1982) spells out the issues in
the introduction to his marvelously insightful and funny book *Real Men
Don't Eat Quiche*:

"Real men don't eat quiche", said Flex Crush, ordering a breakfast of steak, prime
rib, six eggs, and a loaf of toast.
We were sitting in the professional driver's section of an all-night truckers' pit
stop somewhere west of Tulsa on I-44, discussing the plight of men in today's

society. Flex, a 225 pound nuclear waste driver who claims to be one of the last Real Men in existence, was pensive:

"American men are all mixed up today," he began, idly cleaning the 12-gauge shotgun that was sitting across his knees. Off in the distance, the sun was just beginning to rise over the tractor trailers in the parking lot.

"There was a time when this was a nation of Ernest Hemingways. Real Men. The kind of guys who could defoliate an entire forest to make a breakfast fire—and then go on to wipe out an endangered species hunting for lunch. But not anymore. We've become a nation of wimps. Pansies. Quiche eaters. Alan Alda types—who cook and clean and relate to their wives. Phil Donohue clones who are *warm* and *sensitive* and *vulnerable*. It's not enough anymore that we earn a living and protect women and children from plagues, famine, and encyclopedia salesmen. But now we're also supposed to be *supportive*. And *understanding*. And *sincere . . . .*"

Contemporary men face a dilemma. They increasingly are being asked to demonstrate their "feminine" side, that part of their nature that includes the expression of emotion; yet society continues to expect of them the instrumental behavior of "real men." The differences between women and men lie not in the extent to which they experience an inner life, but in the extent to which they reveal it to themselves and others. Since the male role requires that men not reveal themselves, men are under constant pressure to suppress something that is a natural part of their makeup. The inexpressive male who cannot or will not reveal himself to others becomes insensitive to both his own inner life and to the emotional expressions of others. Men who do not reveal themselves to others are not the recipients of other's disclosures, particularly of other men's disclosures, and hence "their concepts of the subjective side of other people—of other men as well as women and children—are often naive, crude, or downright inaccurate" (Jourard 1974).

Women and men both experience pressure to inhibit their feelings, but in almost opposite directions. Women feel pressured *not* to display anger or annoyance; for men, anger or annoyance are considered traditional masculine behaviors, and they feel pressure *to* express them. Women feel pressure *not* to express feelings of love and affection, to avoid rejection or hurt, but also because they sense that men dislike these displays. Men, however, feel pressure *to* express love and affection in sexual relationships and compassion and tenderness in nonsexual ones. Both women and men engage in emotional pretense. Women often express less emotion than they feel; men express more—sometimes as a way of gaining sexual intimacy (Davidson 1981).

Some men can and do, however, express their most intimate feelings to the women in their lives. They are more likely to reveal intimate information, particularly about personality and body concerns, the most sensitive of all, to a woman friend than to a male friend or a relative (Komarovsky 1976).

Feelings have been described as "the real male terror" (Goldberg 1976). To a greater or lesser degree, men block all feelings. Dependency is avoided, sometimes to an extreme; men are expected to be winners, not losers, to "make it on their own" without help from others. Passivity is related to dependency; men are expected to be active, to do something, anything, but not to be idle. Leisure becomes associated with passivity, then with laziness; so men fill their nonwork time with activities and feel uncomfortable if they are not busy all the time. Even such supposedly stress-reducing activities as sports or exercise programs become competitive. Active, independent males, of course, cannot ask for help, even for directions to the nearest gas station, without threatening their masculinity. If the problem becomes asking for help on a major undertaking, or for help with a mental or physical problem, it is even more threatening. Men who express fear are called by feminine names; they are "gutless," "wimps," they have "no balls."

Sadness also is incongruent with masculinity, and crying has historically been absolutely prohibited. President Bill Clinton may be the first world leader to cry in public and not lose all credibility, but he is already suspect in many quarters both because of his anti-war record and because of his stand on gays in the military. That is, to his critics, the fact that he displays sadness does not destroy his masculinity because they see it as lacking already.

The one emotion that men are free to express is anger, but even here there is a taboo. While little boys are expected to be aggressive, the expression of it is expected to be directed impersonally, against strangers, enemies, or competitors. At home or in school, in personal relationships, they are expected to be polite, considerate, and conforming. If they are aggressive to other boys or, worse, to girls, they are called bullies. From boyhood on, males are expected to treat girls and women as fragile and delicate creatures dependent on men for protection. The male is allowed to get angry at a woman only if she gives him some "righteous" cause for doing so, that is, only if she behaves in some unfeminine way. This repression of anger has the effect of stifling spontaneity and creating emotional distance between women and men.

Even gestures of pleasure may be seen as unmasculine. Expressions of high spirits, of freedom and spontaneity, are childlike behaviors, and real men are serious, they are stable and settled, they are goal-oriented. Impulsiveness, spontaneity, even loud and uninhibited laughter, are irrational. Would Flex Crush laugh out loud? Would he jump in the air, pour champagne over the coach's head, swat his teammates on the fanny with a towel when his team won the game?

Finally, the masculine role requires men to be objective and rational, so abstractions or paradoxes may be threatening. Men are expected to see the world in absolute terms, as black and white, as good and evil, as masculine and feminine. Gray areas or logical paradoxes create anxiety and distrust.

The Origins of Male Inexpressivity

The origins of male inexpressiveness are unclear, and there are at least two schools of thought. The first postulates that it has its roots in *homophobia*, the fear of homosexuality. Homophobia, in turn, stems from Christian prohibitions against the enjoyment of sex. The second approach argues that it is actually an instrumental role used to maintain male dominance and power over other men and especially over women.

Homophobia is "the irrational fear or intolerance of homosexuality" (Lehne 1976). It is generally associated with the fear of male homosexuality, and should more correctly be called *homosexism*, or sexism between individuals of the same sex. Homophobia is related to stereotypes about homosexuals that are not grounded in reality, stereotypes which suggest that homosexuals are afraid of the opposite sex, that they act like the opposite sex, that only certain occupations are appropriate for homosexuals, that homosexuals molest children, and that homosexuality is "unnatural."

The roots of homophobia go back to the beginning of Christianity. The Bible (particularly the New Testament) contains some prohibitions against homosexuality, and indeed against many forms of heterosexual behavior. The church, from the beginning concerned for social control and stability to insure its continued survival, was troubled by man's sexual drives and appetites. St. Paul, for instance, allowed that marriage could be good, but truly strong and good men would remain celibate. St. Augustine, like St. Paul, felt that sexual intercourse was fundamentally disgusting, degrading, shameful, and unclean. Therefore, celibacy was the desired state; but those who were too lustful to remain celibate should use sex without passion for the begetting of children. Sex within marriage was permitted, although it was not considered an integral part of marriage. Contraception was the major sin, more serious even than abortion.

St. Thomas Aquinas, more than any other Christian scholar, extended St. Augustine's views of sexuality in general to homosexuality and made it responsible for the fire and brimstone that brought down Sodom and Gomorrah. His case was based on St. Augustine's proposition that sexual organs were designed for and could only legitimately be used for procreation (Tannahill 1980). Prohibitions against nonmarital sex, contraception, and abortion generally have been relaxed except among Roman Catholics and fundamentalist Christians, but homophobia has persisted.

As religious beliefs have waned, the social sciences, particularly psychology, have taken their place in justifying homophobia. Psychology and psychiatry have consistently regarded homosexual behavior as deviant and have argued extensively as to whether it constitutes mental illness. Although the American Psychiatric Association has removed homosexuality from its list of mental illnesses, many Americans continue to look on it as a pathological condition capable of being cured (Lehne 1976).

For whatever reasons, homophobia is pervasive. A majority of people believe that homosexuality is "bad for society." Recent efforts by gay and lesbian activists to ban discrimination have met with enormous backlash. Colorado recently passed a statewide referendum forbidding local governments from passing gay rights legislation; and an even more stringent bill has barely failed twice in Oregon. Arguments against removing occupational discrimination against homosexuals center on the fear that they will "corrupt" their fellow workers, especially in occupations that require sharing living quarters, like firefighters or the military. Another concern is that removing the sanctions would allow homosexuals to molest or convert children. Fundamental religious groups argue simply that a homosexual lifestyle is an "abomination" and that the government ought not to be supporting or condoning it. While none of these views is supported by evidence, they continue to be held by a fairly substantial proportion of the population.

Highly homophobic individuals tend to be more status conscious, more authoritarian, and more sexually inflexible than low homophobic individuals. Homophobic individuals tend to support political repression and a double standard of sexual morality, and not to support equality between the sexes or civil rights for women and minorities. *Homosexist* individuals (those prejudiced against homosexuals) share a belief in the importance of rigid sex roles for the continuation of society, and they believe in the acceptability of authoritarian techniques to enforce their social beliefs.

Homosexist individuals, even those whose lives are not generally affected by homosexuality, are often also homophobic. Such prejudice persists, perhaps, because homophobia is used as a technique of social control to enforce norms of male sex-role behavior. Since men devalue homosexuality, homophobia becomes a norm that can be used to control men in their male roles. Any man can potentially (latently) be a homosexual, and as long as there are social sanctions against homosexuality, the fear of being labeled a homosexual is powerful enough to insure conformity with male roles, since there is no way to prove that one is not a latent homosexual (Lehne 1976).

The irony of homosexism is that it is not just gays and lesbians who are its victims. All males, and all females, have their behavior controlled through the negative social sanctions that await them if they deviate from traditional sex-role norms. Men are reluctant to enter into close relationships with other men, and when they do they are afraid to express their love for their men friends. Men are reluctant to enter into feminine activities or female-dominated occupations for fear of being labeled homosexual.

An alternative hypothesis to the homophobia explanation, however, argues that male inexpressivity is a tool that men use to maintain power. These alternative explanations are not, however, mutually exclusive. In itself, male inexpressiveness is of no particular value in our culture, but it is a requirement for assuming male roles of power. In other words, little boys learn to be inexpressive, not simply because of social expectations, but because the culture is preparing them to become decision makers and wielders of power (Sattel 1976). There are three points to consider in this argument.

First, inexpressiveness in a role is determined by the corresponding power (actual or potential) of the role. The more powerful the role, the less free the male is to express his feelings. We know that men are more expressive in some situations than in others, and that they can unlearn inexpressivity with women, particularly their wives (Narus and Fischer 1982; O'Leary and Donaghue 1978). But we do not know *how* power affects the equation.

Second, male inexpressiveness may represent an effort to control a situation and to maintain position. Communication is by definition a two-way process. If one person refuses to enter into a dialogue, the second cannot continue. Hence the nontalker has controlled the interchange. He has controlled not only what is *not* said but what *is* said.

Third, male inexpressiveness is an intentional manipulation of a situation when threats to the male position occur. Silence and inexpression are the ways men learn to consolidate power. By revealing only strategic portions of oneself, one never reveals the extent of one's resources, efforts, or rewards. Men talk about issues and ideas, not personal concerns, not because they are uninterested in the latter but because revealing themselves would give away power to the competition.

Inexpressiveness in males is probably a function of both homophobia and power building. Its cause is not as important as its effect, which is not only to cut men off from awareness of and sensitivity to the feelings of others, but also to cut them off from themselves.

Sex roles and sex-role stereotypes, then, characterize women and men as being polar opposites of each other. Literally from the moment of birth on, males and females are subjected to social approval or social sanctions, according to the extent to which their behavior corresponds to social expectations. But in spite of these forces, not all individuals conform to sex-role expectations, and not all conform to the same extent. We turn now to the study of individual adaptation to sex roles and particularly to some of the consequences of sex-typing.

PSYCHOLOGICAL ANDROGYNY

Social scientists have always looked at masculinity and femininity as bipolar ends of a single continuum. A person could be one but not the other. Personality tests that measure sex roles give one score. A man who tested as feminine, or a woman who tested as masculine, is considered a sexual deviant and might very well be treated for his or her disorder.

However, philosophers, poets, and playwrights have long recognized that every individual has both masculine and feminine traits and qualities. In literature, as in life, the most independent and inexpressive male could be touched by the love of a child or moved by the plight of an animal; the most helpless and frivolous woman could cope with danger or save her family from disaster when the occasion arose.

In recent years, psychologists have recognized that the bipolar system of sex-role differentiation "has long since outlived its usefulness, and it now serves only to prevent both men and women from developing as full and complete human beings" (Bem 1975). Instead, they have recognized that individuals should be "encouraged to become androgynous . . . they should be encouraged to be both instrumental and expressive, both assertive and yielding, both masculine and feminine, depending on the situational appropriateness of the various behaviors" (Bem 1975).

The concept of androgyny required new methods of measurement, and several have been developed. Probably the most frequently used is the Bem Sex Role Inventory (BSRI), which contains a list of sixty positive traits that have been divided equally into masculine, feminine, and neutral on the basis of sex-typed social desirability. Individuals' sex-role orientation is determined by their endorsement of masculine and feminine personality characteristics (Bem 1974). Individuals are considered masculine or feminine if they score above the mean on just one scale, "undifferentiated" if they score below the mean on both, and androgynous if they score above the mean on both (Bem, Martyna, and Watson 1976). Another frequently used measure is the Personality Attributes Questionnaire (PAQ) (Spence, Helmreich, and Stapp 1974). Although measurements and definitions have varied over time, the similarity of results suggests that androgyny is an important concept in understanding sex-role behavior.

Androgynous individuals differ from sex-typed individuals in one important aspect: They seem to have a larger repertoire of behaviors; they are able to adapt their behavior to the situation, even when doing so requires behaving in ways that might be considered inappropriate to their sex role. In a series of experiments with students at Stanford University, for example, researchers found that masculine and androgynous individuals were very much alike in terms of independence from social pressure, a masculine behavior. In a standard test of conformity, these subjects conformed in significantly fewer test trials than did the feminine ones (Bem 1975). On the other hand, feminine and androgynous individuals were more nurturing, both toward an infant and toward a fellow student with a personal problem, than were the masculine ones (Bem, Martyna, and Watson 1976). Androgynous individuals of both sexes were able to perform cross-sex behaviors with little reluctance. Sex-typed people avoided a wide variety of simple, everyday activities (nailing two boards together, winding a package of yarn into a ball) when those activities were stereotyped as more appropriate for the other sex. They also reported more discomfort and temporary loss of self-esteem when they were required to perform such tasks (Bem and Lenney 1976).

Androgynous people, whether male or female, tend to be alike; sex-typed ones tend to be different. Androgynous males have been found to be high in both the instrumental and expressive domains; androgynous females are high in both independence and nurturance. On the other hand, feminine males are low in independence, and masculine males are low in nurturance. Feminine women are low in independence, and masculine women are low in nurturance.

A major tenet of the androgyny literature has been that androgynous individuals are better adjusted mentally than sex-typed people, but this claim has not been entirely supported by the evidence. Instead, it appears that perhaps it is masculinity, not androgyny, that contributes to adjustment. In other words, androgynous women and both androgynous and masculine men all report high adjustment (Silvern and Ryan 1979). Feminine women appear to have lower self-esteem than androgynous or masculine women, and to be more introverted but not to differ particularly in physical or mental health. Contrary to popular belief, younger women do not seem to be any more likely to be androgynous than their middle-aged sisters (Hoffman and Fidell 1979).

Androgyny is as important for its impact on life choices as it is for its effect on behavior. And indeed sex type and life choice seem to be related. Feminine-typed women tend to have conservative attitudes about the role of women, to like housework (more than any of the other types), and to take full responsibility for child care and homemaking. They tend not to be employed outside the home, they are less educated, and are less economically advantaged than the other types. Masculine women, and to some extent androgynous women, seem to display an almost opposite pattern. They tend to exhibit a feminist pattern in their choices: to have higher education, to work outside the home, to have higher socio-economic status, and to have more liberal attitudes (Hoffman and Fidell 1979).

As we move to the study of management and organizational behavior, we will return repeatedly to the concept of androgyny. Again and again we will see that it is sex-role orientation, not sex, that seems to be significant in the way in which individuals behave, and the way in which they perceive and evaluate the behavior of others.

SUMMARY

To a greater or lesser extent, each of us is shaped by the larger society of which we are a part into attitudes, beliefs, and behaviors based upon our biological sex. Those attitudes, beliefs, and behaviors, in turn, serve to form the shape of our lives, affecting not only the roles we adopt but also our attitudes towards those roles. They affect not only the choices we make on a daily basis but also the choices that we make about careers and marriage, the two most important arenas for self-expression for most of us. As we will see throughout the rest of this book, they shape the way in which we present ourselves to the larger society, our motivations, our satisfactions, and our ambitions. They affect not only the way we perform but the ways in which our performance is evaluated by ourselves and others. They affect not only our expectations of ourselves and others, but the expectations that others have of us.

Sex-role theories often are used to explain the differential experience of women and men in organizations. They are used to support the argument that the problem is not discrimination but socialization. Women, taught from the cradle on to be passive, dependent, and nurturing, fail to make the kind of educational or career choices necessary to achieve success or fail to exhibit the kind of behavior necessary to be successful in male-dominated occupations. This explanation lays the problem anywhere but on the organization. Women can be blamed for failing to take the initiative to overcome the effects of historical discrimination; society can be blamed for socializing women and men into these roles. The solution is to train women to be more like men, confirming once again the "male is normal" hypothesis.

Sex roles and sex-role stereotypes should not be viewed as hopelessly deterministic. What has been learned can be unlearned; changes in social values follow changes in behavior, albeit slowly. Nothing has been more apparent in recent years than the extent to which women's lives are changing. What is less apparent, but certainly still visible, is the extent to which men's lives also are changing. If change persists, roles and stereotypes will adjust. What is seen as unusual or inappropriate behavior in one generation tends to become the norm that governs the next one. We already are seeing an erosion of the feminine stereotype, with more women incorporating masculine traits into their personalities without relinquishing their positive feminine traits. Perhaps some day we will also see an increase in the number of men who can maintain the positive qualities of masculinity and at the same time internalize the best of what is feminine.

But sex roles and sex-role stereotyping, which certainly do exist, cannot explain away the discrimination that continues to exist. Androgynous women and masculine women, willing and able to assume roles that include the positive masculine traits, still find themselves the victims of subtle, and sometimes not so subtle, discrimination. There is certainly a need to change stereotypes so that they more accurately reflect the reality of contemporary lives, but simply changing stereotypes will not bring an end to sex discrimination. Much of the responsibility for that lies within the organization.

6

Working Together

The relationships among and between the sexes have been the subject of confusion, concern, and conjecture for as long as civilization has existed. In song, poem, novel, and drama, as well as in the social sciences, writers both scientific and artistic have explored the dynamics of friendship, family, and love.

The entertainment media have often glorified men's friendships and ridiculed women's. They have presented male–female relationships in every conceivable form from every imaginable standpoint. The scholarly literature is small by comparison; it attempts to separate myth, stereotype, and legend from reality. Unfortunately, little is yet known or understood about these vastly complex relationships, and even less is known about the impact and importance of these relationships on organizational behavior.

Organizational research has examined informal relationships within informal structures, but little study has been done on how sex and gender affect these relationships. We know by observation that few rules about gender-appropriate work place behavior have evolved. Instead, the norms of the social world have prevailed. We observe that women relegated to low-paid, dead-end jobs seem to put a high value on their friendships with co-workers, but so also do men in low-level jobs. We observe that men in upwardly mobile careers tend to compete with male peers, and that women on a career track often look to women peers for encouragement and support. We are aware that women have often served as "office wife" to men managers, while women managers have been denied the same loyalty and attention from their female subordinates. We know that social and organizational taboos have discouraged romantic or sexual relationships, but we know that office romances and affairs occur.

This chapter will look at relationships between women and men, between women and women, and between men and men. It will attempt to describe the nature of these relationships and their implications for management.

MALE/FEMALE RELATIONSHIPS

Whenever women and men interact with each other, whether at work or at play, there is some level of sexual tension. How they choose to deal with that sexuality is determined by a great many factors. Often, appropriate and mutually agreeable sex roles are adopted, virtually unconsciously. At other times, however, behavior that might be appropriate and acceptable in a social situation is offensive or inappropriate in the work place. It often reflects both the inequality and the reciprocity of sexual roles in the larger society.

As social and organizational changes disrupt traditional status hierarchies, they also disrupt traditional sex-role relationships. We need to understand better both the nature of the nonromantic, not-sexual relationships between women and men in organizations, and the nature and consequences of romantic, sexual attraction relationships.

Nonromantic Relationships

Doctors have nurses, lawyers have legal secretaries, and managers have executive secretaries or administrative assistants. Occupational segregation puts men and women into reciprocal roles at work not unlike their reciprocal roles in the family. In these reciprocal roles, status and behavior expectations are clearly understood.

The metaphor of the office wife is a case in point. Secretaries or administrative assistants tend to take their status from the man they work for, in the same way that women have traditionally taken their status from their husbands. Secretaries, like wives, form attachments with a particular man; they treat him in a deferential manner and remain loyal to him over a long period of time. Secretaries often derive their rank and level of reward from the position of their bosses, not from their own skills or abilities. The higher the boss's rank, the higher the secretary's rank. A secretary achieves promotion by being assigned to a boss who gets promoted. In return, the boss receives a measure of status from his secretary. As with a corporate wife, the secretary has to be well dressed and well educated and make a pleasing impression, for her behavior reflects on her boss (Kanter 1977).

But in addition to these reciprocal characteristics of formal organizational roles, men and women tend to enact a reciprocal set of social roles in the informal structure of the organization. These roles also are an extension of socially sanctioned male–female roles played out in the larger society. One typology of roles humorously but quite accurately describes these interactive roles (Bradford, Sargent, and Sprague 1975).

The Macho Male and the Seductress. The male in this role is constantly asserting his male potency. Interactions with women usually have a sexual component to them. He asserts his dominance by calling attention to the woman's sexuality by commenting on her dress or appearance, then minimizing or denigrating her competence in other areas. His message is that she is a sexual object, not a competent person. The female reciprocal role, the seductress, is played by the woman who constantly asserts and reaffirms her sexual desirability through her dress, manner, or behavior. She exerts a certain power over the men by her ability to confer or withhold sexual favors. A woman may not consciously or deliberately play this role; it may be assigned to her by the men in the organization if she is seen as sexually attractive and potentially available (Kanter 1977). Both participants in these roles may gain satisfaction by reaffirming their sexuality.

For the seductress, attention is focused on her female status, rather than on her status as a competent member of the organization. Tension is generated between other women and men as well. She is recognized for her social role, not for her organizational role. When the woman is an unwilling or reluctant participant, she also may lose self-esteem.

This set of roles has become particularly troublesome with the extension of legal protections against sexual harassment. His conduct, if it creates a hostile, intimidating, or offensive work environment for his co-workers or subordinates, may cause him and his employer to face sexual harassment charges. Even if the seductress is playing her role voluntarily, the employer can be held liable for the harassment of other—less willing—victims.

The Chivalrous Knight and the Helpless Maiden. An important aspect of the masculine role in western cultures is that of provider and protector of women; men in the higher social classes in particular are expected to be polite, kind, and gentlemanly. They open doors for ladies; they help them out of cars and across the street; they refrain from using profanity around women and even avoid conversations about serious concerns like politics and business. They are polite, tolerant, and respectful. Further, they are taught such behaviors at an early age and are rewarded for them. Little wonder, then, that in the work world they tend to treat women in the same way. They protect them from tasks that require technical ability, skill, or responsibility. They protect them from any events that might create a conflict between their jobs and their marriages, such as raises, promotions, transfers, or travel. The woman who plays the reciprocal role of the helpless maiden, like the seductress, may find it useful in the short run. She may be protected from onerous duties or, more importantly, she may be protected from making mistakes.

The helpless maiden also may be protected from taking necessary and useful risks. She may surrender the opportunity to become, and to be seen as, a competent person. The woman who exploits the role of helpless maiden, by appearing helpless or inept, may be able to manipulate males to do her bidding, but in the long run she will pay a price. His beliefs about her helplessness or dependency may make it impossible for him to avoid being manipulated. If he confronts her, he is admitting that she is capable of performing on her own, without his help or protection. Yet, an admission of her competence challenges his perceptions of his own masculinity. It is little wonder that these men find themselves angry and frustrated.

The Protective Father and the Pet. This relationship is akin to a father–daughter relationship. The pet is not seen as sexually available, yet she serves as a kind of cheerleader or mascot for the older male. Pets are valued for their support of male humor and displays of prowess. They are expected to observe and approve from the sidelines but not to participate. Occasional displays of competence are tolerated, even approved, because of their rarity. The pet may get a certain amount of visibility in this role, but the attention is again on her femininity, rather than on her competence.

Young women sometimes may confuse this role set with a mentor/protégé relationship. However, the protective father often lacks the organizational power necessary to be an effective mentor. Not recognizing his powerlessness, the woman may welcome the attention of an older man who seems to take an interest in her career, introduces her to other important people, and so on. The protective father, rather than sponsoring her continued achievement, is mainly involved in protecting her, sometimes to the point of overprotection. The mentor encourages his protégé to take risks, to express opinions, and to develop competence and independence; the protective father values his pet for her childlike qualities and encourages her to be dependent on him.

The Tough Warrior and the Nurturant Mother. The tough warrior is the quintessential inexpressive male. He is independent and self-sufficient, suppressing all emotions; he may carry this role to such an extreme that he becomes isolated from peers or subordinates, to the dysfunction of the performance of his duties. The nurturant mother becomes a source of solace and support. She fills a kind of saintly role, not sexually available and not subject to sexual pursuit; instead, she serves as the confidante, the counselor, and the nurturer (often in a real sense, as in bringing the coffee).

While this role is relatively safe, it too has negative consequences. The mother is rewarded for service, rather than for action, and she is perceived as being an "emotional specialist," a stereotypically feminine characteristic that may be interpreted as being sentimental or irrational (Kanter 1977). Further, the woman in this role must avoid being seen as a dominant or controlling mother, so she must avoid criticism and deal solely in support, approval, and encouragement. She thereby forfeits the opportunity to demonstrate her critical or evaluation skills.

The most serious outcome of these feminine roles is that they emphasize the woman's feminine role over her organizational role. They all have the effect of suppressing her competence as well as her confidence.

Either party can, of course, refuse to play the reciprocal role, but it is not always easy to do so. The feminine role expectancy includes being compliant and cooperative; the masculine role includes being sexually aggressive. When the macho male flirts, the expected feminine response is to flirt back. When the seductress flirts, the expected masculine response is to escalate the flirtatousness. Women sometimes engage in a "pseudoseduction plot," manipulating male colleagues by subtly suggesting that they are sexually interested and available but yet always avoiding any sexual activity (Hively and Howell 1980). Other women, who proclaim that they only want friendship with a man, then feel rejected and offended if he does not indicate at least some sexual or affective interest (Safilios-Rothschild 1977). Refusing to respond to these behaviors requires overcoming long years of social conditioning.

The situation gets even harder when the intent is to be genuinely helpful. When the chivalrous knight, with only the kindest of intentions, assumes that the woman could not, and would not want to, understand the budget, it is very difficult indeed to risk offending him by refusing to play the helpless maiden. The alternative that seems safest may be the mother role, but this may not be available to young women.

The best alternative is to abandon these inappropriate modes of behavior and to insist upon sex-neutral organizational roles, but that, too, is no simple task. The traditional male/female organizational roles are to a great extent a mere extension of the social roles that have evolved as an intrinsic part of the industrial/Victorian era. So long as these roles were accepted and acceptable to all, few problems arose. They represented comfortable and familiar ways of interacting in a nonsexual way.

But in recent years the social order has been challenged. Many women are moving into nontraditional occupations, and some of them wish to adopt nontraditional sex roles as well. Recognizing that the traditional roles restrict their behavior and limit their options, they actively seek to abolish the remnants of patriarchy that persist in organizations.

Other women, however, have achieved new organizational positions but have no desire to discard old social roles that they find comfortable and effective. Many men, feeling highly threatened by the "new" women who demand equal treatment, deliberately cling to old behaviors that keep women in a submissive and passive role. Other men, however, genuinely and sincerely wish to help and not to hinder. But they face a real dilemma. If they hold the door open for a woman, she may be offended; and if they do not hold it open, she may be offended. Common sense says that whoever gets to the door first, or is carrying the smallest load, would open the door, but common sense does not always prevail. If a man compliments a woman on her appearance, is it a harmless, friendly gesture? Is it a sexual approach? Or is it a subtle put-down, emphasizing her feminine characteristics rather than her competence? If he doesn't express some sexual interest in her, will she feel rejected and insulted? If he compliments her on her work, is he being patronizing? If he criticizes her work, is it a valid critique or a sexist attack? If he invites her to join him at an important business lunch, is he acting as a mentor or as a protective father? If he includes her in an important business trip, is it business or monkey business?

The problem is real for both women and men. The old roles are no longer appropriate, the emerging ones are ill-defined. Roles function in our society to provide order and stability, and they are derived through consensus. Those who are bound by roles must agree on at least the basic elements of expectations and behavior. And this is where we are at present. Many people, but by no means all, have rejected the existing role expectations for masculine and feminine behavior at work, but no consensus exists as to what new role expectations should replace them. In the meantime, a lot of confusion, pain, embarrassment, and anger are occurring.

Romantic Relationships

As long as the sexual segregation of organizations kept women in subordinate positions, the issue of overt sexual involvement was kept at bay. It is true that women often have been treated as sexual possessions in an organization and prized for their sexual attractiveness. Many work places are characterized with a great deal of sexual energy and activity. Clearly, the office romance has always existed, as has the problem of sexual harassment. But taboos against sexual relationships between high-ranking males and low-ranking females also existed. If these taboos did not prevent office romances, they did serve to keep them discreet.

In recent years, women have increasingly moved into occupations and organizational levels formerly dominated by men. Taboos that prevented a male manager from a sexual liaison with his secretary no longer apply when differences in status and power are reduced. Further, the propinquity of working relationships, plus the shared emotions of working together, may arouse a powerful attraction. When two people work together on tasks that involve high levels of ability, close coordination, and intense competition, a good deal of emotional energy is generated (Mainiero 1986). When the co-workers are women, they may develop a strong friendship. When the co-workers are men, they may enjoy a sense of comradeship, or they may compete for dominance in the situation. If the co-workers are a man and a woman, a number of outcomes are possible. They may experience differing emotions. She may feel a strong sense of friendship, as she would toward a woman colleague, while he experiences a sense of competition. However, since workers do not leave their sexuality at the door when they enter the work place, one or the other or both may experience a strong sexual attraction.

Sexual attraction, of course, may or may not lead to a romantic involvement. People may refrain from entering into a romance because they fear the consequences. A senior person entering into a romance with a subordinate may lose respect in the organization and jeopardize his/her career; for the junior member, the fear may be damaging to one's own self-image and esteem, or the esteem of others, especially if doubts are raised as to whether the person is receiving organizational rewards in exchange for a personal relationship. Finally, of course, a romance may jeopardize the participants' home and family, especially if one or both is married or involved in a committed relationship (Anderson and Hunsaker 1985).

Even when there are no hierarchical differences, a person who is attracted to a co-worker may fear that any sexual advance will be misinterpreted, rejected, or perceived as inappropriate, and could even lead to charges of sexual harassment. Although for many people the work place offers the primary setting for making new acquaintances, most people are there, in fact, to do their jobs and to earn a living. They typically plan to be there for a long time, so any awkwardness associated with sexual advances, or perceived sexual advances, is apt to have long-term consequences. Further, differences in status or hierarchical level affect the ability of individuals to make or respond to sexual overtures. As a result, people often make these overtures in ways that are indirect, ambiguous, and susceptible to multiple interpretations (Gutek, Morasch, and Cohen 1981).

A study conducted in the waiting areas of two metropolitan airports offers some insights to the potential problems of organizational romance. Respondents were individuals who acknowledged that they had been a third-party observer of a romantic relationship between two people in the same organization (Quinn 1977). It tells a great deal about the sensitivity of the subject that these essentially anonymous people, killing time between flights, were the only subjects available to talk about office romances.

When the perceived motives of male and female partners in office romances were compared and evaluated, three types of relationships appeared:

- *The Fling* occurs when both the male and female have "ego" motives, that is, a desire for excitement, ego satisfaction, or adventure. The fling is characterized by a high level of excitement on the part of both participants, who often believe that the relationship is going to be of short duration.
- *True Love* occurs when both participants have love motives, that is, people with sincere motives seeking companionship, love, and a spouse. True love usually, but not always, occurs between two unmarried people and leads to marriage.
- *The Utilitarian Relationship* occurs when the male has ego motives and the female job motives. He meets his needs for excitement or ego satisfaction while she meets her needs for advancement, job security, or increased power (Quinn and Lees 1984).

Even if proximity and motive are favorable to the start of a romance, certain characteristics of the work place may serve as deterrents. The important work group characteristics, which often are interrelated, are rules and expectations, closeness of supervision, closeness of interpersonal relationships, and intensity of the work. Many organizations have explicit rules against romantic entanglements, more or less strictly enforced, and others have rather firm expectations. On the other hand, in some organizations, the expectation is that sexual activity will occur, and women are hired as much for their sexual attractiveness as for their work skills. Close supervision and the existence of a spouse or a committed relationship act as deterrents, and the work group sometimes expresses disapproval. The lovers may respond by breaking off the relationship or by becoming more discreet. Finally, very intense or critical work is usually, but not always, a deterrent. Relationships may flourish because there is not enough work to do and people are bored. However, on occasion, great pressure that includes long hours and intense concentration leads to romantic involvement (Quinn 1977).

Inclination or opportunity for a sexual liaison does not necessarily mean that one will occur. But the man and woman who work closely together may suffer from the suspicion that they are romantically or sexually involved, and suffer the consequences of that suspicion. It is clearly a fallacy to assume that whenever a woman and man are seen enjoying each other's company either that there is a sexual attraction between them or that attraction always leads to bed. In reality, a series of stages lies between attraction and sexual consummation, a developmental sequence that varies in duration:

- *Curiosity*: The couple is interested in getting to know each other.
- *Exploration*: When proximity occurs and curiosity is aroused, the couple looks for ways to spend more time together, either socially or professionally.
- *Friendship*: The couple finds mutual interests, begins to share thoughts and feelings. They make time to be together.
- *Intimacy*: The couple takes the risk of revealing their vulnerability, admitting weaknesses, failures, ambitions, and expectations to each other.
- *Sexuality*: Strong sexual desires and passions are aroused; the intimacy is consummated.
- *Commitment*: The pair decides to build a future together (Josefowitz 1982).

Most relationships stay within the first two stages. And of course the first four stages could be used to describe same-sex friendships as well as mixed-sex ones. It is possible for people to have intimate friendships, even to be sexually attracted to each other, without having intercourse. Nevertheless, their attraction, whether consummated or not, will not go unnoticed and will have consequences for the individuals and for the organization (Bender 1979). The impact on the organization will depend on a combination of four factors: visibility of the relationship, behavior changes in the participants, reactions of other members of the organization, and the over-all impact on the system (Quinn 1977).

Couples usually try to keep their relationships secret, either because of rules forbidding fraternization or because of the fear of gossip or disap-proval. However, efforts at secrecy usually are doomed to failure. Work groups are highly sensitive to even slight changes in behavior. Being seen away from work together, having longer or more frequent conversations, or lunching together may arouse curiosity and gossip, even in the absence of direct evidence like being caught in the supply closet. Of course, if either person is operating out of ego motives, it will be necessary to reveal the relationship, which sometimes is done subtly but effectively.

Behavior changes can be positive or negative. Some people become en-ergized; they are happier, easier to get along with, more willing to work. Others change for the worse; they become preoccupied, make costly errors, increase their absences or tardiness. They may become either indifferent to or highly sensitive to criticism. In a utilitarian romance, changes of power may occur. The male in the higher position is able to give the female her desired rewards, favorable treatment, increased power, or advancement; at the same time, he may become less accessible to other subordinates.

Reactions of other members of the organization may run the gamut from approval and encouragement to strong disapproval and punishment. If each person in the couple is unmarried and no power shifts are involved, others may enjoy a vicarious romantic relationship or at least remain indifferent. But if the affair is not perceived as legitimate, or when competence and power changes are pronounced, members begin to develop strategies for coping with the relationship (Collins 1983). These might include anything from counseling or advising one or both members on the negative effects of their behavior, to blackmail, ostracism, and quitting.

A number of points can be made in summarizing the sexual element of contemporary organizational life. The work place is increasingly a primary setting for establishing new relationships. As women increasingly move into new levels in the hierarchy and into nontraditional female occupations, the old rules and taboos against organizational romances are no longer effec-tive. Competent, ambitious people find each other attractive; and when women and men are together, that attraction can turn to sexual desire, and that desire is sometimes consummated. Whether or not a couple is sexually active, any changes in their behavior or performance will be noted by other members of the organization. They will be the subject of office gossip and, if others in the organization feel resentful or disapproving, they may be subject to negative sanctions. Although there is the possibility for the de-velopment of sincere love relationships leading to marriage, a consequence that would meet with organizational approval, there is also the possibility that the attraction will cause problems for the couple and have negative impacts on the organization, in the form of disruption, loss of productivity, and increased turnover.

A corollary to this concern is that people may avoid working together for fear that a mutual romantic attachment might develop; that a nonmutual, nonreciprocated attraction might cause embarrassment; or that, even in the absence of any involvement, speculation or gossip will hurt careers or reputations. To the extent that such fears discourage males from working with competent females, there can be serious damage to the females' careers and serious loss of productivity.

From a management perspective, office romances have become even more troubling since the Supreme Court's decision in *Meritor v. Vinson*. Employers may be found guilty of illegal sexual harassment, even if the couple has had an ongoing sexual relationship, particularly if one party (usually the man) is in a position of power or authority. The issue the courts will consider is not whether the relationship was voluntary, but whether it was unwelcome or unwanted.

Management is not very good at dealing with these situations. In the past, when rules or taboos discouraged fraternization, management might have taken steps to end a romance that became public knowledge, usually by firing, transferring, or demoting the woman. That remedy still is used frequently; but in cases where the couple is on equal levels or the woman is higher in rank, it is less likely that she will be the one punished (Collins 1983). The most frequent managerial response is no response, but there are times when management cannot or should not ignore the matter. In those cases, several specific remedies should be considered:

- reevaluating and clarifying fraternization, nepotism, and sexual harassment policies, communicating them clearly to members, and applying them consistently and fairly;
- making counseling or other resources available to members having difficulty dealing with feelings of attraction;
- raising the topic as a legitimate issue as a part of team-building efforts (Driscoll and Bova 1980);
- treating the relationship as a conflict of interest rather than a moral issue;
- persuading the couple that the person least essential to the company (in reality usually the woman) or both should leave the organization and helping the ousted person find other employment (Collins 1983).

None of these remedies is easy to implement. The nepotism/fraternization policy issue becomes increasingly complex as co-habitation, homosexuality, and singleness become increasingly common lifestyles. The company must create policies that are realistic and enforceable, and that provide the protections against abuse which such policies were designed for originally (Bender 1979). The other remedies require that management acknowledge and discuss the issue of sexuality in their organizations, and most of them are poorly equipped for such a task (Jamison 1983).

Individuals can take some steps to avoid having sexual attraction interfere with their working relationships. First, they must recognize that their actions will not go unnoticed. Women and men who work together, especially if their work requires meals or travel together, must be like Caesar's wife: they not only must avoid sin, they must avoid the appearance of sin. Women can refuse to play "the seductress" or to play out the "pseudoseduction plot." Both men and women must be sensitive to the concerns of spouses and recognize that, legitimate or not, there inevitably will be some curiosity, at the least, about a work partner who is a potential sex partner (Bender 1979). Good working relationships often require social as well as task-related interactions. But couples who spend time alone together increase the likelihood that they will be the subject of gossip. Three's a crowd, according to an old axiom, and a crowd may protect reputations.

So far we have been talking about ways to avoid gossip. But what happens to couples who feel a strong attraction but who cannot or choose not to consummate the relationship? The conventional wisdom (or pop psychology) suggests that couples can resolve this problem, like any problem, by acknowledging it and talking openly about it. However, such an approach seems fairly unrealistic. Women are so thoroughly socialized to be sexually passive that few women would be willing or able to broach the subject to a male co-worker. Men who are taught to be sexually aggressive have little experience in articulating feelings of any kind, much less feelings of sexual ambivalence or restraint. Either party, however, may find some help in talking out the situation with a trusted same-sex friend, preferably one who is not a member of the organization.

FEMALE/FEMALE RELATIONSHIPS

There are two opposing paradigms of women's relationships with other women, and to at least some extent each is grounded in reality. On the one hand, women are seen as having close, supportive, long-lasting and intimate nonsexual relationships with other women; and on the other hand, women often are viewed as treating other women with distrust, suspicion, or outright dislike; women can be friends or foes. In some ways, these two types of relationships are analogous to the two female stereotypes of women: as devoted wife or as temptress. In organizational settings, each of these types of relationships exists and to some extent is detrimental to the advancement of women.

Women as Friends

Studies of children's relationships show sex differences from preschool age on. Little boys are more "sociable" and more "affiliative" than little girls, in the sense that they interact more frequently in a positive social way with other children in their age groups. Girls have fewer of these interactions, but they are more apt to like the people with whom they interact, even if their friends' behavior occasionally disappoints them. In the early school years, girls focus their play in intensive relations with one or two "best friends," while boys play in larger groups. At the junior high school age, young girls establish a closer degree of intimacy in their friendships and reveal more personal secrets than do boys; possibly because of this self-disclosure they may be less likely than boys to accept a newcomer into their "inner circle," although they may be friendly toward her (Maccoby and Jacklin 1974).

This pattern of intimacy in friendship continues at least through college age. Women and men tend to have equivalent numbers of friends and to put the same value on friendship, but their interactions are different. Women prefer getting together with friends "just to talk." Men prefer activities such as sports. Women are more likely to talk about people and relationships; men are more likely to talk about work, money, and leisure activities, including sports (Bischoping 1993). While members of each sex say they value intimacy and having intimate friends, they seem to have different standards for assessing intimacy (Caldwell and Peplau 1982).

Adult women tend to continue the pattern of intimate friendships with their "best friends," although by college age they seem to have expanded the scope of their acquaintances. The number and the intensity of relationships depends on factors such as age, employment, and marital status (Wright 1982; Caldwell and Peplau 1982). Nevertheless, the media often portray women continuing these childhood patterns, not only sharing intimate secrets with other women but conspiring with them against men, usually their husbands. Thus, Lucy continually plotted with Ethel to manipulate Desi, and *Thelma and Louise* was a box office hit. To what extent these depictions reflect reality for adult women is unclear. Much more attention has been focused on the hostility between women.

Women as Foes

It is frequently argued that women must depend on men for their support, survival, and status. Men are valued for their ability to provide and protect, and women must compete with each other for the attention, and ultimately the marriage, of the most desirable men. This perception is also reflected in the media, most often perhaps in soap operas, where men constantly are portrayed as sex objects over which beautiful but desperate women compete in the most aggressively manipulative ways possible. If this view is accurate, then it would support the suggestion that the "best friend" sharing of intimacies begins to disappear after puberty.

A psychoanalytic view posits that there are indeed barriers between women and argues that they are rooted in the mother/daughter relationship (Caplan 1981). As young girls become conscious of gender identity and the rules of behavior that are governed by one's sex, they recognize their similarities to their mothers, both physically and in the way that they are viewed by society. How they are viewed, of course, is as nurturant, and little girls recognize very early that they will be valued primarily for their success in this role. This recognition plants the seeds for feelings of both alliance and hostility between mother and daughter, which in turn generalizes to all relationships between women. The barriers between women come from several sources:

1. The nurturant role is taught to young girls so early in life that they may be expected to become nurturers while they still feel the need to be nurtured. As adults, their husbands may maintain an emotional distance, and they turn to other women or their daughters to satisfy their need to be nurtured. Geographic mobility may further cut them off from extended families and networks of friends. When a woman turns to a friend, it is with a real sense of need and also with a conviction that the woman ought to be available to nurture her. If she is not, the rejection produces a sense of rage.

   The nurturant role also can explain jealousy between women. Some girls are taught that their activities are restricted to their ability to "look attractive, act nice, be helpful, and take care of others;" they are discouraged from doing anything active, productive, or pleasurable outside those limits. When they grow up, they must rely on a man to take care of them, but they cannot approach or request a commitment from him directly. They must achieve a commitment by being as conspicuously attractive, nice, helpful, and nurturant as possible. The only things that can get in the way of success are failure to be as attractive, nice, helpful, and nurturant as necessary, or another woman, or both. Women come to direct their anger and fear both at themselves and at other women, not at the men they compete for.

2. The devaluing of women, which is so pervasive in our society, causes both women and men to place less value on the friendship, judgment, and opinions of women than of men. Women spend time with other women only when there is no chance to spend it with a man. Since women tend to put a low value on their own worth, they tend to put the same low value on the worth of others like them. This devaluing of women explains the oft-heard statement by women that "I really don't like women; I prefer the company of men." Perhaps what they are really saying is that they want to be like men, superior to women.

3. Constraints are placed on the behavior of girls that are not placed on boys. Limits are placed on physical activity, sexual play and exploration, and the expression of anger and aggression, because they are inconsistent with the nur-

turant role. In adult life, women who deviate from these restrictions are viewed negatively and are ostracized by other women. These reactions are fueled by fears that untraditional behavior might be threatening to men or, even worse, might be attractive to them.

4. The fear of homosexuality, or the fear of rearing a homosexual child, limits the physical interactions between a mother and daughter in ways that do not apply to mother/son, father/son, or father/daughter relationships. There is, of course, a certain amount of unconscious sexual content in the daily interactions of parents and children, especially small children. Despite incest taboos, the norm of heterosexuality and the higher value put on male children permit a good deal of physical intimacy and eroticism between a mother and her infant son. Between mothers and daughters, however, the homosexual taboo may limit these expressions. Fathers, on the other hand, are in general less nurturant and spend less time in caring for children of either sex. So while the fear of homosexuality might inhibit his relationships with a male child, the issue is moot since he does not tend to the child anyway. And the daughter, who receives less nurturing from her mother and might benefit from heterosexual contact with her father, is denied it.

The preference for heterosexuality also may explain hostility between adult women. Female expressiveness and male inexpressiveness are seen as a sort of divine plan occurring in nature. It follows that relationships between females will acquire a level of emotional intensity not found in male/male or male/female relationships. Both women and men subscribe to this myth of the greater emotionality of women and fear the emotional energy generated in relationships between women. While a man may tolerate a woman's emotional outbursts, a woman may respond with an equally intense outburst of her own. In order to avoid arousing feelings that they cannot suppress, they may avoid close relationships with women all together.

5. The very similarity between women, both physical and emotional, is a source of hostility between women. Because of this similarity, women see other women as a kind of mirror image of themselves. Daughters look at their mothers and say "That's me in thirty years" and to the extent that what they see is limited and repressed, they experience disappointment and resentment. The similarity exacerbates the feeling that children generally have that their parents can read their minds. Since the mother spends the most time with the children, and since she is most like the girl child, the child may experience feelings of intrusiveness and of loss of privacy. She may find it particularly difficult to break away from her mother at adolescence (Caplan 1981).

These five sources of hostility create barriers between all women, not just mothers and daughters. One could question the Freudian determinism of the argument, but there is a certain compelling logic about it nonetheless. There is little evidence that this hostility is universal, but that may be irrelevant. To the extent that such hostility does exist, this psychological explanation for it is probably as good as any. It does seem to explain why the "best friend" behavior of prepubescent girls sometimes turns into suspicion and hostility at adolescence.

Women in Organizations

In organizations, evidence supports both paradigms of female relationships. Women tend to form very close, stable relationships with their coworkers, but they also experience conflict and competition with peers, subordinates, and superiors.

Women as Friends. Often women at work, particularly those in occupations with little opportunity for upward mobility, form very cohesive peer groups. For these women, peer group acceptance may be more important than other aspects of their job and as important a reward as pay. This behavior is sometimes threatening to out-groups in the organization and leads to the perception that "women always stick together."

This behavior, however, may be a function of the blocked upward mobility of these occupations, rather than of their being female. People get "stuck," that is, reach the top of their career level, in organizations for a variety of reasons, but women are stuck almost from the beginning. Their career ladders tend to be short, and the differences in pay and other rewards between the bottom and the top are relatively small. For "stuck" employees, peer group norms are likely to develop around and support the generally lower level of aspirations. For one thing, these people stay together on the job longer than people who are moving upward, so the group membership is fairly stable and very important.

Powerful others in the organization have little to offer "stuck" employees in terms of rewards, and so group members tend to focus attention on each other, rather than on higher status people. In fact, group solidarity is often maintained by criticizing or ridiculing higher level groups or individuals. These groups can be compared to adolescent gangs that develop norms of mutual aid and loyalty. Pressure to remain loyal to the group is sometimes so strong that the offer of a promotion may create a dilemma. Promotions for clerical workers often carry small rewards, either intrinsic or extrinsic, and accepting the promotion often means exclusion from the group. Since for women, especially, there may be no comparable group at the next level, the result may be isolation (Kanter 1977).

The existence of these groups can be explained as a function of rewards; women fail to find intrinsic rewards in the kind of work that is permitted to them and turn instead to the rewards that come from group membership (Kanter 1977). However, it also may be that women form and maintain these close-knit groups because they are seeking (and finding) nurturance. If, in fact, women fail to find the desired level of emotional intimacy and support in their primary relationships with their husbands, they may find it instead in their secondary relationships with their co-workers. And since

these relationships endure over long periods and absorb a substantial portion of time, and since women's relationships tend to be intense, it is not
at all surprising that these groups become extremely important and at least
potentially satisfying.

Women as Foes. On the other hand, many upwardly mobile career
women report conflict and competition with women peers, indifferent or
hostile reactions from support staff, and hostility from senior women in
their organizations, all of which would support the notion of hostility
among women. A number of explanations can be offered:

Women Subordinates. If it is true that women look to other women for
support and nurturance and feel angry and frustrated when they fail to get
it, then surely women who find themselves virtually isolated in organizations could be expected to experience such feelings. As women break into
new occupational areas, they find themselves simultaneously isolated and
visible. They must not only be highly competent, but also must be able to
understand and participate in the political and strategic processes of the
organization. Organization change tends to occur very slowly, and management may move very cautiously in appointing and promoting women.
So, while there may be promotional opportunities for many men, there may
be far fewer for women. In reality, the only real competition that an ambitious woman encounters may come from the other women at her level.
She finds herself wishing for support and friendship from the people who
are least available to give it to her.

If the young woman executive looks to her secretary or administrative
assistant for support, she may not find it there either. It is almost a truism
that clerical staff are less helpful to women than to men bosses. The reasons
probably have more to do with the devaluing of women than with a need
for nurturance.

First, workers in general prefer to work for people with power. Especially
for women in the clerical ranks, the only avenue to advancement may be
to attach oneself to a powerful and upwardly mobile employer. If a female
subordinate perceives her female boss as being less powerful or less pro-
motable, there is little incentive to provide the level of support and services
that she would to a similarly placed male.

Second, there is a traditional role involved in the boss/subordinate relationship which requires that the boss be dominant and the subordinate
submissive. This relationship is possible between a male boss and a female
secretary, even if the woman is considerably older than the man. The
woman playing the office wife or mother not only provides direct job services but also may serve as both his listening post and spokesperson, giving
and receiving information that is important to him. However, among
women, the only basis for dominance/submission is the mother/daughter
relationship, one that often is filled with conflict. In effect, the subordinate
woman responds to her female manager as she would to her mother; she

may, for instance, withhold information from her and spread gossip about her. The situation tends to be further exacerbated if there is a considerable age difference between the two.

Third, clerical women may feel that the woman manager's position or behavior is sex-role deviant or inappropriate. She may perceive the woman as neglecting or abandoning her role as wife or mother, in effect denigrating those roles. If, for instance, a woman has sacrificed her own abilities or ambitions for the sake of her family, she may strongly resent a woman who sacrifices her personal life for the sake of her career.

Fourth, women in professional or managerial positions often must distance themselves socially from the secretarial ranks in order to achieve legitimacy in the organization. They may have to reject offers of friendship from the very women that they count on for administrative services. If they have no peer group at their own level, they will seem very aloof and isolated to their subordinates.

Finally, a woman's work often is seen as less important and less urgent than a comparable man's. In a situation where managers must share the services of a secretary or a steno pool, the clerical staff may give the man's work higher priority than the woman's. For all of these reasons, and probably many others, women in nontraditional roles often find themselves abandoned or sabotaged by the people they most expect to support them.

Women Superiors. Women at entry and middle-management levels find that they meet with competition from women at their own levels and antagonism from women at lower levels. Often in their search for support, they turn upward in the organization to the women who have "made it," only to find that there, too, they are unwelcome. One might expect that these women, of all women, having struggled to achieve success in a male-dominated culture, would willingly offer a helping hand to rising younger women. Usually they do, but sometimes they do not. Some of these women respond with an attitude that says "If I can do it, anybody can. I didn't need anyone to help me, and neither do they." There are a number of reasons why this attitude occurs.

First, these women may have been co-opted by the system. In order to survive and flourish, they have taken on the attitudes, behaviors, and protective cover of the male culture.

Second, these women enjoy not only the benefits and perquisites that come to all successful people, but also the attentions that come from being the only woman in an all-male group. They see other women as competitors and as threats to their privileged position. They certainly do not want other women to enjoy the fruits of success without having to go through the same struggles that they did (Staines, Tavris, and Jayaratne 1974).

It would be a mistake, however, to conclude that this behavior is a sex-related trait. Many men believe that success is a product of individual effort and achievement, take pride in the fact that they have worked very hard to reach success, and take pleasure in seeing that younger people struggle just as hard or harder than they did. Maccoby reports in *The Gamesman* (1976) that 40 percent of the male managers he interviewed believed that "the fittest should survive." Once again, a double standard exists. Successful women, but not men, somehow are expected to "pave the way" for those of their sex who aspire to follow them.

The conclusion we come to is that the structure of most organizations encourages women to remain in low-opportunity positions and rewards them for doing so with important and satisfying peer group relationships. The woman who seeks achievement in a nontraditional occupation may find herself alternatively cut off from and in competition with other women, at her own level, at the subordinate level, and at the top-management level.

MALE/MALE RELATIONSHIPS

Men's relationships with other men have always been seen as being characterized by warmth, good fellowship, laughter, and caring. Men are assumed to prefer the company of other men and to have significant and long-lasting friendships. As we saw earlier, organizations like the Boy Scouts and the YMCA were successful in the early part of the century because they gave men a legitimate reason to spend time away from the influence and domination of women. Throughout history, men have cherished and protected their right to participate in all-male groups. The hunting party of tribal societies may have been organized for the purpose of providing food, but some sociologists maintain that it was more important as a social phenomenon since, for one thing, the women and children had to continue to gather food while the hunting party was away. The hunting party has almost exact replicas in the hunting, fishing, and camping trips that some men enjoy for recreational purposes today. The men's hut in tribal societies was a place where women were excluded, and where the men could both talk "men's talk" and discuss the important issues facing the tribe. Today, men withdraw to their clubs, lodges, and sometimes the neighborhood tavern for the same purposes.

One of the most visible vestiges of the men's hut is the Bohemian Grove in northern California, where for two weeks every summer men of great wealth and influence from all over the country, and even the world, gather in secrecy to do whatever it is they do. Women are excluded entirely from the camp, although apparently not from the nearby towns and resorts. Reports from "the grove" suggest that during the encampment, these men, heads of state and captains of industry all, dress and behave in a variety of bizarre ways, drink and eat lavishly, participate in a variety of musical and dramatic entertainments, and discuss major political and economic issues.

This preference for and enjoyment of members of one's own sex has been called *homosocial* behavior (as opposed to homosexual behavior) because it does not necessarily involve erotic sexual interaction. Socio-biologists assert that the tendency for males to congregate in groups began with the hunting party and with the need for males to cooperate in order to protect not only themselves but also their women and children. Because those who were successful in forming and maintaining groups were the ones who survived, the tendency to group behavior has become part of the genetic code so that now "male bonding" is an innate quality in males (Tiger 1969). Although this explanation of the origins of homosocial behavior, which is based largely on animal studies, has been widely criticized, the existence of the behavior is unquestioned (Tavris and Offir 1977).

Men can and often do satisfy most of their needs—intellectual, physical, political, economic, occupational, social, power, and status—with other men. Men, it has been argued, need women only to satisfy their need for paternity, "the ultimate claim to masculinity." The homosocial world gives men access to unequal power and resources in the society (Lipman-Blumen 1975).

Nevertheless, since masculinity in our culture is characterized by inexpressiveness, men tend to have a pattern of friendships that is different in character from that of women. Men may have a wide circle of acquaintances but few real friends (Fasteau 1974). Among even very young boy children, the attraction of group membership and the lack of intimacy is apparent. Boys, as opposed to girls, have more social interactions with children their own age. Unlike girls, they do not seem to care very much whether they like their playmates. The important element is the game, and when they have the chance to choose partners or teammates, they will choose on the basis of skill or ability rather than personal attraction. Among very young children, boys tend to form more intense relationships than girls, in that they always seem to play with the same children and to avoid others. However, by about age seven, the pattern shifts. Girls focus their attention to one or two best friends, while boys play in larger groups. By junior high, boys are more likely than girls to welcome a newcomer into their group, which suggests that their friendships involve less self-revelation (Maccoby and Jacklin 1974).

By college age, differences between women's and men's friendships are apparent. Men's relationships are characterized by a great deal of joking, much of it both sexual and hostile. Acceptance in the group is won in part by flaunting social norms or rules and also by "being cool" in the face of aggressive teasing. Men view the solidarity engendered by this behavior as a prelude to friendship and intimacy, but they are more likely to talk to their friends about impersonal topics than about feelings or relationships (Lyman 1987). When they do reveal themselves, they are more likely to disclose their feelings to their closest woman friend than to anyone else, including either their male friends or their parents (Komarovsky 1976).

Even men who report fairly intense and long-lasting relationships tend to emphasize external interests and mutual activities. They also tend to see their friends in differentiated ways—different friends for different activities or interests (Wright 1982).

When men reach adulthood, boyhood and college friendships are lost and seldom replaced. Men often report having many friends, but only because they tend to label as a friend anyone with whom they share an activity. Men seldom have a *best* friend, and when they do it is likely to be a woman. Men talk to their male friends about work, women, and marriage, often jokingly, but rarely about their own problems with these subjects. Men may assert that they have male friends to whom they can reveal themselves, but they seldom do (Rubin 1985).

The camaraderie of men in all-male or predominantly male work groups, as reported by the men themselves, is similar to that observed in other settings. Groups of comparative strangers rely on stories about sexual adventures and exploits, off-color jokes, stories about either work or sports prowess, and stories about capacity for food and drink. When a woman is present, rather than tempering their inclination to tell these stories, the men may become more boisterous, show off for her, and increase the degree of sexual or business prowess contained in their "war stories." Men occasionally will use sexual innuendoes, locker-room humor, or business successes to test a woman's acceptance of the dominant male culture or to underscore the woman's exclusion from the group (Kanter 1977).

However, even though males prefer the company of other males and turn to them for gratification of most of their needs, they often fail to find their needs for friendship or intimacy satisfied. This estrangement has been called "the lost art of buddyhood" (Goldberg 1976). Men are constantly "checking each other out," comparing themselves with other men, competing not only in sports and business but also for women. They often fear that a friend might "do better" at something like career or sports, which could spell the end of the friendship.

As a consequence, men are blocked on both sides from friendship with other men. They cannot share their failures for fear of being seen as weak, and they cannot share their successes for fear of being boastful or of inciting jealousy. The only safe conversational topics are cars, sports, sex, and politics; the only safe friends are women. In fact, close friendships among men often are looked at with suspicion. The need for a buddy often is perceived by others as adolescent or immature or, worse, as a sign of latent homosexuality. Wives often resent the time spent with a buddy and interfere whenever possible. Friendships become acceptable only when they involve some business "trade-off" or when they are directed toward some external goal.

Men may, as some argue, have a biological predisposition to "male bonding," and they may have the same need for nurturing and intimacy that women have. Whatever their propensity, it appears that their needs are rarely met.

SUMMARY

Women and men differ biologically and socially. They also differ in the nature of their social interactions. Men and women tend to interact with each other in ways that enact their stereotypical roles and at the same time reinforce their differential power and status. They often bring these social roles into the organization and adapt them to organizational roles in non-sexual ways. However, organizational taboos against office romances are increasingly being relaxed, as are sexual mores in general. And increasingly the office romance, or the potential office romance, is causing problems not only for individuals but for management as well.

Women's relationships with other women have been the subject of a good deal of study, mostly by psychologists. Women are capable of, and often have, close, intimate, and enduring friendships with other women, relationships that often are characterized by a high degree of self-disclosure. But women also often find themselves in competition with other women, for nurturance, for the attentions of men, and, more recently, for job opportunities. Women in organizations often supply much needed help and support for each other, but they also often provide antagonism or outright hostility.

Men from the youngest ages tend to have wide circles of acquaintances, and their preferred method of interacting with them is in the sharing of interests or activities. They put a high value on membership in these groups, whether they are exclusive clubs or street gangs. Acceptance by the group and loyalty to the group are essential. Some evidence exists for the theory that men have an innate need to have some sort of relationship with other men, but the exact nature of the need or the ideal kind of relationship is unclear. Men may crave a more intimate, sharing, and supportive relationship with a true friend or buddy, but social and sexual norms of competitiveness and homophobia make that virtually impossible in adulthood.

Men come to the work place, a primary arena for the validation of their masculinity, with a need to belong to the dominant group and perhaps with a need for intimate friendship. Their work relationships tend to follow the pattern established in social roles. They compete within the group through "male verbal dueling," taunting each other with tales of their sexual conquests, their sports achievements, and their business successes. They avoid friendships with other men that might involve self-disclosure or that might be perceived as having a homosexual potential. They form safe, cohesive groups that exert power within the organization, and they use the power of these groups to control the culture and to exclude and isolate individuals who constitute a threat, such as women and minority group members.

Men's relationships to other men at work are not, as most of the literature of organizations implies, devoid of sexual content. Men in organizations, like men everywhere, are constantly in the process of competing with, comparing themselves with, and seeking validation from other men. The entry of women into the "men's hut" means that men now must compete with women as well as with men. The nature of the contest and the value of the outcome are greatly changed, in much the same way that the value of prizefighting would be changed if women competed with men in the ring. Or if women played football. Or if women were allowed into combat in the army. The value of these activities, in allowing men to exhibit their prowess in order to win the respect, admiration, or friendship of other men, and in order to validate their own masculinity, is lost. After all, how can you validate your masculinity by going 15 rounds with a woman? And what would happen to your masculinity if you lost?

7

Communication

Whenever conflict arises, whenever carefully laid plans go awry, whenever hopes are frustrated and dreams shattered, someone is sure to attribute the problem to a breakdown in communication. And indeed there is always some truth in this attribution. But the statement is often so vague as to be meaningless. What is communication and why is it important in organizational life? Why does miscommunication occur so often? How does it occur? And, of course, how do gender and role contribute to communication or miscommunication?

Communication is the process of exchanging meaning, and is the life-blood of organizations. Communication consists "of a sender transmitting a message through media to a receiver who responds" (Kotler 1980). An organization consists of two or more individuals working toward the accomplishment of a common goal. It typically requires some division of labor, which then requires coordination and control of the activities of the members. That coordination and control, in turn, requires the ability to exchange meaning. It requires communication.

Communication requires three sets of behaviors: sending, receiving, and responding. Miscommunication can occur in several ways. One, the sender simply neglects to send, that is, the person with some vital piece of information neglects to transmit it to the relevant others in the organization. Two, the sender sends the information, but the receiver fails to receive it. Again, two errors are possible. Either the receiver receives no message at all, or, usually worse, the receiver receives a message but misapprehends it, that is, the meaning that the receiver attaches to the message is not the same meaning that the sender intended. Third, the receiver can fail to respond or, once again, the response can be misunderstood. In any of these cases, the results may be costly for the individuals and for the organization.

Let us take an example. Mary Jones is production manager for the Sicilian Pizzeria and Gelateria. Jim Smith, a catering salesperson, has sold a large order of anchovy pizza and kumquat gelato for the Republican fundraiser on a Sunday afternoon in the suburban town of Griede. He processes the order so that it comes to Jones' attention two days before the scheduled event. She is awaiting a shipment of anchovies from Nepal, kumquats are out of season, and the delivery person is getting married on Sunday and has been promised the day off. Clearly, this is a case of failure to communicate. Smith will no doubt argue that he should have been told that these products and services were not available at this time. Jones will argue that he should not commit the firm to extraordinary orders without checking first to see that they are feasible. Each, of course, is partially right, but that does not undo the damage that is done to the firm or to each of them.

Sometimes, of course, messages are sent and not received. In this case, Jones has issued a routine memo to all department heads indicating which gelato flavors would be available for the next six weeks and which would be in short supply. But the memo is piled on the desk of Smith's boss; salespeople do not have time to read a lot of paperwork. Instead, Smith had called Jones' office and talked to her secretary, who said he thought for sure they could manage it. Smith did not ask him to check with Jones, and he did not. Smith perceived his question as a formal request and the answer as an assurance that his order could be filled. The secretary, who was a temporary worker hired through an agency, perceived Smith's question as a request for his opinion, so he gave his opinion for what it was worth—not much—and saw no reason to pass on the information to Jones. In this case, the miscommunication is more complex, but the result is the same—an unhappy customer, an angry salesman, and a frustrated production manager.

This example is highly simplistic, of course. The dynamics of the communication process involve the shared meaning of a great many symbols, both verbal (written or spoken words) and nonverbal (all message carriers other than words). And in both verbal and nonverbal communications, gender differences confound and increase the problems of clear communication.

VERBAL COMMUNICATION

Much attention has been focused in recent years on the extent to which language reflects the inequities that exist between the roles of women and men. Women, it has been argued, experience discrimination in language in two ways: "in the way they are taught to use language and in the way language use treats them" (Lakoff 1975). In each case, women are relegated to subservient functions, and for this reason certain words have different meanings when applied to men or to women. These different meanings rely exclusively on the different roles played by the sexes in our society.

It also is argued that women and men use language differently. Men speak in forceful ways that are considered unfeminine for women. Women use words, phrases, or intonations that would be considered effeminate if used by men. To the extent that these differences actually occur, women are caught in a double bind. If they talk as men typically do, forcefully or emphatically, they may be labeled as unfeminine; if they talk as stereotypical women, they may be ridiculed as unable to think clearly, as unable to take part in a serious discussion, and in some sense even as less than fully human.

Lakoff (1975) argues that:

It will be found that the overall effect of "women's language"—meaning both language restricted in use to women and language descriptive of women alone—is this: it submerges a woman's personal identity, by denying her the means of expressing herself strongly, on the one hand, and encouraging expressions that suggest triviality in subject matter and uncertainty about it; and, when a woman is being discussed, by treating her as an object—sexual or otherwise—but never a serious person with individual views. The ultimate effect of these discrepancies is that women are systematically denied access to power, on the grounds that they are not capable of holding it as demonstrated by their linguistic behavior along with other aspects of their behavior: and the irony here is that women are made to feel that they deserve such treatment, because of inadequacies in their own intelligence and/or education. But in fact it is because women have learned their lessons so well that they later suffer such discrimination.

Not all the research on the subject supports this pessimistic view, yet none completely contradicts it, either. The differences are only a matter of degree, not of substance.

The Ways in Which We Speak

Clearly, great differences exist between individual women and individual men in their speech patterns. If there were such a thing as "men's language" and "women's language," many similarities still would exist. Nevertheless, some generalizations are allowable about sex differences in content, linguistics, and syntax:

- Women's speech tends to be more person-centered, more concerned with interpersonal matters, to deal more with the feelings of both the speaker and the listener, to be more polite, and more indirect. It employs more fillers, qualifiers, disclaimers, and other softening devices to avoid strong or direct statements.
- Men's speech tends to be more concerned with external things and to involve more factual communication. It is more literal and direct, employs stronger statements and stronger language, and tends to exert power over the listener (Eakins and Eakins 1978).

Many of the words that women use are different from the words that men use. For example, women use adjectives that discriminate in great detail about nuances of color or feeling—words like *mauve* or *puce* that men would never use and that they consider to make irrelevant distinctions. Women use certain adjectives that would be ludicrous (or effeminate) if used by a man, words like *adorable, lovely, charming, divine* (Lakoff 1975). Women make greater use of "intensive" adverbs such as *so, such, terribly, quite,* or *awfully,* as in "The dinner was s-o-o-o delicious." They also tend to use emphatic forms like *fantastic, ghastly, amazing* and reduplicative forms such as *itsy-bitsy* or *teeny-tiny* (Key 1975) except in the company of men (McMillan et al. 1977). The effect of these syntactical differences is that men's speech has more strength and impact, they get listened to and heard more often, and they get reinforcement for their position of power.

The expletives, exclamations, and expressions used by women often take forms that are considered meaningless, such as *Oh, Dear,* or *Oh, Fudge.* Men in similar circumstances are more likely to use stronger expletives— *Oh, Shit,* or *Oh, Damn.* The male language expresses feelings a great deal more forcefully. There is clearly a difference between "oh, dear, I've pricked my little finger" and "oh, shit, I've cut my hand," although both might describe the same injury. This double standard of language permits men to use the full range of vocabulary, including sexual and profane terms, except in front of women and children, but denies the same freedom of expression to women. Linguist Mary Ritchie Key (1975) reports being advised not to use the word *damn* in a linguistic example because "it made me sound like a feminist." Obviously, many people of both sexes feel little need to express themselves using profanity or expletives. Indeed, many will argue that those who must rely on these terms suffer a paucity of language. However, the point here is not that women should be as able as men to curse and swear, but that women are denied the opportunity to express thoughts and feelings with the force and energy that is permitted to men. Women are not seen as feminine if they permit themselves the luxury of strong expressions of feelings.

Women not only use different words from men, they also use different syntax. Women are more likely to use "tag lines" or "tag questions," lines midway between an outright statement and a yes–no question—less assertive than the former, more confident than the latter—for example, "John is there, isn't he?" Another syntactical form is a difference in patterns of intonation in women's speech—a declarative answer to a question that has the rising inflection of a yes–no question and is uttered hesitantly, as though one were seeking confirmation for his answer. "What time is dinner?" "Oh . . . around six o'clock . . . ?" The answer is really saying "we'll eat at six o'clock if that's all right with you." These patterns are part of a larger pattern of politeness associated with femininity. They avoid forcing an opinion on the listener and leave the door open for either agreement or contradiction. However, they have the effect of making women seem indecisive and unsure of themselves. They also can be used on requests. A direct order, "close the door," can be turned into a compound request with the addition of particles, "won't you please close the door?" The more particles that are added, the more polite the request, and the more polite, the more powerlessness is conveyed, and the more characteristic it is of women's speech (Lakoff 1975; Key 1975). Both women and men expect women to use these polite forms, whether they are attempting to achieve feminine or masculine goals, and whether they are speaking to women or men (Kemper 1984).

Men use tag questions, too, but they more often use them to add force or emphasis, as in "You aren't going to stand in my way, are you?" (Eakins and Eakins 1978). Men are expected to speak like women and use polite forms of address when speaking to women or attempting to accomplish feminine goals; but on masculine tasks, especially when speaking to men, they are expected to be impolite (Kemper 1984).

Women use more "modal constructions." A modal construction occurs when a speaker expresses possibilities, probabilities, or doubtfulness about events that did or will take place. The modal words are *can, could, shall, should, will, would, may, might*, or verb auxiliaries such as *have* and *been*. An example would be a statement such as "I think I may have gotten a higher score than Arnold" (Key 1975).

Women's speech also is made more uncertain and hesitant than men's by the use of qualifiers and fillers (Eakins and Eakins 1978). Qualifying, softening, or mitigating words and phrases often are added to statements to soften or blunt their impact. They are used to avert or avoid negative reactions to our words and have the effect of making statements less absolute in tone. They can be found at the beginning, at the end, or sprinkled through the statements. Such words and phrases as *well, let's see, perhaps, possibly, I suppose, I think, it seems to me, you know,* or *do you understand what I'm saying* all have this effect. The statement "That's not true," has a very different impact from the statement "Well, I really wonder if that's true." A statement may be further qualified by adding such softeners as *rather, somewhat, sort of,* and *to some extent.* We might say "Well, I wonder if to some extent that's not always true."

Another form of qualifier is the disclaimer. These usually come at the beginning of the sentence and explain, excuse, or ask forbearance of the listener. They include such phrases as "I hope you won't be angry, but . . . ," "This may sound a little silly, but . . . ," or "I don't know much about it, but . . ." (Eakins and Eakins 1978). While men also use disclaimers, particularly in discussing feminine topics, women tend to use them more frequently, particularly the forms that indicate poor logic, ignorance of the facts, or tentativeness and hedging. While these disclaimers have a positive effect in softening the impact of negative messages and seeking concurrence of opinion, they also make the speaker seem less knowledgeable or self-assured. Disclaimers like "Well, I don't really know very much about this, but I wonder if . . ." may make the listener prejudiced against an opinion even before it is expressed.

In male–female conversations, women use fillers—words and sounds like *well, You know, I mean,* or *like*—more than men do (Eakins and Eakins 1978). In female–female conversations, women use fewer fillers, suggesting that women are more fluent, more at ease, and less hesitant talking to other women than they are talking to men.

Women and men vary not only in their choice of language but also in their conversational behavior. Differences have been found in turn-taking (who speaks when), expressivity, the selection of topics, and the use of humor (Eakins and Eakins 1978).

Lapses occur in a conversation when one member falls silent. In male–female conversations, women fall silent more frequently than men. These silences come in response to one of three male conversational behaviors: overlap, interruption, or delayed minimal response. Minimal responses are those that do not count as a turn, "stroking" behaviors such as *MMHMM* or *Oh* or *Yeah* that display continuing interest or participation in the conversation without attempting to break in. Displaying or postponing these minimal responses may signal disinterest, inattention, or lack of understanding. Silence following a delayed minimal response suggests that the speaker is uncertain about the listener's continued participation in the conversation. These silences are found much less infrequently in same-sex conversations (Eakins and Eakins 1978).

Men have been found to take more turns and to talk more in mixed groups, in part because they interrupt women more often and answer questions not addressed to them. Turn-taking violations may take several forms: overlaps—two people speaking at once because the second speaker has started before the first one finished; interruptions—two people speaking at once before any signal that the first is near the end of the statement; and delayed minimal response. In same-sex conversations, turn-taking violations seem to be fairly equally divided; but in male–female conversations, practically all of the overlaps and interruptions are by male speakers, a general disregard by males for female speakers. In a study of turn-taking among university faculty members, this pattern was quite evident. Males interrupted more than females; the female who interrupted the most did so to other females. The person most often interrupted was a woman, the one person without a Ph.D. degree; the person interrupted least was the department chair. These observations would suggest that status had a good deal to do with turn-taking (Eakins and Eakins 1978).

The content of conversation also differs along gender lines. Women's conversations tend to be more expressive or relational, while men's contributions are more instrumental and goal-oriented. These styles generally reflect social roles in which men tend to be more instrumental and women more nurturing. In mixed-sex groups, women seem to take concern for group maintenance, for relief of tension, and for ego protection of other members. In choosing conversational topics, women choose to talk about persons about twice as often as men do. Men's preferred conversational topics are business and money, followed by sports and amusements. Women's preferred topics are men and clothes (Eakins and Eakins 1978).

A final sex difference in conversation has to do with the use of humor. Women are generally less able than men to tell amusing narratives, especially in mixed-sex groups. Spontaneous humor, wit, and laughter in organizations seem to be distributed by status, with those at the lower end of the spectrum making many fewer witticisms than those with more authority. A pecking order prevails in which jokes or witticisms are never directed at persons higher in authority or rank. Women rarely make jokes, but they laugh hard at the jokes told by men (Eakins and Eakins 1978).

Social and situational factors other than sex also affect the use of language. The use of hesitant or uncertain forms may be influenced by individual psychological factors (for example, communication apprehension or low assertiveness), or by familiarity with the topic or with the listener. Speakers of both sexes also tend to use more intensifiers when they are familiar with the topic (McMullen and Pasloski 1992). In an interesting, if not reassuring, twist on the issue, women were found in one study to be more tentative in their speech when talking to men than when talking to women. However, contrary to expectations, women who spoke tentatively were more influential with men and less influential with women than those who spoke assertively (Carli 1990). Clearly, more research is needed to fully understand how men and women differ in their use of language, what variables affect their choice of language, and how differences in language are perceived by others (Smythe and Schlueter 1989).

The Ways in Which Women Are Spoken About

Language communicates messages at a number of different levels simultaneously. It conveys not only the substantive message contained in the meanings of the words themselves, but also a great many social and cultural messages about the speaker, the listener, and the subject of the words. Thus, language tends to reveal a great deal of the disparity that exists in the social attitudes toward masculinity and femininity. These values are revealed in the euphemisms that we use for the sexes, the differences in meaning attributed to seemingly parallel terms, and in the use of names, titles, and pronouns.

Several years ago, a county sheriff in California was running for reelection. In a campaign speech to a women's group he made several references to the positive advantages he had brought to the "girls" and the "ladies" in the sheriff's department (sworn officers). When a listener suggested to him that these terms were offensive to some voters, he asked what terms he should use instead. "Why don't you just say women?" he was asked. With that the sheriff grew red in the face, drew himself up to his full height, puffed up his chest, and responded heatedly "I was raised to respect the fair sex. If I had ever called my mother a woman, my father would have whipped me."

The word "man" has very positive connotations in our society. It is a compliment to a male person to say "he is a real man," "he took it like a man," or "he is a man's man" (whatever that means). Young boys are admonished to "*be* a man" and are praised when they are called "*little man*." The word *man* in this context symbolizes strength and maturity. Women, however, are rarely complimented by a phrase like "she is a real woman." The word *woman* in this case suggests sexuality, rather than strength. We might say, instead, "she is a real lady." *Lady* then becomes a euphemism for *woman*, a polite substitute for offensive and undesirable terms like "broad" or "dame." The parallel term *gentleman* is used far less frequently than *lady*. It is not a euphemism for man, which has no negative connotations and therefore needs no substitute.

The word *girl* often is used as a euphemism for woman. It often is applied to women of all ages, as in "my office girl" or "the girls in the bridge club." Many women find the term flattering, and indeed comments about a woman's youthful appearance are usually intended as compliments. Others, however, take offense on the grounds that *girl* suggests immaturity or helplessness. For the sheriff, however, *girl* is quite obviously like *lady* in that it removes the suggestion of sexuality which is present in the word *woman*.

Some interesting research supports the notion that these words are used euphemistically. Respondents reported that they would expect a woman to have interesting and important things to say; ladies were seen as more frivolous, having more wealth, and concerned mostly with social or charitable interests. However, older respondents in particular preferred *lady* to *woman*. *Lady* signified dignity, respect, and refinement, it brought better treatment, and it was seen as a desirable thing to be. *Woman*, by contrast, seemed earthier and more common. Younger women and, to a lesser extent, younger men, however, saw *woman* as being less pretentious, less prudish, and less stilted (Eakins and Eakins 1978).

In addition to euphemisms, language tends to offer a semantic reflection of the general sexual polarization that characterizes society. Words that seem to be pairs actually have quite different implications in use. The words themselves are neutral, neither pejorative nor oppressive; their meanings are anything but parallel. The words *manly* and *womanly*, for instance, tell a great deal about how society views masculinity and femininity. To be *manly* is to have the positive qualities of a man, and the word usually applies to a man. But to be *mannish* is quite another thing; the word typically refers to aberrant women. *Womanly*, on the other hand, suggests feminine traits of decorum and modesty; but *womanish* usually is used to describe a man as weak, effeminate, or petulant (Miller and Swift 1976).

Other examples include *bachelor* for an unmarried male, whether or not he has been previously married, *spinster* for a never married woman, and *divorcee* for a previously married female. (There is no comparable term to divorcee—although a previously married man may be referred to as a *divorced man*.) The word *sir* implies respect for a male; the parallel term *madam* may suggest the keeper of a brothel. A man who is a *wizard* is clever, even magical, but not so the woman who is referred to as a *witch*. A *brave* is seen as strong, youthful, and courageous; *squaw*, like *witch*, often is used disparagingly to suggest women who are old, ugly, or aggressive. Still other examples are *King/Queen, Governor/Governess, Patron/Matron,* or *Prince/Princess*. A *master* is one who is skilled in an art of profession, but a *mistress* normally is used only in a sexual sense, that is, as a woman who has a sexual relationship with a man to whom she is not married.

Adjectives sometimes have different meanings when applied to women and to men, and different adjectives are applied to equivalent characteristics. A woman is *brainy*—not usually a compliment—but a man is *smart*. *Smart* applied to a woman usually refers to her appearance. She is a *hooker*, a *slut*, or a *roundheels*; he is a *Don Juan*, a *Playboy*, or a *Casanova*. He is a *hard drinker*; she is a *lush*. He is a *man of the world*; she *has been around*. He is *self-confident*; she is *conceited*. He is *exacting*; she is *picky*. And so on. The language discriminates between masculine and feminine traits and behaviors, and tends to put negative connotations on the female words.

Names and titles are different for women and men. Women typically give up a good deal of their identity when they marry. The once traditional marriage ceremony reflected this when the couple were declared "man and wife." He retained his status as man; she exchanged her status as woman for that of wife. (Many contemporary couples now substitute the more egalitarian "husband and wife," and modern brides prefer to vow to "cherish" rather than to "obey".) Up until that moment she has been known as Miss, now she will be known as Mrs.; he remains Mr. She may give up the surname that she previously has been known by and take up the name of her husband; for many purposes she will take on her husband's full name, that is, she will become Mrs. John Smith. Even after his death she may continue to be known as Mrs. John Smith or as John Smith's widow. Men, by contrast, are rarely identified as Mr. Jane Doe, wife of Jane Doe, or as Jane Doe's widower.

Women who choose to be addressed as Ms., or who opt not to use their husband's name, will come in for criticism despite their own personal or professional achievements. Hillary Rodham, for instance, a highly successful Wellesley College and Yale-educated attorney, changed her name to Hillary Clinton after her husband lost his bid for reelection after one term as governor of Arkansas. Polls indicated that the voters resented her decision to retain her pre-marriage name. Only after she became first lady did she become Hillary Rodham Clinton, a choice that was severely criticized in some quarters. No one, apparently, questioned Bill Clinton's decision not to become Mr. Hillary Rodham or even Bill Rodham.

Much more frequently than her husband, a woman will be called by her first name or by familiar titles (honey, doll, blondie) by those whom she meets quite casually (Eakins and Eakins 1978). Men on the other hand often are referred to by their last name only, a form of familiarity that is considered rude and disrespectful when applied to women (Lakoff 1975).

Occupational and organizational descriptors differ. The domain of most occupations is assumed to belong to men, so that when women enter they must be identified. We do not specify a *male* firefighter or *man* astronaut, but the woman who becomes a doctor or a race driver must be semantically differentiated by the use of a "marker." She becomes the *woman* (or worse, the *lady*) doctor or the *female* driver. In the same way, in those rare instances where the occupation is a female-dominated one, we may designate the occupant as a *male* nurse or *man* teacher. Unfortunately, these terms tend to demean the individuals and trivialize their accomplishments. As an example, a California newspaper story about a long-running strike by members of the Teamsters Union carried the headline "Grandmas Striking at Walnut Plant Begin a Fast" (*San Francisco Chronicle* 1993). The fact that the strikers were long-term employees and had grandchildren had nothing whatsoever to do with their decision to strike.

Another kind of differential nomenclature is adding suffixes such as -*ess*, -*ette*, or -*trix* to distinguish male from female occupations. A man who writes poetry is a poet; a woman who writes poetry is a poetess. Other examples include *steward/stewardess, waiter/waitress, aviator/aviatrix,* and *drum major/drum majorette* (Eakins and Eakins 1978). These modifications feminize the titles and detract from them the sense of competency or power normally associated with them. In most cases, the differential titles cannot be justified on the basis of semantic necessity or clarity.

A final and most difficult area of language differentiation comes in the use of exclusionary language, the exclusive use of the noun man and of masculine pronouns and possessives. Linguists argue that the term *man* is grammatically correct as the generic term for mankind which includes both women and men. The difficulty, of course, is that it is nearly impossible to distinguish this meaning from the more common meaning of the word as the opposite of woman. Research provides some convincing evidence that when the word *man* is used generically people tend to think *male* and not to think *female*. Surprisingly, terms like "Urban Man," "Industrial Man," and "Economic Man" tend to evoke strong images of power and dominance. When the terms are replaced with gender-free words like "Urban Life," the reactions are quite different.

Studies of children from preschool through high school all show that the word man produces a masculine image, almost no matter what the context. When the wording is changed to substitute such words as *people* and *humans*, the image that is aroused includes both men and women (Miller and Swift 1976). These semantic differences apparently cause little problem for children. They learn relatively early that the word *man* has a dual meaning and learn to make the distinction when necessary. However, in the absence of clear indications to the contrary, they tend to apply the specific meaning of the word rather than the generic one. The fireman, the postman, the policeman are all perceived as males, not as either males or females. Hence, the use of markers or of exclusionary language reinforces occupation stereotypes and affects occupational choice, even of very young children (Rosenthal and Chapman 1982).

An even more pervasive problem arises when it comes to pronouns. The rules of English grammar assert that *he* must be used when the referent is singular and indefinite or unknown. Grammatical purists argue that substituting "he and she" is a form of sexism, since the use of *he* alone loses its sexist connotations if used consistently. If you never qualify the generic pronoun, it always will be understood to stand for "he and she"; insisting on the distinction has the effect of making women a special category, excluded unless they are specifically mentioned. The difficulty, of course, is that the generic term and the specific term are identical, so women are already excluded (Miller and Swift 1976). The other, more equitable, approach would be to use "he or she" in all cases except when one or the other is specifically excluded (Eakins and Eakins 1978).

The generic use of *he* might be acceptable, even if it is exclusionary, if it were used consistently. Indefinite referents such as *manager, engineer,* or *astronaut* would appropriately take the masculine pronoun *he*, but so also would equally indefinite referents as *secretary, nurse,* or *housewife*. But that rarely happens. If generic terms are indeed acceptable and nonexclusionary, then the marriage partner who cares for the home and children and does not seek paid work outside the home would be called a housewife regardless of gender, and there would be no need for the word *househusband* (Persing 1977). If the language were truly consistent, the deity surely would be referred to as *he* but so also would ships and hurricanes. If we cannot have equity, the very least we should insist upon is consistency. Some have even argued for the acceptance of *they* as a singular pronoun (I see an educated person as . . . (one who) uses *their* knowledge . . .) so long as consistency is maintained (Meyers 1989).

Verbal communication distinguishes men and women in two ways—the way we talk and the way we are talked about. So far in this chapter we have seen that women and men talk differently. The many differences in semantic, linguistic, and grammatical patterns show that men's speech tends to perpetuate masculine positions of power and dominance. Further, semantic and linguistic distinctions in the words that are used to describe and define women and men also reflect cultural stereotypes and biases. Because language is such a powerful force in shaping and controlling society, it is essential that these language differences be addressed and inequities reduced if there ever is to be anything approaching equality between the sexes. Some linguists argue that it is nearly impossible to change language, and there is no question that change will come only with great difficulty. However, it is possible to insist on certain fundamental rights. Women can insist that the written language, at the very least, be free from exclusionary language. They can reject the euphemisms that demean womankind. They can insist on being recognized as autonomous individuals, professionally independent from the possession of the primary males in their lives. And they can continue to insist on the same semantic rights and privileges as their brothers.

NONVERBAL COMMUNICATION

Defining verbal communication is fairly straightforward. The term refers to words and their usage. Defining nonverbal communication is more difficult. In a general sense, it refers to all of the ways in which meanings are exchanged other than with words. We cannot claim a clear distinction between the two, for verbal communication often is influenced by the nonverbal—"It is not what you said, it is how you said it." The words themselves, particularly spoken words, take on different meanings depending on such things as facial expression, tone of voice, or posture; and the nonverbal message greatly overpowers the verbal one (Argyle et al. 1970).

There are some important distinctions between verbal and nonverbal communication. Language, that is verbal communication, is used most often for communicating information about events external to the speakers, whereas nonverbal codes are used to establish and maintain interpersonal relationships. Another distinction is that nonverbal communication need not be, and often is not, either intentionally sent or consciously received (Donaghy 1980). Like verbal communication, however, nonverbal cues differ in use and in meaning between women and men. To an even greater extent than verbal cues, they reflect differences in status and power between the sexes (Henley 1973–74).

The study of nonverbal communication is particularly important to the study of women and men in organizations because of the implications for social control. Since we most often respond to nonverbal behavior unconsciously, and since people in dependent positions have been found to adapt their behavior to the nonverbal messages of dominant ones, the result is a self-fulfilling prophecy that keeps women dependent. For instance, when a woman or a minority is expected to perform less well than others in a situation like a job interview, and the dominant person (the interviewer) communicates that expectation in a number of nonverbal ways, the submissive individual adapts to the expectation and does in fact perform less well, and the prophecy is confirmed. The problem then is compounded when research focuses on the reasons why members of the stereotyped group perform less well, rather than on the interactions (Henley 1977).

The elements of nonverbal communication that have significance for women and men in organizations include physical appearance, posture, facial expression, eye behavior, body movement, touch, and space.

Physical appearance refers both to clothing and to body characteristics, including height; weight; the color, style, length, and thickness of hair; the presence or absence of facial hair; the color, texture, and condition of skin; the color and shape of eyes; and much more. Most healthy people take a good deal of interest in their physical appearance; it reflects how we see ourselves and how we would like others to see us. In a larger sense, each of us has an overall self-image—an image of the kind of person we are that we would like to pass on to others. An important part of this self-image is the body image—the picture we have of our own body and its appearance. Since most of us are aware that initial impressions are formed largely on the basis of physical appearance and tend to be fairly long-lasting, we take a good deal of care about our appearance.

The feminine stereotype depicts women as being more concerned than men about their bodies, their clothing, and their appearance in general; as is often the case, there is both truth and reason to the stereotype. Women are subject to a great deal more observation than men; their figures, their clothing, their general attractiveness are the criteria by which they most often are judged. Not surprisingly, then, women are more conscious than men of their visibility. This difference translates into both a power and a sex difference. In a situation where one person is observing and the other is being observed, the observer dominates the situation. When a woman is judged by a man on the basis of her dress and appearance, the man is able to assume dominance over the situation (Henley 1973–74).

Posture refers to positions in which we place our bodies for a relatively long time. Our bodies are active at all times, that is, we are always in some position, either standing, sitting or reclining, whether or not someone else is around. The postures that we assume tell a great deal about us. Society imposes both sex-role and status requirements on our posture, and once again sex differences translate into power differences.

In general, men's stances tend to be more open than women's. Women tend to stand or sit with their legs close together and crossed; men tend to stand with their legs apart and to sit with one knee bent and their foot on the opposite knee. Women tend to tilt their heads to the side, indicating coyness or submissiveness; men tend to tilt their heads forward, signaling aggressiveness. Women keep their arms close to the trunk or crossed over the chest, while men move their arms away from the body, sometimes with hands clasped behind the head. Men tend to adopt more relaxed and informal positions, that is, to slouch or recline. These differences are not trivial. One of the earliest lessons that female children learn is to walk, stand, and sit "like a lady." Female clothing adds to the lesson, since dresses restrict movement and increase the problem of maintaining decorum. Women who assume masculine postures are seen as unfeminine and unattractive, but also may be seen as sexually uninhibited.

In situations of nonequal status, people of higher status are allowed a great deal more relaxed posture than their subordinates. The boss can slouch on the subordinate's desk, but the subordinate does not slouch on the boss's desk. In meetings, people of high status will recline in their chairs, sit on the floor, turn sidewise, or assume whatever level of casualness makes them comfortable. But low-status people will sit straight in their chairs. They may take their cues from the higher status individual, and follow their behavior up to a point, but they will always remain more formal than their superiors.

The comparison is obvious. Acceptable, role-appropriate feminine posture is the posture of submissiveness and vulnerability. The postures of dominance and self-confidence that are embodied in more relaxed stances are seen as inappropriate to femininity. Women who adopt them may be seen as sexually available, rather than as powerful.

Facial expression can convey a number of messages simultaneously and very rapidly, almost subliminally. Our facial expressions tend to convey messages about our emotions, rather than our status, and can reflect happiness or sorrow, approval or disapproval, acceptance or rejection. Most of us learn to some extent both to follow certain social conventions and to conceal certain feelings. We learn, for instance, to look solemn at solemn occasions and to smile at happy ones; we learn not to show undue pleasure at another's pain or discomfiture.

Men and women differ a great deal in their use of facial expressions. Women are more prone than men to reveal their feelings in nonverbal ways, just as they are in verbal ways. For men, the "strong silent type" image requires remaining inscrutable, and the ability to maintain a "poker face" is greatly admired. The same inexpressiveness from a woman is perceived as unattractive and unfeminine.

Smiling is one of the most frequent facial expressions. Women smile more often than men, but not necessarily because they are happier than men. A smile can mean many things: happiness, greeting, appeasement, approval seeking, warmth, and liking. It can be a buffer against aggression, a release of aggressive tension, or a counterforce to aggressive or hostile words. To a great extent the meaning is derived by the context (Frieze et al. 1978). Women are expected to smile a lot and are considered deviant if they do not. Their smiles may really mean merely conformity to convention, approval seeking, or submissiveness; the smiling woman may be expressing not her pleasure or happiness but her inferior status in the situation. In this respect, the woman's smile has been compared to the servant's shuffle (Firestone 1970).

Eye movements as we look at someone may be a sign of liking or approval, but a stare may be an aggressive threat (Frieze et al. 1978). Eye contact is one of the areas where the greatest sex differences in nonverbal communication are found. Women look more at others than do men; they look more at each other while speaking, while being spoken to, and while exchanging glances. Regardless of the gender of the receiver, they look more often and they look longer at the other person. Why? Is it because they are generally more open to emotional expression and interpersonal relationships? Or is this another manifestation of women's greater submissiveness?

Once again, the differences are related to status. Among unequals, the subordinate is more likely to seek approval, and people have more eye contact with those from whom they are seeking approval. Women may get important feedback on their own behavior by seeking nonverbal information from the facial expressions of men, a source of information not particularly valued by males. In conversations, speakers tend to look away while listeners tend to look at the speaker; and men tend to talk more frequently and longer and to interrupt more often than women in mixed-sex conversations. Hence, women would tend to look more at men. Further, there is more eye contact when the person being addressed is of high status or when the speaker has a positive attitude toward that person. The reason that women seek eye contact more than men may be that both women and men perceive women to have lower status (Eakins and Eakins 1978).

Prolonged eye contact, however, may express something quite different. Instead of some mutual expression of warmth or understanding, it may represent a struggle for dominance. The first person to look away has demonstrated submission. Most children are familiar with the meaning of a parent's prolonged gaze when he or she is caught in some unacceptable behavior. Usually the child senses the gaze of the adult, perceives its meaning, casts down his or her eyes, and stops misbehaving. The threat is implicit but clear; failure to change the behavior will result in punishment. As adults, women tend to show submission by averting their gaze, particularly when they are stared at by men.

Contradictions are cleary operating here. Looking at someone may be seen as a sign of dominance or as a sign of submission; looking away can also signal either dominance or submission. The disparity can be reconciled by understanding that eye behavior characterizes dominance and submission in different ways: dominant staring and looking away, and submissive watching and averting the gaze. Staring can be used by a superior in some situations to communicate power and assert dominance. But in other situations it may not be needed. When the superior's power is secure, it becomes unnecessary to express dominance or scan an inferior's face for approval or feedback. Instead, the superior can look away or gaze into space. On the other hand, an underling can communicate submission and attentiveness, as well as gather feedback, by careful watching. But in some cases, as when receiving a fixed stare from a dominant person, the subordinate signals submission by averting the eyes (Eakins and Eakins 1978).

Body movements (kinesics) are movements of various parts of the body— arms, hands and fingers, leg and foot, head and shoulders, or the torso— that can communicate universal messages or can be unique to the individual. Movements can be classified into their uses as follows:

- *Emblems* are hand or finger gestures that are generally and easily understood. For instance, a hand gesture with fingers curled and thumb extended and pointed sidewise to the body indicates a request for a ride; the same hand with the thumb pointing downward indicates disapproval, and the same hand with the thumb pointed upwards and the hand moved forward away from the body conveys approval.

- *Illustrators* are movements that emphasize the words being spoken, such as raising five fingers while you enumerate five points in an argument.

- *Regulators* help to facilitate interaction between individuals by nodding, gesturing, or shifting the torso.

- *Affect displays* demonstrate our emotions by clenching hands, squirming, or pacing.

- *Adapters* are unconscious habits that are unique to an individual; they have usually been adopted first as a method of achieving comfort or convenience but have become habitual over time; examples are such things as stretching or pushing the hair back from the face. These adapters may have little significance to strangers but may convey subtle messages to the sensitive observer or to close acquaintances (Donaghy 1980).

Sex differences in kinesics seem to be less pronounced and less significant than in other nonverbal behaviors. Men shift their posture more frequently than women, make hand gestures of longer duration than women, and move their feet somewhat more (Frances 1979). Women tend to tilt their heads to the side (Key 1975). Women tend to use more adapters, particularly arranging or playing with their hair or touching ornamentation. Men use sweeping gestures, use their arms to shift position, and stroke their chins. Both females and males tend to use a greater number of gestures with the opposite sex than with the same sex.

These differences support the notion that males and females use nonverbal methods to display gender traits, although alone they are less compelling than some other modes. Women's lesser use of gestures can be seen as a function of passivity or submissiveness. Men's greater use of gestures, including such power gestures as pointing or sweeping hand gestures, may reflect their greater dominance.

Touch, or the differential use of touch, is of much greater significance. Touching has different meanings depending on who initiates or returns the touch, the part of the body being touched, the environment in which the touching occurs, and the length or duration of the touch. Certain forms of public touching—handshaking, backslapping, dancing, or casual bumping—are usually of short duration and may be fairly impersonal. More prolonged or more intimate touching is generally reserved for nonpublic places.

Of all forms of nonverbal language, interpersonal touching shows the greatest sex differences. Both gender and status differences occur in who touches whom. Men may touch other men only in public and only very briefly—with a handshake, a back or arm slap, a mock punch. Women often hug or kiss each other—also briefly—in public and are generally allowed a great deal more touching than are men. Men touch women a great deal more than women touch men; they help them out of cars, guide them across streets and through doors, playfully touch them on their hair or other parts of the body, and in many instances treat them in the same way they treat objects or possessions (Eakins and Eakins 1978). Women, even as children, are generally touched a great deal more than men and boys are.

Status, more than sex, explains why women and girls are touched more frequently than men and boys. A high-status person may touch a lower status person in situations where it would be presumptuous for the lower status person to return, let alone initiate, the touch. In these situations, the touch serves as a "status reminder," or a "power put down." In an equal relationship, on the other hand, the touch is seen as a gesture of solidarity, closeness, or support (Summerhayes and Suchner 1978). But even in reciprocal sexual relationships, for instance, between a dating couple, male dominance may be demonstrated by the fact that it is the male who is expected to initiate intimate touch (Henley 1973–74; Major, Schmidlin, and Williams 1990).

Since males in general have higher status than females, the effects of messages of power and dominance in touch are compounded. The supervisor may approach the subordinate's desk and lay a hand on his or her shoulder while he or she talks. In this gesture, the status of the subordinate is diminished. The subordinate, however, is unlikely to approach the boss's desk and touch him or her. And even if this happens, the status of the subordinate will not be raised appreciably, regardless of gender. However, gender cannot be ignored when the boss is male and the subordinate is female. She accepts the touch of her male superior as normal behavior; it is part of the power that he possesses. If the situation were reversed, however, the male subordinate would be unlikely to touch his female boss, but it is also unlikely that she would initiate touch with her male subordinate. If she did, it would be perceived as a gesture of sexual intimacy, rather than of power (Henley 1976).

Status, however, may not be the only explanation for the greater frequency of cross-sex touch initiated by men. Such touching may in fact be linked to sexual intent, at either a conscious or unconscious level, or merely may be linked to a desire for warmth and intimacy (Major, Schmidlin, and Williams 1990). Even attractiveness has been found to affect how touch is perceived (Burgoon 1991).

Space (proxemics) involves three aspects: personal space, territory, and social space. Personal space is the psychological space that surrounds us and that we consider to be our own. It varies in size with the nature of the people and the situation we are in; for example, the amount of personal space we require in a classroom may be quite different from what we require at a movie theater, in a crowded tavern, or walking down the street. Whatever our personal space, we tend to be protective of it and to resent invasion of it by others. Territory is similar to personal space. It is the space that we have staked out and claimed as our own. Primary territories are the exclusive domain of the owner—a home and particularly one's bedroom; secondary territories, the living room or dining room of the home or private clubs, can be used only by a few select people. Public territories— restaurants, parks, libraries, the streets—are available to anyone for temporary use. Territories often are staked out with a marker, any object that signifies our possession—a fence around our property, our books and notebooks spread over a library table.

Social space is conversational distance, the distance between ourselves and others around us. It can be divided into four categories: intimate distances—0 to 18 inches; casual/personal distances—1 1/2 to 4 feet; social/ consultative distances—4 to 12 feet; and public distances—from 12 feet out. As the titles suggest, the nature of interaction will change based upon the distance from the person with whom we are interacting. We will not attempt to discuss intimate matters at social/consultative distances; we will either change the nature of the conversation or the distance. The social space is a matter of negotiation between the parties and will vary depending on age, sex, culture and ethnicity, and subject matter (Donaghy 1980).

Both territory and personal space are associated with status, and behavior reflects the lower social status of women. The amount of territory that one controls and the extent to which it can be violated is an indicator of status. High-status people have bigger homes, bigger cars, bigger offices and desks, all of which tend to keep them at a greater distance from others.

Even people who frequently occupy a particular public place—a church pew, a park bench, a particular seat in a classroom—come to think of it as their own and will protect it against invasion.

In organizations, higher status individuals are accorded larger offices. This symbol of status is so important that some organizations have devised formulas that determine the number of square feet allocated to each hierarchical level. Further, the extent to which the space can be violated is also a mark of status. A private office connotes greater status than a shared office or open work place. A private secretary to limit access, both in person and by phone, further enhances status. The high-status person may work in a private office that cannot be entered without the permission of a secretary, or at the very least without first knocking and receiving permission to enter. On the other hand, the high-status person may enter the territory of the lower status person without permission.

High-status or powerful people also, perhaps unconsciously, violate the personal space as well as the territory of lower status persons, but the privilege is not reciprocated. The boss may come close to the subordinate, even touch him or her, when asking a question or giving a direction; the subordinate could not and would not approach the boss at the same distance.

Once again, status differences often are reflected in gender differences. Women tend to control less territory than men and their personal space tends to be smaller. In the house, mothers are less likely than fathers to have a special room that is off limits to other members of the family. A den or workshop may be reserved for the father; the kitchen is generally regarded as the woman's private space, but it usually can be entered by anyone. Men often have a special chair reserved for them and usually sit at the head (the end) of a rectangular dining table. Women, in fact, often have no place in the home that is exclusively theirs, where they can work undisturbed and in privacy (Frieze et al. 1978). The brilliant feminist writer Virginia Woolf (1932) understood the importance of territory. Speculating on the lack of women's achievements in the arts, she fantasizes that if Shakespeare had been a woman, the plays never would have been written. Every woman, she declares, has a right to "500 (pounds) a year and a room of her own."

Men and women also have different access to personal space. Women stand closer to each other, and men stand closer to women than to other men. When women and men approach each other on the street, women more frequently than men move out of the way. As was noted above, women tend to sit in postures that command a smaller amount of space. They condense; they sit or stand erectly and keep their elbows close to the body and their legs crossed. Men expand; they sprawl, keep their arms away from the body on the arms of chairs or behind the head, and they keep their legs apart or put one foot on the other knee (Eakins and Eakins

1978). When men intrude on the personal space of women, women tend to yield the territory; it is perceived as a legitimate expression of dominance.

As with other nonverbal cues, behaviors associated with space and performed by high-status persons and males are perceived as appropriate gestures of power and dominance, but the same behaviors performed by women are seen as inappropriate or as sexual. When women and other powerless people attempt to usurp nonverbal symbols of power, they often are ignored, denied, or punished, rather than accepted, and denial often takes the form of attributing the gesture to sexual advance. Women have been found to be particularly apt at reading nonverbal messages and tend to respond by adapting their behavior to the males' characteristics. The result is that behaviors that seem meaningless or trivial have the effect of sustaining the social control of women in submissive roles (Henley 1977). Hence, a good deal of women's self-limiting behavior may be the end of a sequence in which assertion was tried and suppressed on the nonverbal level.

SUMMARY

Communication is the lifeblood of organizations; without it, activities would grind to a halt almost before we could measure the passage of time. Communication is both verbal and nonverbal; it carries both direct and indirect messages. In our roles as senders of communication, we reveal a great deal about ourselves and our perceptions of our receivers. In our roles as receivers, we are affected by both the sender and the message.

Significant differences exist between women and men in both verbal and nonverbal communications. Women tend to convey messages of passiveness and powerlessness. In language, women and men use different words, and masculine language is considered unfeminine and inappropriate for women. Different words are used to describe women and men, and apparently parallel words have very different connotations. Men and women tend to talk about different subjects. Women tend to listen more and give more encouragement, while men tend to talk more and to interrupt more. Women and men send different nonverbal messages; feminine behavior conveys messages of submission while masculine behavior conveys messages of dominance. When women do use status or power behaviors, they often are misinterpreted as sexual messages.

Thus our language, both verbal and nonverbal, tends to perpetuate stereotypes and to sustain the image of the high status and power of males and the submissiveness and sexuality of females. Communication problems present a particularly difficult dilemma for the woman manager. If she uses verbal or nonverbal language consistent with her status, her behavior may be perceived as inappropriate for her sex, or it may be interpreted as a sexual advance. But if she uses stereotypically feminine language and behavior, she may be perceived as passive and dependent, which is appropriate to her sex but not to her position. Either way, her effectiveness is impaired.

There are no easy solutions. Managers can start by removing exclusionary language from all written organizational documents and materials. They can exclude the word "girl" from the organizational lexicon unless it refers to young female children. They can insist upon sex-neutral terms wherever possible and nonsexist language at all times. They can be aware of sexually discriminatory assumptions and sexist connotations in seemingly innocent usage. They can educate employees to the significance of these distinctions. If women are ever going to receive equal treatment with men in organizations, they must receive equal treatment in language.

8

Motivation and Rewards

An axiom that women often quote says, "Unfortunately, a woman must work twice as hard and be twice as good as a man in order to get half as far. Fortunately, that's not hard." Unfortunately, there is a lot of truth in that statement. Since women workers are widely perceived as being less "career-oriented," more committed to home and family than to jobs, or less motivated by organizational rewards than men workers, they may have to work harder to demonstrate their competence. If, however, women do not differ significantly from men in their motivation or their preference for organizational rewards, managers may be underutilizing their women employees to a significant extent.

What we are concerned with here is the extent to which stereotypes are supported, whether men and women differ in their commitment to work, their preferences for job attributes or organizational rewards, and their motivations. We will start by looking at the notion that women work for different reasons than men, that they have different expectations from their jobs or less commitment to either their jobs or their organizations. Next we will look at theories of motivation as they apply (or do not apply) to both women and men workers. Finally, we will look at the differences in outcomes, the extent to which expectations are met and job satisfaction achieved.

COMMITMENT: CAREER VERSUS FAMILY

There for many ways of defining commitment. For our purposes, we will consider commitment to be "the extent to which an individual accepts and internalizes the goals and values of an organization and views his or her organizational role in terms of its contribution to those goals and values" (DeCotiis and Summers 1987).

In the popular view, women are seen to be less committed to work than their male counterparts and to prefer extrinsic job attributes, such as hours, working conditions, or congenial co-workers. Men, on the other hand, are presumed to value intrinsic career-oriented job attributes such as responsibility, promotion, or opportunities to use one's skills. Recently, researchers have devoted a good deal of attention to these perceived differences and, not surprisingly, their conclusions often differ (Lacy, Bokmeier, and Shepard 1983).

Some studies have found global differences between women and men in terms of work involvement, commitment to work, or the centrality of work. But when variables such as hierarchical status, career salience, family status, education, income, or age are considered, the sex differences become much less important. A major study, using data from five national samples over an 8-year period, found that differences in job attribute preferences were more likely to be related to factors such as education, age, and occupational prestige than to sex. Both men and women were most likely to prefer work that was important and meaningful and gave one a feeling of accomplishment. Income and promotion were the second job attributes most preferred by both sexes. For neither sex was job security or working hours the most important criterion (Lacy, Bokmeier, and Shepard 1983).

This is not to say, however, that there are *no* gender differences in expectations or commitment. Both men and women experience conflicts between work and other roles, but they experience them differently, leading to preferences for different job attributes. People are in the work force for any of three different reasons: because they *have to*, they *want to*, or they *are expected to* (Chusmir 1982). The common perception is that men have to work but women do not. However, in reality, few women have the luxury of remaining out of the paid work force. Nevertheless, the expectation that they will work falls more heavily on men than on women. Marital status does make a difference. Among unmarried persons there are no sex differences. But unmarried women are more committed to continue working than married women, and married women are less committed to continue working if it is not economically necessary (Lacy, Bokmeier, and Shepard 1983).

Both wives and husbands report that family responsibilities negatively affect their careers and ability to advance, as well as their ability to concentrate and to make judgments at work. Women, however, continue to bear primary responsibility for care giving at home, and tend to experience greater stress than men. Women also bear a greater societal burden. Society continues to view the "good" mother as one who is physically present to meet the needs of her children. Employed mothers are viewed as less dedicated to their families, less sensitive to the needs of others, less affectionate, and more selfish. Further, they are expected to have poorer job performance (Covin and Brush 1991).

However, the relationship is more complex than a simple married/not married equation. Men and women in dual-career (as opposed to dual-earner) marriages appear to be very alike in the degree of commitment to and importance of their careers. Women who planned before marriage to combine career and married life are more committed to their careers than women who had not planned that lifestyle (Sekaran 1982). Even so, these women do not perceive themselves as being as high on job commitment as do their husbands (Sekaran 1983). Both women and men with employed spouses appear to have less job involvement and organizational identification than those who carry the breadwinner role alone (Gould and Werbel 1983).

Women do have a higher turnover rate than men, when turnover is measured globally, which tends to confirm the perception that women are less committed. But these conclusions, too, are subject to challenge. First, they assume that preference to leave the organization or the work force is somehow a sex-based personality trait. Second, the data typically ignore the relative position of women within an industry or the economy—occupations, wages, promotional opportunities, or age distributions. When individual characteristics are controlled, differences in intention to leave the organization or the work force can be explained by work-related factors or by characteristics of occupations, rather than by sex (Miller and Wheeler 1992).

Another approach to perceived differences can be found by looking at values, specifically by separating those values associated with work from personal values. A survey of men and women managers found very similar work values but substantial differences in personal values. Men ranked a sense of achievement (a work value) as number one; women ranked self-respect (a personal value) at the top of the list (Chusmir and Parker 1991). These value differences, unquestionably socially learned, reflect differences in role expectations. Work organizations assign similar expectations to male and female managers, who internalize similar values. Society assigns different personal roles to women and men, and their values differ as well. What that suggests is that their work behavior may not be much different, but the role conflict they experience is.

Kanter (1976) has argued that perceived sex differences in the work place are really a function of the power and opportunity structures in organizations, rather than of gender. She asserts that:

people in low mobility or blocked mobility situations tend to limit their aspirations, seek satisfaction in activities outside of work, dream of escape, and create sociable peer groups in which interpersonal relationships take precedence over other aspects of work.

These behaviors and preferences are equally characteristic of women and men. Because women are so frequently placed in low-status positions, the behaviors are attributed to their sex rather than to their position on the hierarchy, and once again the stereotype is reinforced. This view is partially supported by research. When studies control for hierarchical level, differences between women and men are greatly reduced (Golembiewski 1977). However, for women but not men, the longer they stay in an organization, the greater their job involvement, irrespective of their occupation or organizational level (Gomez-Mejia 1983). Surprisingly, organizational commitment is lower among women who feel that they have received preferential treatment because of their sex than among women who perceived themselves to have been judged on ability alone (Chacko 1982).

It is clearly unwarranted to make any assumptions about the commitment or preferred job attributes of women workers as a class. We can conclude that any global perceptions that women, married women, or women with children differ in commitment or preferences for job attributes are greatly oversimplified. The differences that exist are mitigated by occupational and organizational status, age, education, income, marital and family status. In fact, women may have more job involvement and men less than what usually is assumed.

JOB SATISFACTION

Job satisfaction is concerned with expectations and outcomes. It is a measure of the degree to which valued and expected rewards, extrinsic or intrinsic, are realized on the job. The relationship between job satisfaction and performance is a complex one that still is largely unexplained by theory or research. While a positive correlation clearly exists between the two, the degree and direction of the interaction is unclear. Whether satisfaction causes good performance or the reverse is even less clear (Petty, McGee, and Cavender 1984). Appealing as the idea may be, it has never been satisfactorily demonstrated that "a happy worker becomes a productive worker." Job satisfaction is, however, demonstrably related to absenteeism and turnover, problems that are perceived as having greater impact on women workers.

Although the results of job satisfaction studies are contradictory, one conclusion stands out. Women workers to a very significant extent receive smaller rewards, both intrinsic and extrinsic, than corresponding males in their organizations, yet they are equally satisfied or only marginally less satisfied (Weaver 1978); and the factors that contribute to dissatisfaction differ remarkably little (Andrisani and Shapiro 1978). Satisfaction with the job seems to be closely correlated with life satisfaction for both women and men (Kavanagh and Halpern 1977), and what sex differences in satisfaction do appear diminish when hierarchical level or occupations are included. Men seem to become more satisfied with age; but for women, the length of time on the job rather than age seems to be a major factor (Hunt and Saul 1975).

A study of the link between sex discrimination in pay and job satisfaction, based on data from a national probability sample, found that women workers were in fact victims of discrimination when it came to the assignment of organizational rewards. They were discriminated against dramatically in terms of income, and somewhat less so in terms of the "quality of their jobs." However, even though 95 percent of the women workers were found to be the victims of objectively measured discrimination, less than 8 percent reported themselves dissatisfied with their jobs (Levitin, Quinn, and Staines 1971).

A decade later, a decade in which women's awareness of discrimination had ostensibly increased dramatically, very little had changed. A study of college students in management courses found that women students expected lower pay than men students, not only at the entry level but at the peak of their careers as well (Major and Konar 1984). When this study was replicated and extended to students from other disciplines, and still another decade had passed, the differences had increased rather than decreased. Regardless of occupational field, women had lower expectations than men for career peak pay, and, with the exception of social science majors, for entry-level pay. In the male-dominated field of engineering, women expected to earn about $35,000 less at career peak than men. But even in female-dominated fields such as education or nursing, women expected to earn $20,000 less at career peak than men. Further, they expected other women to earn less than men, both at entry and at career peak, and they believed this disparity was fair (Jackson, Gardner, and Sullivan 1992). A number of factors helped to explain the differences. Women expected to take more time out for childrearing than men, regardless of their career field, and put a higher value on job accommodations to family life.

Even women in low-paid, low-status jobs seemed to have high levels of job satisfaction, which may be explained by their perception of the occupational choices available to them. People who have achieved success—as they have defined it for themselves—report high levels of job satisfaction, even though their achievements may not spell success to others (Lewin and Olesen 1980). For some women the significant choice is not between jobs or careers, but between paid work and full-time homemaking; hence they compare their inputs and outputs not to male co-workers or even to female co-workers, but to women who are out of the paid labor force. Among working-class women, for instance, even low-status work makes an important contribution to their self-image. The work place provides a source of friendship and camaraderie that is not available to the homemaker. Further, a job has clear requirements and clear payoffs—both in money and in a sense of accomplishment. Housework, by contrast, tends to be lonely work, and relatively few women feel competent at it (Ferree 1976).

Whether a woman works from choice or necessity may have an impact on both her job satisfaction and her life satisfaction. Career-oriented and noncareer-oriented women are equally likely to feel stressed and overwhelmed, but the noncareer-oriented women are more dissatisfied with being spread so thin. In either case, employed women feel greater satisfaction when their husbands share in household chores (Stokes and Peyton 1986).

The evidence, then, tells us that there are few differences between women and men in terms of job satisfaction, even though women's jobs tend to have many fewer rewards and many more negative features. The disparity is probably explained by the fact that women have lower expectations than men; they expect to earn less and they expect to make more accommodations to their family responsibilities.

Also, women workers seem to compare themselves with other women workers or with full-time homemakers, rather than with men workers. Women who work outside the home, whether at professional careers or low-skilled jobs, experience a good deal of role conflict and stress, yet they are more satisfied than full-time homemakers who would rather be working, and they also experience higher self-esteem and a more positive self-image (Aldag and Brief 1979). The important question would seem to be not what the actual rewards are for working women, but how they perceive those rewards and what they consider to be the alternatives.

MOTIVATION

We will examine two theories of motivation where gender differences may operate: *achievement motivation*, which is based on the broader category of *needs theory*, and *attribution theory*, a cognitive theory. Needs theories focus on the job itself. They consider the psychological needs that individuals bring to the job and attempt to motivate workers by designing jobs that provide opportunities to achieve need satisfaction. Cognitive theories attempt to explore the internal process by which individuals interpret the outcomes of their efforts.

Needs theories are based on the work of Abraham Maslow (1943), who posited a "hierarchy of human needs," which progressed from physiological through safety, affiliation, and esteem needs to something called "the need for self-actualization." According to the theory, only unmet needs have a motivating effect, and needs are arranged in a hierarchy of "successive prepotency" that individuals climb in their search toward everhigher and more abstract needs. The theories concentrate on rewards that are intrinsic to the job itself—the opportunity for personal growth, recognition, or a sense of achievement—and discount extrinsic needs such as pay, benefits, and working conditions.

Although Maslow's theory has come in for a great deal of criticism

(Miner 1980; Yankelovich 1981) and has never been empirically validated, it has nevertheless served as the basis for a good deal of motivation theory and management experimentation (Argyris 1957; Herzberg 1966; Mc-Clelland 1965; McGregor 1960).

Needs Theories

Achievement Motivation. This theory is a narrow version of needs theory. Rather than attempting to identify the whole range of human needs and the factors associated with jobs that satisfy those needs, achievement motivation theory concentrates on only three motives: achievement (n-Ach), affiliation (n-Aff), and power (n-Pow). The theory was first articulated by McClelland (1965), who developed a thematic apperception test (TAT) to measure the presence of these motives. The test asks subjects to look briefly at a series of pictures showing an ambiguous situation involving men alone or women and men in a work situation. The subject is asked to write a paragraph describing what is going on in the picture. The assumption is that subjects will project their own motivations onto the figures in the pictures. Hence, the responses are scored for evidence of the presence of the three motivations.

According to the theory, all motives are learned, and over time each individual arranges his/her own motives in a kind of hierarchical order that influences subsequent behavior. As children develop, positive or negative feelings become associated with certain events. If pleasure is associated with achievement, the person develops a strong motivation to achieve in order to experience the pleasure. As achievement moves to the top of the motivation hierarchy, it takes only minimal cues to arouse the expectation of pleasure. An achievement cue, such as a challenging task, is associated with pleasure. The cue arouses the achievement motivation and the individual responds by striving for success.

Men and Achievement Motivation. McClelland viewed n-Ach as closely linked to the Protestant Work Ethic and essential not only for personal success but also for economic progress. He was concerned with the process of how male children acquire this motivation. Unlike Maslow, who believed that human needs were inherent and immutable, McClelland argued that achievement motivation is learned in situations where a person achieves success through his own effort and ability (rather than through chance), characterized by intermediate levels of difficulty and risk, and in which clear and unambiguous feedback on success is received (Miner 1980).

Sex roles and stereotypes once again influence both perception and reality. McClelland failed to find a consistent pattern of n-Ach among women. In some cases, women were found to be low in achievement motivation, which was consistent with the feminine stereotype and with the expectations of the researchers. However, in other cases, women subjects were found *not* to differ from males on achievement motivation. So pervasive is stereotypical thinking that the researchers concluded not that the stereotype or the expectation was wrong, but that the test was not valid for women. As a result, most of the research was conducted only on male subjects.

Women and Achievement Motivation. A great deal of research, however, has been applied to two aspects of women's motivation. First, are women more motivated by the need for affiliation (n-Aff) than by the need for achievement? And second, do women experience a *motive to avoid success* (MAS) that causes them to decrease their performance on tasks where success might induce jealousy or a loss of femininity?

One view argues that when women perform well on tasks such as school work, they may do so because they are motivated not by achievement but by affiliation motives. They may work for good grades, for instance, not because they seek mastery of the task, but because they are rewarded by approval (Hoffman 1972). Another view argues that women are indeed motivated to achieve, but that the areas of achievement are different from males because of cultural definitions of femininity. Women are motivated to develop the skills for which women are valued, that is, social skills. Women express their achievement motivation by achieving in social settings where they receive praise, rather than in traditional masculine areas, where they may experience negative reactions (Stein and Bailey 1975).

Still others assert that women often fuse the affiliation and achievement motivations, expressing pleasure and reward both in achievement *per se* and also in achieving in activities that "make other people happy" (Hoyenga and Hoyenga 1979). Women with high n-Aff tend to spend more time with others and to develop good social skills. However, rather than seeing themselves as dependent, they tend to see themselves as dominant and influential (Wong and Csikszentmihalyi 1991). These views are certainly the least deterministic of all of those concerning achievement in women and perhaps best explain the conflicting evidence of other studies.

Two other theories closely related to n-Ach are *motive to avoid failure* (MAF) and *motive to avoid success* (MAS). Motive to avoid failure suggests that a person who fears failure may avoid activities that might lead to failure, even when they might also contribute to success. Motive to avoid success posits that some able individuals are ambiguous about success.

According to theory, for some individuals the MAF becomes the primary motive and hence suppresses n-Ach. The person with a high MAF associates stronger negative feelings with failure than positive feelings with success. Given an achievement situation such as a challenging task, this person's expectation of success is low and negative feelings associated with failure arouse a motive to avoid failure. The response is to avoid situations or activities that might lead to success, since they also could lead to failure.

Fear of failure individuals tend to prefer situations where the chances for success are either very high or very low. When the chance is very high, there is little likelihood of failure; and when the chances are very low, the individual did not really fail because the task was so difficult that no one could have succeeded. In either event, the individual inhibits his performance and trades the chance to succeed for the chance to avoid failure (Miner 1980).

MAF is more common among men than among women. Because of the very high expectations of success that are placed on men in our society, the penalties for failure are high. Men who have inadequate experiences with success tend to develop a high MAF.

The motive to avoid success was first described as "a latent, stable personality disposition acquired early in life in conjunction with standards of sex-role identity" (Horner 1972). The theory suggests that, when an individual anticipates that the consequences of success will be negative, anxiety will be aroused. The anxiety, in turn, inhibits the action expected to give the negative consequence. Since for women success often has negative consequences, women will have a motive to avoid success. MAS is not a motive to fail, the theory asserts. Women do not seek failure, they seek achievement; but success carries the expectation of negative consequences and arouses anxiety. If MAS does occur, it would be more characteristic of high-ability, high-achievement–oriented women.

A thematic apperception test was developed to test the theory. It used a verbal cue describing a high level of accomplishment in a mixed-sex competitive achievement situation. For females the cue was "After first term finals, Anne finds herself at the top of her medical school class." For the men, the clue was the same but the name was changed to John. The original research tested only for the arousal of MAS in same-sex subjects. MAS was considered present if the subjects' responses to the success of someone of their own sex showed evidence of conflict, expectations of negative consequences, denial of effort or responsibility for achieving success, denial of the cue itself, or some other response.

The original research, which was conducted on students, found very dramatic differences between women and men in their level of MAS; fewer than 10 percent of the males, but over 65 percent of the females, showed evidence of MAS. Partly because of these dramatic findings, and perhaps because the theory has an intuitive appeal, it has been widely cited and frequently replicated, with mixed results (Tresemer 1976). The original observed gender differences in MAS and MAF between males and females have decreased to the point where they have become small or nonexistent.

However, researchers continue to explore the phenomenon of success avoidance behavior. A slightly different theory argues that success avoidance is not based on internalized needs but merely on a belief that sex-role inappropriate behavior is deviant. The individual does not actively seek to avoid success in general, but only to avoid success in those specific circumstances where success is, by social rules and conventions, considered inappropriate. In fact, success avoidance in some circumstances may be rational behavior, since individuals really are seeking to achieve a hierarchy of goals. If goals are in conflict, the individual may elect to forego a lower level goal in order to achieve some superordinate goal (Hyland 1989).

What we have learned, briefly stated and oversimplified, is that there is some combination of sex-role socialization and situational constraints that leads some women and some men to inhibit their performance in some circumstances. The relationship is a great deal more complex than Horner's original work suggested. The motive, if indeed it can properly be called a motive, is a good deal less stable and certainly less pervasive than her work suggested. But all of that is the nature of theory building. It is from the continual process of theorizing and testing that understanding and knowledge arise.

Both MAF and MAS have been highly controversial. As the debate continues, attention has turned to the concept of power motivation (n-Pow). While achievement motivation is related to entrepreneurial success, managerial success—particularly in large, complex organizations—is more closely associated with n-Pow than n-Ach.

Power Motivation. After years of study of n-Ach, McClelland concluded that achievement motivation "leads people to behave in very special ways that do not necessarily lead to good management" (McClelland and Burnham 1976). Achievement-oriented people, who like to do things for themselves and who seek short-term feedback on their performance, are well suited to entrepreneurial endeavors. Management, however, requires the ability to delegate tasks and to accomplish organizational goals by influencing the behavior of others.

Effective managers must have a greater need for power than need to achieve; they also must be disciplined and controlled so that their exercise of power "is directed toward the benefit of the organization and not toward the manager's personal aggrandizement. Moreover, the manager's need for power ought to be greater than his need for being liked" (McClelland and Burnham 1976).

Good managers are high on power motivation, low on affiliation motivation, and high in inhibition and control. Managers high on affiliation motivation have a need to be liked and want to stay on good terms with everybody; they may behave in ways that enhance their popularity but which are detrimental to the overall goals of the organization. They often make decisions based on what is best for the individual and ignore orderly procedures and long-range goals. However, this is not to argue that the best manager is insensitive or self-serving; a distinction must be made between "personal power" and "socialized power." The individual who abuses power or seeks personal aggrandizement is using personal power;

Figure 8.1
McClelland's Stages of Power Development

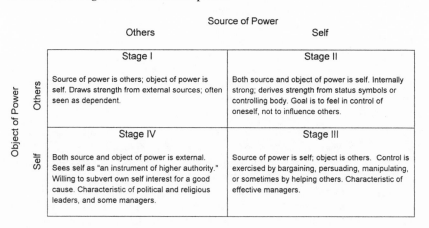

Source of Power

	Others	Self
Stage I	Source of power is others; object of power is self. Draws strength from external sources; often seen as dependent.	**Stage II**
		Both source and object of power is self. Internally strong; derives strength from status symbols or controlling body. Goal is to feel in control of oneself, not to influence others.
Stage IV	Both source and object of power is external. Sees self as "an instrument of higher authority." Willing to subvert own self interest for a good cause. Characteristic of political and religious leaders, and some managers.	**Stage III**
		Source of power is self; object is others. Control is exercised by bargaining, persuading, manipulating, or sometimes by helping others. Characteristic of effective managers.

Object of Power — Others / Self

managers who combine power motivation with "controlled action or inhibition" are using socialized power. Those high on personal power often exercise their power impulsively; they are rude, try to exploit others sexually, and collect such status symbols as fancy cars and big offices. Those high on socialized power, found to be the most successful managers, are more "institution minded" and want to serve others (McClelland and Burnham 1976).

Because people experience power in different ways, McClelland (1975) has developed a typology of power that fits into a developmental model. (See Figure 8.1.) Using the two dimensions of "source of power" and "object of power," either of which is either internal (self) or external (others), he identifies the following four stages of power development:

Stage I: The source of power is others, and the object of power is self. The person derives his strength from others. In infancy, the child derives strength from a caretaker who nurtures and protects and in so doing makes the child feel strong. In adulthood, the person continues to draw strength from external sources—from friends, spouse, or others he admires. S/he wants to be around such people to draw strength from them. People in this stage often are described as being very dependent, but they are only dependent in the sense that it makes them feel strong to be near a source of strength.

Stage II: Both the source and the object of power is self. The person becomes internally strong. As children develop, they learn that they can gain control over their own bodies and minds and can decrease the control by and dependency on their mothers. In adulthood, the person in this mode feels powerful by accumulating possessions which are a part of the self—status symbols such as an expensive car or home—and by controlling the body through dieting, exercise, or yoga. The goal here is to feel strong and in control, but not necessarily to influence others.

Stage III: The source of power is the self and the object is others. Soon after children learn that they can control themselves, they learn that they can control, or at least maneuver, others. As they grow older, they learn more subtle methods of control—bargaining, persuading, manipulating. Adults in this stage are often competitive and exploitive. However, somewhat surprisingly, some kinds of helping behaviors also fall into this quadrant. Giving and receiving help can be looked at as a two-way interaction not unlike winning and losing. People who receive help from others tacitly acknowledge that they are weaker than the givers, at least at that point. The person who gives help without a reciprocal receiving of help achieves a kind of dominance over the receiver.

Stage IV: Both the source and the object of power is external. In this most advanced stage, the person sees him/herself as an instrument of higher authority (God, law, the larger group) which moves him to try to influence or serve others. The religious or political leader at this stage, and many business managers as well, willingly subvert their own self-interest for the greater good of the collectivity. People in this stage are more responsible in organizations, less ego-involved, more willing to seek expert help when appropriate, and more open to intimates. However, the person who has reached this state of maturity has the ability and the opportunity to use power behaviors in any of the three stages.

It would appear at first glance that effective managers would fall into Stage IV, but McClelland argues that they more likely represent an advanced phase of Stage III. The leadership motive pattern, that is, the set of motives most associated with effective management at high levels of organizations, includes being at least moderately high in n-Pow, lower in n-Aff, and high in self-control. McClelland's theoretical explanation for this pattern is

High n-Pow is important because it means the person is interested in playing the "influence game," in having an impact on others; lower in n-Aff is important because it enables the manager to make difficult decisions without worrying unduly about being disliked; and high on self-control is important because it means the person is likely to be concerned with maintaining organizational systems and following orderly procedures (McClelland and Boyatzis 1982).

Are there sex differences in n-Pow? Women and men do not appear to differ in the extent to which they are motivated by the opportunity to use power (Van Wagner and Swanson 1979), but they do differ in the way they express power. In a general and oversimplified sense, men high in n-Pow tend to be "assertive in one way or another and emotional." They get into arguments, share information (boast) about their sex lives with family and friends, and have difficulty sleeping. Women tend to focus more on themselves and to be concerned about their bodies, in the sense both of disciplining the body through diet and exercise and of being concerned with clothing. McClelland concludes that women and men in a sense revert to sex roles in a reciprocal expression of power motivation. Men with high n-Pow have an emotionally assertive approach to life and find strength in action; women with high n-Pow focus on building up the self and on being internally strong.

McClelland and others have demonstrated that this leadership motive pattern is correlated with successful management careers for men in non-technical management positions, but not for men in technical management positions. Whether it holds true for women is yet to be tested. In Chapter 9 we take a detailed look at the differences in the way men and women perceive, attain, and use power.

Attribution/Aspiration Theory

Attribution/aspiration theory is a cognitive approach that categorizes the way women's successes or failures are perceived, to what causes they are attributed, and the effect of those attributions on future performance (Frieze 1975). It is based on the following three premises:

1. men and boys consistently hold higher expectations for personal success than do women and girls;
2. women and men consistently attribute their own successes and failures to different causes; and
3. other people attribute success or failure to different causes depending on the sex of the performer.

Attributions of Self. Four attributional causes are possible: ability, effort, luck, and task ease or difficulty. A person may be seen as having achieved success because of unusual ability or unusual effort, or simply because of good luck or because the task was relatively undemanding. Failure may be laid to incompetence or lack of effort, or to bad luck or difficulty (Miner 1980). Attributions differ along two dimensions: whether they are stable or unstable, and whether they are internal or external. The stable, internal causes are ability and effort; they lie within the individual. Success or failure attributed to stable factors might be expected to be repeated. The unstable, external dimensions are luck and task difficulty. It is difficult to predict whether success or failure will reoccur when they are attributed to unstable causes (Frieze 1975).

In a very general sense, men tend to attribute their successes to internal and stable causes (ability and task difficulty) while women tend to attribute their successes to external and unstable causes (good luck and exceptional effort). On the other hand, men tend to attribute their failures to external and unstable causes (bad luck and lack of effort) while women attribute their failures to internal and stable causes (lack of ability and task difficulty). To the extent that this statement is true, it could support an argument that women, failing to attribute their success to their own ability, would be less likely to seek to repeat their successes. However, as is so often true, a number of situational variables serve to reduce the sex differences in attributions.

- When job level is held constant, no sex differences were found in attribution to luck, effort, or task. But men rate their own performance more favorably, see themselves as having higher intelligence and greater ability, and attribute their success more to ability than do women (Deaux 1979).
- Women with high masculinity scores (on the BSRI) attribute their success to skill more than do feminine women. Women who score low on masculinity (feminine or undifferentiated) attribute their success to luck more than masculine or androgynous women (Orlofsky 1981).
- When a task is labeled as masculine, males tend to expect success and females failure. When these expected outcomes are achieved, they are likely to be attributed to stable causes, while unexpected outcomes a ∍ more likely to be attributed to unstable causes (Weiner et al. 1971)

Attributions of Others. The third element of attribution/aspiration theory speaks to the attributions of others, and again the evidence is mixed. When objectively equal performance is being evaluated by observers, men are consistently rated higher than women by both male and female raters. The same bias that exists with self-attribution persists with the attributions of others, that is, the success of males is attributed to internal causes and of females to external causes, while the opposite holds true for failure (Galper and Luck 1980). But once again, there are situational variables:

- When a male is successful in a task that is labeled masculine, his success is likely to be attributed to skill, while the same performance by a female is likely to be attributed to luck. But the reverse does not hold true. If the task is seen as feminine, attributions for women and men are about the same (Deaux and Emswiller 1974).
- Attributions and judgments support the notion of a double standard, that is, identical behavior by males and females is attributed to different causes and judged by different standards. Behavior by males that is seen as incongruent with the masculine role is attributable to internal causes. However, for women role-deviant behaviors are attributed to external causes (Galper and Luck 1980).
- Expected outcomes tend to be attributed to ability, while unintended outcomes will more likely be attributed to luck (Feather and Simon 1971).
- Males who hold an essentially negative attitude toward women as managers are inclined to attribute the success of a woman manager to the external factors of luck or an easy job, while men with a positive attitude toward women managers are more likely to ascribe their success to internal factors of ability and effort.

Success or failure of the women managers does not change the attitudes of the subjects toward women managers in general (Garland and Price 1977).

- Inadequate performance due to family demands is viewed by both male and female managers as being external to the person, variable, and beyond the individual's control. However, it is viewed as a more stable cause for women than for men (Wiley and Eskilson 1988).

Aspirations. Both sexes tend to err when it comes to predicting success or failure. Men tend to have higher expectations than women, especially when the task is a masculine one. When objective measures of ability are available, men tend to overstate their expectation of success relative to their ability, whereas women tend to understate theirs. On the whole, however, even though women tend to be less optimistic, they tend to be more accurate (Frieze 1975).

Attributions are important to motivation because they affect our aspirations. If success is attributed to ability and effort, one can take pride in the achievement and assume that it will be repeated. If success is attributed to luck or simply an easy task, there is little sense of achievement and little expectation of future success. If failure is seen as the result of too little effort or bad luck, one can hope to achieve better results with increased effort or a change in fortune. But if the failure was the result of incompetence, little improvement could be expected on future tries. Hence pride of accomplishment is closely related to the internal and stable factors of ability and task difficulty, and success leads the performer to expect that future effort would lead to future success. Failure attributed to external and unstable causes also could lead the performer to expect that future tries will result in success. Either of these cases should induce the individual to attempt future success, since he or she could reasonably expect to succeed. The opposite set of conditions, however, success attributed to external and unstable causes and failure attributed to internal and stable causes, would lead not only to a loss of self-esteem but also to an expectation of future failure, or at best of a lack of control over future outcomes.

If there are sex differences in attributions, it could be argued that women are less motivated than men. But what sex differences do appear in self-attribution or the attributions of others are very slight (Frieze et al. 1982) and are largely explained by situational and "dispositional" variables. The basic connection remains clear: Expectations of success or failure are related to effort and outcome, and these expectations in turn are a function of the attributions of cause of past outcomes by oneself and by others. To the extent that, and under the conditions that, women and men make different attributions in like circumstances, their aspirations and their outcomes also will be different. And that is a difference that has profound implications for both individuals and for management.

SUMMARY

In this chapter we have reviewed theories of motivation with the hope of identifying sex differences. We have found repeatedly that neither men nor women can be treated as a homogenous group. Men and women differ in terms of the values they attach to various organizational rewards; their commitment to work; the satisfactions they receive from work and the sources of that satisfaction; the extent to which they are motivated by achievement, affiliation, or power needs; and the sources to which they and others attribute their successes or failures. However, all of these differences are eliminated or greatly mitigated by a number of variables.

Occupation and organizational level are major factors in explaining motivation differences. Individuals in low-status jobs, with little power and little opportunity for promotion, tend to value extrinsic rewards and the social aspects of the job regardless of gender. Managers and professional workers tend to differ very little from each other but a good deal from other organizational groups in their preferences for rewards, their job commitment, their job satisfaction, and their achievement and power motivation.

Other personal variables include age, education, income, sex-role orientation, tenure on the job, attitudes and feelings associated with success or failure, marital status (including whether the spouse works), the presence or absence of children in the home, and organizational choice. Other situational variables that affect motivation include the sex labeling of the job and the causal attributions of self and others.

The dilemma is compounded by the fact that none of these variables works in isolation; there is clearly an interactive effect between them that has not been, and probably never will be, fully explored. To do so would be enormously time-consuming and no doubt unproductive. Would we be better off if we understood the differences in motivation between a married, college-educated woman with teenage children working as a bank officer and a divorced man with preschool-aged children with a high school education working on an assembly line? Probably not. Would we be better off to acknowledge that any perceived sex differences are much more likely to be a function of individual differences or of some combination of the above variables? Probably so.

9

Leadership and Power

The study of management has alternately concentrated on the study of leaders themselves and styles of leadership. The earliest research focused on the traits of people who were perceived to be effective leaders and, not surprisingly, formulated "the great man theory of leadership." If we could identify those traits common to successful leaders, the theory posited, we could then test aspiring managers and predict which ones would be successful; a highly deterministic view. When trait approaches proved disappointing, the research turned to theories of leadership *style*, which of course could be learned. These studies generally looked at the two dimensions of leadership, task orientation and people orientation. Later yet, when it became clear that no one style of leadership was effective, study turned to an examination of the context in which leadership was exercised.

Only very recently has the study of the acquisition and use of power been a serious concern of organizational research. Even though Max Weber's (1930) work looked at the importance of legitimate power and the acceptance of authority, the issue of power has been mostly ignored until very recently. However, McClelland's findings that power motivation is more significantly related to managerial success than achievement motivation has focused attention on the role and use of power in organizations.

This chapter will review the findings of the literature on the relationship between gender and leadership. It will start with traits and then proceed to the study of leadership styles and situational variables. The final section will look at masculine and feminine differences in the use of power. The study of power, as we shall see, is approached in two different ways. The more traditional approach looks at power from the individual or situational viewpoint; another approach looks at power as a function of the organizational structure.

TRAIT THEORIES

Trait theory starts with the belief that leaders differ in some fundamental way from nonleaders. Early research was conducted in order to determine just what those trait differences were. However, efforts to distill the information proved disappointing. One review found that only 5 percent of all traits thought to be related to leadership or success showed up in four or more studies (Bird 1940). Another showed that while certain traits differentiated leaders from nonleaders, the relative importance of these traits changed from one situation to another (Stogdill 1948). So persuasive were the critics that trait theory was virtually abandoned as research turned to the significant situational and style variables to explain managerial success. However, a subsequent re-review of the literature concluded that researchers had overreacted. While we now know that there are no traits that are essential to managerial success, the personal nature of leadership cannot be ignored (Stogdill 1974).

Literally hundreds of studies of the traits or characteristics of "natural leaders" have been conducted over time. They became particularly popular between about 1920 and 1950, when the rapid development of psychological testing instruments made personality assessment more available. The kind of traits most frequently studied included physical characteristics, personality, and ability (Yukl 1981). Certain traits were found to be common among leaders, for instance, they tend to be tall; of high socio-economic status; intelligent, exhibiting superior judgment, decisiveness, knowledge, and verbal ability; have good interpersonal skills; and have high achievement needs (Aldag and Brief 1981). Actually, these traits are more related to the probability of being selected as a leader, so they tell us something about why women are less likely to be chosen as leaders. On the average, women are shorter than men and are seen stereotypically as being less intelligent, decisive, and motivated. Women are perceived as having good interpersonal skills, as people-oriented, as task-oriented, but they are not seen as being powerful or influential.

Managerial Traits: Differences Between Women and Men

The effective manager is overwhelmingly perceived as masculine. Men managers, women managers, and even personnel directors, when asked to select the adjectives that best describe a man and a woman, describe both the woman and the man as having the stereotypical traits of their sex. When asked to choose the traits that best describe a successful manager—sex unspecified—they chose the same traits that describe the stereotypical male (Schein 1973; Schein 1975). Women were seen less favorably in terms of the knowledge, aptitudes, skills, motivation, interests, temperament, and work habits that are demanded in most managerial roles (Rosen and Jerdee

1978). Women also were seen to "cry easily," perhaps with good reason. Contrary to conventional wisdom, younger men show no less stereotypical attitudes than older men. Older men managers, who are more likely to have actually worked with a woman manager, have been found to be less traditional in their perceptions than their younger colleagues (Massengill and DiMarco 1979).

A surprising variation occurs, however, when women use the simple expedient of electing to be addressed as Ms., rather than Miss or Mrs. A woman who prefers to be addressed as Ms. has a better chance of being seen as a successful manager than women who choose the more traditional forms of address (Dion and Schuller 1990).

The concept of psychological androgyny once seemed to offer a fresh prospective. If the androgynous individual is a more effective individual in nonorganizational settings, perhaps the good manager would be perceived as androgynous. However, the hypothesis was soundly rejected by both males and females, who concurred that good managers are masculine (Powell and Butterfield 1979). However, bad managers are not perceived as feminine but as undifferentiated, that is, low on both masculine and feminine qualities (Powell and Butterfield 1984).

Self-Perceptions of Traits. While the argument persists that stereotypical feminine qualities are essential to good management, and some research supports that argument, managers themselves, both men and women, tend to subscribe to the "great man" theory of leadership. One study explicitly included sex role as a variable and found it to be of no importance to managerial success. Ghiselli (1971) used a "self-description inventory" to measure leader traits and then correlated these traits with success on the job. At the very bottom of the list, showing no part in managerial effectiveness, was masculinity-femininity. However, since these were self-descriptions, and since the managerial stereotype so closely parallels the masculine stereotypes, it seems unlikely that successful managers would describe themselves as having feminine traits.

In reality there are few, if any, trait differences between women and men managers. One extensive study found differences on only two minor variables: women scored highly on "social and work incentive" and men on "interpersonal competence between managers and their peers" (Donnell and Hall 1980). Actually, individual masculinity scores are much more highly correlated with level in the organization than with sex. Labeling these traits as masculine may be a misnomer; they may simply be the traits of high-level managers (Fagenson 1990).

Traits and Emergent Leadership. If the trait approach has any validity at all, then it should be able to explain "emergent" leadership, that is, in a group in which no individual is assigned the role of leader, what are the traits of those who emerge by consensus as the leaders. It is widely believed, and often demonstrated, that in groups where no leader is designated, men will emerge as leaders more frequently than women. The qualities most frequently found amongst emergent leaders are dominance, intelligence, and masculinity–femininity (Dobbins et al. 1990).

In single-sex groups, the person with the most dominant personality will most likely emerge as the leader. In mixed groups, however, a dominant woman may exert her influence not by taking the leader role herself but by making the decision about who will lead (Megargee 1969). When the task is perceived as a masculine one, she may defer to a less dominant man. When the task is a feminine one, she is more likely to assign herself as leader. In other words, the leadership role lies in who makes the decision, not in who is anointed leader, and the high dominance woman makes the decision based on her perceived competence in the task (Carbonell 1984). If the task is sex-neutral, interpersonal attractiveness and a masculine sex-role orientation, but not sex, are also important determinants (Goktepe and Schneier 1989).

Self-monitoring—the ability and willingness to read verbal and nonverbal social cues and alter one's behavior accordingly—is also associated with emergent leadership, and it may be the most important trait. Although this seems to be a sex-neutral skill, males still emerge as leaders more frequently than women, for reasons that are still unclear (Dobbins et al. 1990).

Managerial Traits: Differences Between Women Managers and Nonmanagers

If there are few differences between women and men managers, there are fairly clear differences between women managers and nonmanagers. *The Managerial Woman*, a well-known and influential trait study, compared the life experiences of twenty-five top-level women managers to a matched group of nonmanagers. The women managers had achieved their positions through progressive career advancement, and their current positions were ones not regarded as feminine. The question being addressed was how they had managed to depart from traditional female roles to achieve success in "a man's world" (quotation marks in original) (Hennig and Jardim 1977).

Remarkable in-group similarities were found. All twenty-five successful managers were first-born children. Each was either an only child or the eldest in an all-girl family of no more than three children. Each had a happy childhood in a very traditional, warm and loving, upwardly mobile middle-class family. Each identified more with her father than her mother and received support and encouragement from her father to succeed.

The career development of the group was also remarkably homogenous: each had gone to college, each had started her career in a secretarial position, each had spent her whole career in one firm, none had married before age 35, none had children of her own. Each had had at least one male mentor and each had gone through a "midlife crisis" in her middle thirties. By contrast, there was no similar pattern amongst the nonmanagerial group.

The similarities within this group are certainly surprising. But what does all this tell us? First of all, these women were all born during the period in which the first women's movement was at its height. They went to college during the 1930s, and the financial hardships that kept many depression-era young people out of college seems not to have affected their lives at all. Much of their early career progress took place during World War II, when a shortage of men workers created unusual career opportunities for women and when fewer young men were available for dating and marriage. We could conclude that these women had traits that were essential to managerial success, or we could as easily conclude that they reached career maturity at a fortuitous time.

Other research, though, does confirm that there are more differences between women managers and nonmanagers than between women and men managers. A comparison of women in nontraditional occupations (20 percent or fewer female occupants) and women in nursing found that the nontraditional women were more achieving, emphasized production more, and saw themselves as having characteristics more like managers and men. Although they had not foregone marriage, the business women considered the domestic role less important and had fewer children than the nurses (Moore and Rickel 1980).

These trait studies suggest that effective women managers differ very little from effective men managers in terms of their attitudes, motivation, and behavior, but that women managers differ considerably from women non-managers. Finally, and perhaps most importantly, they tell us that the traits that are perceived as being related to managerial success are ones that are also perceived as masculine.

LEADERSHIP STYLE

Studies of leadership style identify two dimensions of leadership behavior that are seen as instrumental to effective management: task orientation and people orientation. People orientation includes such behaviors as leader supportiveness, friendliness, consideration, consultation with subordinates, representation of subordinates' interests, openness of communication with subordinates, and recognition of subordinates' contributions. These relationship-oriented behaviors are all instrumental for establishing and maintaining good relationships with subordinates. Task orientation includes behaviors concerned with directing subordinates, clarifying subordinates' roles, planning, coordinating, problem solving, criticizing poor work, and pressuring subordinates to perform better (Yukl 1981).

Over time it became apparent that leadership style alone was insufficient to explain leader effectiveness; the contexts in which the leader performed were equally important. One of the first to introduce situational variables into leadership style theory was Fiedler (1965). He agreed with the basic premise that style could be divided into the two categories, but he argued that the effectiveness of a given style was contingent upon situational variables that were not easily manipulated.

Rather than training leaders to adopt new behaviors, which is always problematic, this approach argues that it is easier and more effective to train them to recognize their own leadership style and to identify the situations in which their style will be most effective. Fiedler argues that it is nearly impossible to "turn a cold and hard manager into a warm and fuzzy manager" through training, but you can train people to recognize and avoid the situations in which they are likely to fail. As we will see, situational variables have far more effect on leadership than does sex.

Contrary to predictions based on sexual and managerial stereotypes, women managers do not necessarily adopt a people-oriented style and men a task-oriented style. Most research has found no sex differences. In some studies, women and men managers used a very similar style (Birdsall 1980). In others, women leaders were actually seen as more task-oriented than men leaders (Bartol and Wortman 1975). And in still others, as the number of male subordinates rose, the female leaders' style became increasingly task-oriented (Chapman 1975). Whatever differences appear seem to be a function of situational variables other than sex.

Also, contrary to stereotypical expectations, subordinates are not necessarily more satisfied when a woman adopts a people-oriented style or a man a task-oriented style. For the most part, the leader's sex or leadership behavior itself seemed to make little difference in job satisfaction (Osborn and Vicars 1976; Bartol and Wortman 1975). People orientation has been associated with job satisfaction for *both* male and female leaders (Petty and Bruning 1980). Satisfaction appears to be more related to the work values of the subordinates than to the sex of either the leader or the subordinate. These values vary depending on the gender and occupational position of the subordinate, and employees tend to be more satisfied when the manager's leadership style is in harmony with their own values (Jensen, White, and Singh 1990).

Managerial effectiveness also is unrelated to either the sex of the leader or their leadership style. However, leadership style may be evaluated differently, depending on the leader's gender. Even when performance is identical, women tend to be evaluated more favorably than men on people-oriented behavior and men more favorably than women on task-oriented behavior (Bartol and Butterfield 1976). But the sex of the subordinate also makes a difference in how behavior is evaluated. Women may be judged harshly when they exert authority over a male subordinate or when they are lenient with a female subordinate (Jacobson et al. 1977).

If there is any difference in the way women and men manage, it is not in the difference between task and people orientation but in the choice of influence tactics, that is, the use of an autocratic or democratic decision-making style. Although the differences are slight, women do seem to be more democratic and participative in their approach, possibly as a result of their more skillful interpersonal behavior. This style may help female leaders to win acceptance from others, gain self-confidence, and thereby be effective (Eagly and Johnson 1990). Proponents of this interactive style say that it improves the performance of their subordinates by encouraging involvement, sharing both power and information, and enhancing self-worth (Rosener 1990).

We can conclude that women and men do not differ in terms of leadership styles. Women do not adopt a more people-oriented style; men do not exhibit higher task orientation. Women are not necessarily more effective when they use a people-oriented style; men are not necessarily more effective when they use a task-oriented style. Subordinates are not more satisfied when their manager uses a sex-appropriate style. Women are more likely than men to use democratic or participative styles and are effective when they do. Highly task-oriented managers, female or male, probably will not learn to be "warm and fuzzy," and highly people-oriented managers, female or male, probably will not become cold and hard. Either will be successful if his/her style is appropriate to the situation.

One cannot, however, ignore the implications of the managerial stereotypes. Even though the evidence shows scant differences at most, stereotypes continue to favor the "male is normal" model of leadership. The most encouraging indication we have is that stereotypes tend to become less important as experience increases. In the real world, women and men, leaders and followers, adapt their behaviors and their attitudes to the situation.

LEADERSHIP AND POWER

Interest in the whole area of power has increased greatly in recent years. Power, which once was treated as a taboo, may be a great deal more important than previously thought in understanding managerial effectiveness (Pfeffer 1992). It is the coercive or abusive use of power, not power itself, that we find offensive. We use terms like "Machiavellian" to suggest abuses of power. We often recall Lord Acton's axiom that "Power corrupts, and absolute power corrupts absolutely." We accuse aggressive leaders of being "on a power trip." It is perhaps not surprising, given these negative attitudes, that we have shunned the study of power. And yet, in another sense, the failure of organizational scholars to more seriously consider the dynamics of power is surprising indeed. We saw earlier that the motivation to acquire and use power has been found to be more closely associated with managerial success than achievement motivation.

Management involves a wide range of roles and activities: the focus on leadership traits and style is too limited to explain what differentiates the successful from the unsuccessful manager. The important question, for our purposes, is the extent to which women and men differ in power use. There are two distinct but not mutually exclusive approaches to the issue. One looks at the notion of *interpersonal power*—the use, perception, and effectiveness of given power styles. The other looks at *structural power*—the extent to which organizational structure and processes differentially affect men and women in their search for power.

Interpersonal Power

Interpersonal power can be defined as the ability to get another person or persons to act, think, or feel in a way that they would otherwise not have done (Frieze et al. 1978). Despite its negative connotations, power (or influence) is something that everyone exerts a good deal of the time. The father who insists that his daughter finish her homework before she may watch television is exerting power. The manager who congratulates her administrative assistant when he has done a good job also is exerting power.

A seminal analysis of interpersonal power was explicated by French and Raven (1959). They developed a typology of six power bases, sources of power that exist in a particular relationship between influencer and influencee:

1. *Coercive power* refers to the ability of one person to threaten another with punishment. The punishment might be physical or verbal. It can take tangible forms such as levying fines, firing, or withholding some valued outcome like a promotion or a raise.

2. *Reward power* is the ability to administer a reward which the influencee values. Again, the reward might be tangible, such as a raise or bonus, or it might be intangible, such as praise or gratitude.

3. *Referent power* is based on similarity and liking. If one admires another person and wishes to model him- or herself after that person, then the person has referent power. S/he is a point of reference to the admirer.

4. *Expert power* is based on having superior skills or knowledge in a particular area or on a particular topic. If one is perceived as an expert, others will defer to her or him. Expert power tends to be particularized to the influencer's unique area of expertise.

5. *Legitimate power* is based on one's position in the organization. Power is legitimate when it is based on the legally constituted authority of the office. It is concerned with "rank." Legitimate power depends for its effectiveness on subordinates perceiving the legitimacy of the influencer's authority.

6. *Information power* is based on influencing others by having specific information

or data relevant to a particular issue. If one knows what time the plane leaves, one can influence one's fellow travelers to leave for the airport in time.

These power bases are available to a greater or lesser degree to individuals, depending on a number of factors. When faced with a situation requiring the use of power, one must choose from among the bases available at the moment. How does one choose which to use? First there is a cost/benefit analysis, which may be done consciously or unconsciously. How effective will this strategy be? What will it cost in terms of time, effort, money, or bargaining chips? Second, there is an evaluation of the reactions of others to a particular strategy. This step involves not so much questioning the effectiveness as questioning the subjective reactions. What will others think of me? Finally, one's own attitudes, values and beliefs, and personality affect the choice. How will I feel? What will I think of myself? (Raven and Kruglanski 1970).

Not everyone has access to power in the same way, however. Four factors influence how much power a person can have and use: *status, concrete resources, expertise,* and *self-confidence* (Frieze et al. 1978).

Status is socially determined. Every social system attaches values to certain traits, positions, or achievements. Those with high status have access to a wide range of power bases. Further, they are able to accumulate "idiosyncrasy credits," that is, they are able to behave in ways that would be unacceptable for a low-status person.

Concrete resources include time, money, material possessions, physical strength, and other personal resources, such as sexual favors and warmth and affection.

Expertise is a special form of resources, including knowledge, information, or skills.

Self-confidence is related to possession of status, concrete resources, and expertise. Self-confident people attempt to influence others more; those with low self-confidence expect less success, attempt less influence, and use less risky power bases.

Clearly, on all of these grounds—power bases, power determinants, and power opportunities—men and women have different experiences. Power behaviors that are seen as appropriate for men will not, as we shall see, be seen as stereotypically appropriate for women. The cost and outcomes for women and men of a given power base often will be different, and women and men will feel differently about using them. The opportunities for power use that are routinely available to men often are lacking for women. However, when women do achieve power positions, they tend to use power very similarly to men and be seen as equally effective (Ragins 1989).

Differences exist between women and men in both the opportunity and use of interpersonal power. The theoretical constructs described above are the bases for three dimensions of power styles: *indirect versus direct power, personal versus concrete power*, and *helplessness versus competence* (Johnson 1976).

Indirect power often is called *manipulation*. It occurs when the influencer acts, or attempts to act, without the receiver being aware of the action. Dropping hints, starting rumors, and feigning illness are all examples of indirect power. Men use indirect power but can also use direct power without negative sanctions. Indirect power behavior is primarily associated with women. It may be effective in the short run, but it has negative consequences. If it is effective, the influencer may obtain the objective but will get no recognition and will not be perceived as being powerful. If it is not effective, the influencer may be seen as being manipulative or exploitive. Further, the influencer is not likely to see her/himself as strong and will not build a sense of self-confidence.

Personal versus concrete power refers to the types of resources one controls, those that depend on personal relationships, such as liking or respect, and those that are concrete, such as money, knowledge, and physical strength. Again, sex differences are apparent. Women tend to possess stereotypically feminine personal resources—liking, affection, love, or approval. Men tend to possess and control concrete resources. Personal resources tend to be successful only in the short run. In order to use them effectively, the influencer must have a personal relationship with the influencee, which creates a form of dependency.

Helplessness versus competence rests largely on one's own sense of competency. Women often do not feel competent and are not perceived by others as being competent, except in female-based tasks. Displaying competence in masculine tasks may be perceived as unfeminine. Helplessness can be effective in the short run; even men can use it, for instance, the man who influences a woman to sew a button on his shirt by being unable to thread a needle. The person who trades on weakness may bargain away the right to trade on strength at some later point, and once again may suffer a loss of self-image.

Women, if they act in an acceptable feminine manner, will rely on indirect, personal, and helpless forms of power. The interplay of these sex-role expectations and opportunities form the basis of actual differences between female and male power styles (Johnson 1976).

Reward and coercion are more commonly used by men and are considered masculine behavior. Reward power can be used directly or indirectly and can involve either concrete or personal resources. Men more often have access to concrete resources and are more likely to use them. The use of reward with personal resources is seen as stereotypically feminine and is more frequently used by women.

Coercion can be direct or indirect and also can use personal resources, for example, withholding affection. Men, who usually are stronger and more aggressive than women, more often use physical coercion, usually against other males but sometimes against women as well. Although personal coercion is seen as feminine, men also may use it effectively. Women, then, are limited in their use of this power base to only those situations and relationships where their personal resources are of value, while men have the opportunity for a much wider sphere of influence.

Referent power is based on the psychological process of identification with another person whom we consciously attempt to imitate. It is a purely passive form of power that relies on the perception of similarities. It is not seen as sex-stereotyped; women may have referent power, particularly with other women, but that doesn't necessarily make them appear powerful.

Expert power is seen used often by both men and women. It is the form of power most directly under one's own control, and therefore one that women managers can develop. While men are more likely to be in expert positions, when women use expert power they are perceived as powerful (Ragins and Sundstrom 1990).

Information power differs from expert power in that the influencer does not just state that she or he knows best, but uses information to explain why. It relies on having access to information, rather than to concrete or personal resources. Since women often do not have access to information and are not seen as being as logical or competent as men, information power is seen as masculine and more often used by males. If a woman does have information and uses it directly, she may be seen as acting out of role and may arouse hostility. She may be more effective if she presents her information in a stereotypically feminine manner, using a soft voice or hesitating manner. Men, on the other hand, are seen as effective when presenting information in a direct way.

Legitimate power, or position power, is based on shared understanding of the rules of who has the legitimate right to influence whom. Women have less access to legitimate power than men and use it very little; when they do use it, however, they are seen as equally powerful as their male colleagues (Ragins and Sundstrom 1990). A variation, legitimate helplessness, appeals to the norm of social responsibility; social norms mandate that a person in a helpless position be rescued. Legitimate helplessness is more effective for women, but, as with the missing shirt button, it is acceptable for men to use it in some cases (Frieze et al. 1978).

To recap: there are six bases of power—reward power, coercive power, expert power, legitimate power, referent power, and information power. At least four factors determine opportunities to use power: status, control of concrete resources, expertise, and self-confidence. In addition, several factors determine what power base we will use in a given situation, including the perceived costs and outcomes of a particular strategy, the effect it will have on others, and our own internal reactions. Finally, power strategies operate across a number of dimensions: direct versus indirect power, concrete versus personal power, and helplessness versus competence.

The evidence all points to the same conclusions. Successful managers are those who are able to acquire and use power strategies effectively. Those power styles and strategies that are most associated with being perceived as powerful and competent, with being effective or persuasive, also are associated with being masculine. These also are the strategies that are associated with direct use of power. Further, people who are successful at getting and using power tend to acquire self-confidence and to exhibit fewer symptoms of psychological distress. On the other hand, those strategies that are perceived as being least effective and are least associated with being powerful are those indirect and personal styles commonly associated with femininity. Finally, both masculine and feminine styles may be effective if used by men, but masculine styles may be less effective when used by women. The ineluctable conclusion is that women have the choice of using power in an indirect (manipulative) way and risking being either ineffective or unrecognized, or using direct styles and risking being both ineffective and disliked.

This view of power, as noted above, looks at the relationship between sex-role stereotypes and perceptions of power styles to explain women's relative powerlessness in organizations. Another approach looks, instead, at the structure of organizations themselves for an explanation.

The Structural Approach

The successful performance of the managerial role requires not only the downward use of authority but also the upward and outward use of influence. It requires that managers not only have the legitimate authority of their positions but also that they are seen as having power and influence in the larger organization. It requires, in short, that they be successful at organizational politics. The word politics, like the word power, has negative connotations, but it is used here in a nonpejorative sense to mean the use of aggregate, rather than personal, influence or power. It means the forming of alliances or coalitions with other powerful people in the organization in order to accomplish mutual goals. It implies a synergistic accumulation of individual power, that is, the power of a coalition is greater than the sum of the powers of the individuals (Pfeffer 1981).

Organization members tend to look on power as a finite quality and hence at the distribution of power as a zero-sum game in which what one person gains another must have lost. Organizational politics creates power within the organization, because a powerful person can, by association, empower a less powerful ally without reducing his or her own power. On the contrary, the ability to empower another may in fact increase an individual's perceived power. This kind of structural power is essential to the accomplishment of the organization's goals; it also may be necessary to the accomplishment of individual ambitions. It also is consensual. You can poll any sample of organizational members as to who are the most influential actors and achieve a very high level of agreement (Salancik and Pfeffer 1983).

Productive power is a function of one's connections with other parts of the system, rather than of one's sexual orientation (Kanter 1979). Organizational power evolves from two kinds of capacities: access to the resources, information, and support necessary to do the job; and the ability to get cooperation in doing what is necessary. A manager is seen as being powerful in the organization when he or she can accomplish such goals as interceding on behalf of someone in trouble with the organization or getting a desirable promotion for a talented subordinate, getting regular or fast access to top decision makers, or gaining access to early information about important events.

Thus, people who look like they can command more of the organization's resources, who look like they can bring something that is valued from outside into the group, who seem to have access to the inner circles that make the decisions affecting the fate of individuals in organizations, may also be more effective as leaders and be more liked in the process (Kanter 1977).

Two vital elements of this kind of structural power are credibility and dependency. Executives who were asked to define the characteristics of effective leaders respond that credibility was more important than anything else. Credibility meant competence plus power. People with credibility were able to command the resources of supplies, information, and support necessary to get the job done. Those who had credibility upward in the organization also had it downward. Credibility downward was based on the subordinates' perception of their manager's importance in the organization and was in turn related to their effectiveness. "People sensitivity" was a good thing to have but was of very little value in terms of eliciting subordinate support without the respect that comes with credibility (Kanter 1977).

The degree to which credibility is related to power is a function of the amount of dependency in the situation. If power is related to the ability to acquire and control resources, then it follows that the scarcer and more critical the resource, the greater the amount of power that attaches to it. Leaders who are able to define what resources are critical to the organization and who can control the distribution of those resources are able to make others dependent on them. Their departments or units become critical to the survival and success of the larger organization (Hickson et al. 1971).

Dependency occurs in organizations because of the complexity of the division of labor and because of the uncertainties created by the environment. Virtually no group can accomplish its task without dependence on others—for materials, for personnel, for consumption of output. Virtually no group can control completely all of the uncertainty that arises from the environment, from market or technological shifts, from economic conditions, or from competition. The extent to which one group is dependent on the other for either internal or external control of uncertainty is a measure of the power relationship between those groups and hence between their leaders. It is the reciprocity of these dependencies that makes the exercise of power possible (Kanter 1977).

Hence, organizations have power structures that are not solely a function of job title or of position on the organizational chart, and it is one's position in the power structure, not one's personality traits or motivation, that determines one's leadership style. Power positions are achieved in one of two ways: through activities or through association. In order to increase power, activities must meet three criteria: they must be extraordinary— being first in a new position, taking major risks and succeeding, making organizational changes; they must be visible; and they must be relevant— being identified with the solution to critical organizational problems. However, in addition to activities, power almost always comes from social connections outside the immediate work group: through having or being a sponsor, through peer acceptance, and through powerful subordinates (for example, having a subordinate who is recognized as a "comer" or a "water walker" in the organization). To the extent that women in organizations are few in number and fairly isolated, it becomes very difficult for them to gain control of the critical activities or to establish the essential alliances. Fear of sexual entanglement also is substantially increased when women are "tokens," increasing their isolation.

Certain positions within the hierarchy are associated with powerlessness. The first two, not surprisingly, are first-line supervisors and staff (as opposed to line) managers, positions frequently held by women. (The third is surprising; it is the Chief Executive Officer, a position rarely held by a woman. Chief Executives are rendered powerless when the press of daily activities keeps them from using their power to make long-range planning and policy decisions.) First-line supervisors are people in the middle, caught between higher management and their subordinates. They have little chance to gain power through activities and few chances to make power-enhancing alliances. They have little credibility, since they have little chance for upward mobility. They have moved from the ranks of the workers, but the next ranks, the entry levels of middle management, are generally filled with entry-level college graduates or MBAs. They have little or no impact on the making of policies or rules that affect their workers, they have few rewards to administer, and they may suffer resentment from their former co-workers. First-line supervisors tend to act out their powerlessness by oversupervising, by overcontrolling and by overreliance on rules. Powerless themselves, they deny their subordinates any opportunity for individual autonomy or freedom.

Staff professionals are the people who supply the support services to line departments. They have no direct authority in the larger organization and must use persuasion and bargaining techniques to get line managers to carry out their recommendations. They are perceived as useful (although sometimes as an unnecessary hindrance) but not as critical to the organization's survival. They often are hired because they have expertise in a particular area; they have little opportunity for upward mobility outside of their specialty, so they have little opportunity to reach the ranks of upper management. Their work can be, and frequently is, assigned to outside consultants. They have little credibility and less dependency in the larger organization and little opportunity to form reciprocal alliances. Staff managers tend to respond to their powerlessness by becoming turf minded, creating islands in the organization. They create a false sense of their own expertness and often engage in jurisdictional disputes with other staff departments (Kanter 1979).

Powerless people respond to their powerlessness in a number of ways: by controlling behavior and close supervision, by being rules-minded, and by exerting territorial and domain control. These behaviors are unlikely to produce effective results, and subordinates often respond by slack performance, leading in a vicious downward spiral to more control, more frequent application of rules, more territoriality. These are behaviors typical of all managers in powerless positions, regardless of sex. But since women managers are most frequently found in powerless positions, these behaviors often have been associated with female managers and have contributed to the stereotype of the mean, bitchy, woman boss.

There is a common and well-founded presumption that most workers, male or female, prefer a male boss to a female (Forgionne and Nwacukwu 1977). However, resistance to women as managers is greatly reduced when respondents have actually worked for a woman (Ragins and Sundstrom 1990). The preference for men bosses is really a preference for power, and in most organizations women do not hold positions in the power structure. But when they do, "power wipes out sex."

SUMMARY

This chapter has looked in detail at the research on leadership. It began with a review of trait theories, moved on to leadership style studies, and finally considered power, from the standpoints of both interpersonal power and structural power. The major area of interest is the extent to which differences exist between women and men managers.

The trait literature suggests that successful women managers tend to be more like successful men managers and less like nonmanagerial women. They also suggest some important differences between male and female managers based on sex-role expectations, both in the way women exercise leadership and in the way their leadership behavior is viewed and accepted. While these studies give us some interesting insights into the backgrounds, personalities, and experiences of successful women managers, they tell us little about the situational factors that affected their career development.

Studies of leadership style turn out to be at best inconclusive, at worst contradictory. There are apparently no gender-related differences between women and men, either in what style they adopt or in their effectiveness. The only sex difference is that women seem more likely to use a participative, and men to use an autocratic, style of decision making. The most positive conclusion that one can come to is that, in any given situation, it is the appropriateness of the leadership style to the situation, rather than the gender of either the leader or the subordinates, that is important.

When we look at the ability to acquire and use power, some differences are apparent. The study of interpersonal power suggests that there are strongly sex-linked power styles, power dimensions, power opportunities, and power determinants. Those styles that are closely related to managerial success are direct styles associated with status, competence, concrete resources, and self-confidence, and are based on expertise and legitimacy. They are the styles most closely linked to masculinity. Power styles considered feminine are indirect styles associated with helplessness and personal resources, and are based on referent or legitimate power. These styles are manipulative, they are less effective, and, even when successful, they fail to establish the credibility of the influencer. To the extent that women are able to adopt direct styles, however, their efforts are appropriate and effective.

The final section looked at power as a structural phenomenon. Organizational politics award power to individuals who can exert influence upward and outward in the organization. This power is based on achieving credibility and creating dependency through the control of resources of supply, information, and knowledge. The more critical one's activities are to the organization's success and survival, the more dependent other elements of the organization become, and the more power is generated. One achieves power through activities, which must be extraordinary, visible, and relevant, and, more importantly, through alliances with other powerful people, either of which may be more difficult for women, especially if they are relative isolates. Hence, organizations create informal power structures that are independent of formal organizational charts. Certain positions in these power structures are particularly powerless, including first-line supervisors and staff managers, the kind of management positions most frequently held by women. The leadership style of incumbents in these positions often is characterized by close supervision, strict adherence to rules, and zealous protection of territory and domain. These characteristics often are attributed to the fact that the managers are women and contribute to the stereotype of the mean, bitchy, woman boss. They are, however, characteristic of powerless people regardless of gender.

Women can and do achieve power positions in organizations, and when they do they are as effective as men managers, but for women access often takes longer and is less assured. Power develops over time, throughout one's career development, as one acquires individual and interpersonal resources. The career path for men leads them on a straight course to power positions, but for women it "can best be characterized as an obstacle course" (Ragins and Sundstrom 1989).

Congresswoman Shirley Chisholm once said that women will have to take power, because "no one is giving it away." And taking power may mean overcoming a great deal of social baggage.

10

Performance and Perceptions of Performance

In Chapter 8, we found virtually no sex differences in motivation that did not disappear when situational variables were considered. Men and women similar in age, occupation, and educational level, with equivalent opportunity and power in the organization, varied not at all in terms of their desired outcomes from work and their job satisfaction and very little in terms of their commitment to work. When situational factors were taken into account, they also varied little on their motivation to achieve, their fears of failure or success, and their attributions for their successes and failures.

In Chapter 9, we found a similar lack of significant sex differences in managerial style. Although managers are seen stereotypically to have masculine traits and to behave in masculine ways, in fact very few differences exist in either traits or styles between women and men managers. However, women and men do differ in their ability to get and to use power and in climbing the organizational ladder. This upper limit has come to be known as a "glass ceiling," and it exists for both women and people of color.

Three levels of explanation are available to explain why women fail to achieve managerial success at the same rate as men. One lies in women themselves; it argues that women are less independent and more conforming than men, and/or that they lack the self-confidence to be successful leaders. The second lies in perceptions of women's performance or ability; it argues that others interpret women's abilities differently than men's, based on stereotypical assumptions. The third lies in organizations themselves; it argues that systemic organizational barriers, both overt and covert, keep women out of the domains of power.

This chapter will look at each of these in turn.

PERCEPTIONS OF SELF

As we have confirmed repeatedly, a double standard affects the way women's behavior is perceived by others. If a woman is deferential and passive, she may be seen as feminine but not as competent or powerful. If she is independent and assertive, she may be seen as unfeminine but not as necessarily competent. We turn now to the question of whether women are more conforming and persuasable than men, and whether they have less self-confidence than men. And if they are, under what circumstances are these behaviors most likely to occur?

Conformity/Persuasability

Some years ago, a male author wrote "It has been well established, at least in our culture, that females supply greater amounts of conformity under almost all conditions than males" (Nord 1969), and, indeed, research supports this notion. Women have been found to be, by nature or nurture, more conforming, more easily persuaded, and less independent than men (Sashkin and Maier 1971; Adams and Landers 1978). Women tend to behave differently from men in organizational settings. In mixed-sex groups, men speak more frequently, are more influential, and are more likely to initiate task-oriented actions (Lockheed and Hall 1976).

The differences in behavior may have to do with women's minority status, in which case men also would behave differently when they were in the minority. But "token" males in predominantly female groups behave quite differently from "token" females in predominantly male groups (Webber 1976). In an experiment that sounds realistic to many women, groups of managers were to prepare a final draft of a written report. In the groups where males were in the majority, the men did the substantive work and the women were relegated to typing. The women's input was rejected or ignored, a role that the women seemed to accept. However, when the men were in a minority, they behaved very differently. Every single man in a female majority group claimed that he was the group leader. In both types of groups, far more men than women were seen by others as the group leader. Minority status in organizations may keep women from full participation in the activities of the group, but it does not explain why they are willing to accept second-class status.

But not all of the evidence supports the notion that females are more conforming, and as always, situational variables go a long way toward explaining the apparent differences.

Sex-Typing and Task Difficulty. Males tend to conform more when the task is considered feminine, females conform more when the task is considered masculine, and both conform more as the task becomes more difficult (Sistrunk and McDavid 1971; Sistrunk 1972).

Sources of Influence. On a difficult task that is perceived as masculine, women tend to turn to women peers for advice, even if they are less expert than other sources (Sistrunk and McDavid 1971). In a similar situation, males tend to take advice from whoever is most expert rather than their peers (Hansson, Allen, and Jones 1980). It may be that these differences have to do with sex roles. Men may reject advice from their peers because they want to appear independent, and women may turn to female sources, even less expert ones, to avoid appearing incompetent to their male colleagues.

So men and women do differ to some extent in the circumstances in their susceptibility to persuasion. The vast majority of people working in managerial positions or seeking managerial positions are working in male-majority situations and participating in tasks that are perceived as masculine. Under these circumstances we would expect the men to be more independent and the women more conforming. As the task difficulty increases, the men may become more persuasable, but they would be more likely to turn to a male than a female for advice, unless the female were perceived as particularly expert in the field. Absent such expertise, her suggestions are apt to be rejected or ignored and her efforts resented. Thus it is not surprising that women are more conforming; perhaps their survival depends on it.

Confidence

A lot of the "how-to" literature for women aspiring to management positions urges them to be self-assured and confident—as though that were a matter of choice. In truth, women do not display lower self-confidence in all achievement situations. As is so frequently true, situational variables influence women's self-confidence relative to men's (Lenney 1977).

First, the level of self-confidence for women and men depends on the nature of the specific task. Women have higher expectations for success on tasks they see as feminine, men on tasks they feel are masculine. Women's self-confidence seems to be lower in tasks involving spatial-mechanical ability and creativity, even though their performance is no different (Lenney 1981). Women and men in supervisory positions show no differences in their work-related sense of competence (Snyder and Bruning 1979), and both women and men show more self-confidence at work than in the social/family environment (Chusmir, Koberg, and Stecher 1992).

Second, women often have lower self-confidence than men when they are given minimal or ambiguous feedback on their abilities or performances. In achievement situations where the person is provided with clear information on his/her task-specific abilities, the sexes demonstrate equal levels of confidence. But, when clear, unambiguous feedback is not available, women report lower levels of self-confidence than men.

Third, women's estimates of their own abilities appear to be lower than men's when their work is compared with that of others' in a group or evaluated by the others. For women, but not for men, confidence varies remarkably depending on both the sex and the perceived ability of the person to whom one is being compared (Lenney 1981).

The higher one goes in a career or profession, the more difficult it becomes to receive clear and unambiguous feedback, and the closer the comparison and evaluation of one's work by others. Particularly for women in the professions, clear and specific criteria for judging performance rarely exist. Newcomers learn the ropes by "intense socialization" into the culture of the profession, a process that typically starts in graduate school. Employees who have been excluded from professional networks during college are excluded not only from situations where they can learn to perform, but also from a social system that lets them know how well they perform (Epstein 1970). In organizations as well, to the extent that women are viewed as outsiders, or as interlopers, they are excluded from the socialization process that teaches newcomers the norms of performance and behavior.

Fourth, differences in confidence levels may be a function of differential status. A theory of *Diffuse Status Characteristics and Expectations States* posits that under certain conditions group members expect high-status individuals to be more competent (Lockheed and Hall 1976; Meeker and Weitzel-O'Neill 1977).

According to the theory, the process works like this: Groups expect some members to perform better than others. Members who are expected to perform better receive and take more opportunities to make contributions, have more influence, and get more agreement and approval than those for whom expectations are lower. In the absence of information to the contrary, group members assign performance expectations to themselves and others based on external status characteristics—such as sex—and males have the higher status. A contribution that is accepted by other members of the group will be assumed by the contributors and others to raise the status of the contributor. But raising one's own status in the group is legitimate only for those who already have high external status, that is, for men but not for women.

The "information to the contrary" might be information that the person is motivated to help others in the group rather than to raise her own status, or it could be legitimately assigned higher status, such as being appointed group leader by an outside authority. Thus women must satisfy both themselves and others that they are competent and also that their motives are not self-serving before their contributions will be perceived as legitimate and their contributions accepted (Meeker and Weitzel-O'Neill 1977).

In this section we have looked at the differences in performance between women and men. In certain circumstances, women do tend to take a less active role, to be more conforming and persuasable, and to exhibit less confidence than men. We have emphasized the situational nature of these differences, recognizing at the same time that these situations—female minority status, masculine sex-typing of tasks, lack of clear and unambiguous feedback on performance, and comparison with others—all contribute to greater conformity and lower self-confidence among women. We also have rejected the explanation that women are biologically less competent than men, or even that these differences are the result of sex-role socialization. Instead we have advanced the theory of status characteristics and expectation states to reason that the cause lies in the differential status of women and men, and specifically in the higher status accorded men.

We turn now to a more complex and disturbing problem, the differential evaluations of women's and men's performance. In order for women to gain credibility, their performances not only must be extraordinary and relevant, they must be recognized as such by managers, peers, and subordinates. If women's work is devalued relative to men's, they will never get the opportunities to acquire and use power.

PERCEPTIONS OF OTHERS

Management theorists have struggled for a very long time to devise objective measurements of employee productivity and performance. A variety of methods—some quite simplistic, some very sophisticated—have been developed. But regardless of how carefully constructed the measurement instrument, evaluations are and will always be inherently subjective. Some imperfect human ultimately must decide what tasks or responsibilities adhere to a particular job; what skills, knowledge, and ability are essential to it; what outcomes are desired; and what standard represents acceptable performance. And further, once these determinations have been made, some equally imperfect human being must measure or observe outcomes to determine to what extent the individual incumbent meets the expectations. One of the great fallacies of organizational life is that these evaluations are implicitly valid and reliable measures of individual and relative performance.

Equally problematic is the assessment of future performance, that is, the selection decision. Managers must evaluate and compare candidates on both their competence to perform and their motivation to do so. Before the decision is made, the manager must ask, *Can* this person do the job to my satisfaction? *Will* this person do the job to my satisfaction?

Although there tends to be an overall male bias in evaluation, it interacts with other variables such as the sex-typing of the task, the sex of the rater, similarities between the rater and the ratee, and physical attractiveness. For example, when college and university department chairs in psychology departments were asked to judge the qualifications of applicants, women were rated as less desirable candidates than men with identical qualifications.

The men were more likely to be offered positions at the associate professor level, the women at the lower assistant professor level (Fidell 1970). Identical work—essays, paintings—is rated higher when it is attributed to a male than to a female (Mischel 1974; Pheterson, Kiesler, and Goldberg 1971).

However, sometimes an opposite—and equally discriminatory—effect occurs; women receive higher ratings than equally qualified males. This "you're pretty smart for a girl" phenomenon seems to happen in situations where women achieve in circumstances where expectations for their success are low. For example, women attorneys were rated as more vocationally competent than identically qualified males (Abramson et al. 1977); women responding to an emergency situation were rated as more deserving of a reward than men who performed identically (Taynor and Deaux 1973). In these circumstances, women's accomplishments are not being compared against those of males, but against other women. Because of the lower expectations of women in these male arenas, what is considered average performance for a man is seen as superior for a woman.

Three factors affect these situations: (1) the level of inference required in the evaluation situation, (2) the effects of sex-role incongruence, and (3) the effect of level of qualifications and performance involved (Nieva and Gutek 1980).

Level of inference refers to the amount of speculation involved. At one extreme is the evaluation of past performance. It requires only the scrutiny of behavior or outcome that is exhibited. At the other extreme is the judgment of an individual's qualifications for a job, a situation that requires speculation about the future, about which little is known. The rater is asked to make inferences, based on such information as education, experience, or past performance, on how the person will behave in the future.

The higher the level of ambiguity in the situation, the higher the level of inference required, and the higher the likelihood that stereotypes will come into play. Ambiguity occurs when little is known about the specific job being filled or about the applicant. Hence, the more information available about the task to be performed or about the individual performer, the less likely that sex bias will affect the evaluation. The less specific and concrete information available about the individual, the more likely that judges will make inferences based on what is generally known about the group to which the person belongs.

Evaluation can be affected by very "subtle, nonfocal cues of affect and innuendo." Consensus about a leader's competence can be achieved in two ways—legitimation by an authority figure or expert, and peer group approval. In one study, identical leader performance was evaluated differently when an authority figure expressed (or withheld) confidence in a leader's ability, even though the authority figure never made any direct statements either praising or criticizing the leader. The leader also was evaluated less positively when members of the group revealed occasional subtle, nonverbal cues of either approval or disapproval. The evaluators in this experiment truly believed that their evaluations were based solely on the performance itself; they were completely unaware that their perceptions had been influenced by these subtle cues (Brown and Geis 1984).

Sex-role incongruence seems to be a factor in many cases where a pro-male bias has appeared. Both males and females suffer to some extent when applying for sex-atypical jobs, but women also suffer in other, more fundamental ways. Often norms regarding work-related behaviors are incompatible with the norms of the feminine sex role. A women who is competent, assertive, or competitive may be perceived as lacking in femininity; but worse, her performance may be attributed to chance or some other external cause, rather than to ability. For example, women who were appointed to leadership positions because they were women were rated less positively than those who became leaders through more equitable methods (chance, ability), regardless of whether their groups succeeded or failed (Jacobson and Koch 1977). This may be an example of *over*evaluation, but either way, the woman is being judged by different criteria, and the emphasis is on her sex, rather than her performance.

The level of qualifications and performance: The more demanding the job, the more likely that males will be preferred. When women and men are equally competent, men tend to be rated higher; but when they are equally incompetent, women are rated higher. Competent men are liked better than competent women (Spence and Helmreich 1972); people would rather work with a competent man than a competent woman. In fact, they would prefer an incompetent woman to a competent one (Hagen and Kahn 1975). Bias, then, tends to work in both directions. Competent males are rated more positively than equally competent females, while incompetent males are rated lower than equally incompetent females (Nieva and Gutek 1980).

"Beauty Is Its Own Reward"

Women have always been valued for and judged by their appearance. Looking attractive, looking sexy, and especially looking young are the criteria by which women are evaluated as women. Men as they grow older are thought to become distinguished; women as they grow older are thought to become ugly. Yet stereotypes apply here as well: Women are said to be "beautiful but dumb;" to be blond is synonymous with being a "dumb blond." Surely everyone has heard the story of the man who spends hours interviewing candidates for a secretarial job. He questions each one about her education and experience, her clerical skills, and her administrative abilities. He evaluates each one on her judgment, intelligence, and maturity. And at the end of the process he announces "I'll take the blond with the great legs."

Is there any truth to that? Unfortunately there is. But a peculiar kind of paradox occurs in reactions to physical appearance. Physically attractive people, both male and female, are assumed to possess more socially desirable personality traits than unattractive ones. They also are expected to achieve more prestigious occupations, to be more competent and successful spouses, to have happier and more successful professional lives, and overall to be happier than less attractive people (Dion, Berscheid, and Walster 1972). What is more, physical attractiveness appears to be a more potent factor in the evaluation of females than of males. Males tend to be evaluated on more objective grounds, for instance, the amount of money they earn, while females are evaluated on more subjective grounds, including their perceived ability to attract a successful husband, which in turn is perceived as related to their physical attractiveness (Bar-Tal and Saxe 1976).

These judgments are based on an overall evaluation of the individual's worth. But the evaluation of performance on a specific task is affected by the relative attractiveness of the individual, and once again men and women are treated differently. Male judges rated an attractive female author as more talented than an unattractive one, and they rated her essay as better, although both were actually being rated on the basis of the same essay. The attractive female was also rated higher than one whose appearance was unknown to the raters, and the impact of attractiveness was greatest when the essay was of poor quality (Landy and Sigall 1974). However, one exception was found; males with liberal attitudes toward women rated an incompetent unattractive female higher than her attractive counterpart (Holohan and Cooke 1981). Female judges were less influenced by a female author's attractiveness, and neither male nor female judges were affected by physical attractiveness when evaluating essays attributed to a male author (Kaplan 1978).

These findings should at least bode well for the attractive female. If males evaluate her work more positively than that of unattractive females, especially when the quality of the work is poor, then the effects of other forms of discrimination should be alleviated. But, alas, it is not that simple. Although competent women are judged to be just as attractive as competent men, women who are incompetent are seen as more attractive than equally incompetent men (Rhue, Lynn, and Garske 1984). Further, attractive people are seen not only as more masculine or feminine, but also as more socially desirable (Gillen 1981). Thus, attractiveness may enhance evaluations on sex-typed tasks, but it may work against women when the task is perceived as masculine (Cash and Trimer 1984).

For example, women who are generally agreed to be attractive expect to be successful in social situations, but they show little confidence in their ability to succeed in masculine tasks (Abbott and Sebastian 1981). Attractive men applying for any white collar position and attractive women applying for nonmanagerial positions are rated higher than their less attractive counterparts. But for managerial positions, attractiveness works against women, exaggerating the disparity between their femininity and the typical masculine traits considered relevant to work performance (Heilman and Saruwatari 1979). For women in clerical positions, personal appearance—attractiveness and social skills—is so important that business and secretarial schools teach dress and grooming along with technical skills. But moving up the ranks in these positions still means moving up the clerical ranks, with little chance of moving into management positions (Kanter 1977).

Attractiveness makes women appear more feminine and more appreciated as women. It causes them to be more highly evaluated when they are involved in role-consistent behaviors. But it enhances the incongruities between their sex roles and roles that are perceived as traditionally masculine. The blond with the great legs may have a better chance of getting the secretarial job but a lesser chance of getting one that is managerial.

Similar to Me

Another aspect of evaluation that deserves some attention is what is sometimes called the "similar to me" phenomenon. Managers often give their highest ratings to those employees they perceive as holding values similar to their own (Senger 1971) or as being "similar kinds of people" (Pulakos and Wexley 1983). Candidates are assigned higher ratings of job suitability, intelligence, personal attributes, and attraction when their resumes show biographical information similar to that of their white middle-class interviewers (Rand and Wexley 1975).

We could predict, then, that women would be rated higher by women and lower by men, and the reverse, but of course no such simple conclusion is possible. In fact, it is sometimes argued that women are more harsh in their judgments of women than of men. A frequently cited study found that women value the professional work of men more highly than the identical work of women (Goldberg 1968). However, many repeats of this study have shown that the average differences between ratings is negligible (Swim et al. 1989). In one study, females actually rated an essay allegedly written by a female as better than the same essay written by a male (Levenson et al. 1975). In still others, women rated work by other women higher only when it had already been awarded a prize (Pheterson, Kiesler, and Goldberg 1971) or when it was attributed to a person with high professional status (Peck 1978), raising again the issue of whether women are more conforming than men.

So both the sex and the personality of the rater affect perceptions of performance (Lord, Phillips, and Rush 1980). Women raters also tend to be more consistent in their perceptions of female performance than of male performance, a difference not found among male raters (Wexley and Pulakos 1982). But the strength or direction of these differences remains to be determined. Past experience makes a difference. Both women and men who have been supervised by a woman are more positive about women's motivation to manage, but not necessarily about their managerial ability, than those who have not (Ezell, Odewahn, and Sherman 1981). Androgyny level seems not to make a difference; androgynous individuals were no less affected by stereotypes in their evaluations than nonandrogynous ones; both showed subtle levels of discrimination against women (Gutek and Stevens 1979).

It is not at all clear, however, to what extent men and women see ratees as "similar to me" on the basis of gender alone. More research is needed to determine to what extent sex, biographical similarity, or other characteristics, for example, age, race, religion, or nationality, might affect the perceptions of similarity and how those perceptions might affect evaluations. In the meantime, we are left with the reality that men do seem to rate the work of subordinates more favorably when they perceive them to be like themselves in values and personalities. Men are also more likely to let their judgments of a woman's work be affected by her attractiveness. The potential for discrimination against women is enormous, since men are far more likely to be in the position of making judgments. Even if women do achieve the power, it may not always work to the advantage of other women (Nieva and Gutek 1980). Women evaluators are relatively unaffected by attractiveness, but they are affected by status. They often undervalue the work of other women unless the work or the person performing the work has already achieved recognition.

To recap: Performance evaluation is not and can never be value-free. The sex of the ratee, and to a lesser extent the sex of the rater, has a distinct impact on the judgments of both the performer and the work. Most often this impact takes the form of a pro-male bias, although in some cases the result is an overevaluation of female work. Three factors that affect the level of bias are (1) the level of inference required—the less concrete and specific the situation, the more likely that males will be preferred; (2) sex-role incongruence—males tend to be favored over females in tasks that are perceived as masculine, but the reverse effect is less strong; and (3) level of qualifications and performance—the greater the demands, the more likely that males will be preferred. Being physically attractive helps for males in most situations but only for females in situations that are not perceived as incongruent with the female sex role. Having shared values or personality traits with the rater tends to enhance the evaluation, but gender may or may not contribute to feelings of similarity. The pro-male bias is demonstrated by both sexes, except that women rate other women higher when their accomplishments have already received recognition. And perhaps most discouraging of all, bias can be evoked by very subtle, nonverbal cues of approval or disapproval from either authority figures or subordinates.

So, while we have found so far no significant differences in female competence, we have found differences in the way female performance is perceived and evaluated. The next, and perhaps the most critical, issue is how these differential evaluations enter into organizational decision making.

ORGANIZATIONAL IMPACTS

Despite thirty years of Civil Rights laws, a resurgence of the women's movement, and the enormous growth in women's labor force participation, despite significant gains in women's entry into the professions, women still tend to be clustered in female-dominated jobs in the lower levels of the organization. A number of factors may contribute to that situation, including women's own occupational choices. But it is impossible to ignore the evidence that confirms that organizational structures and decision-making processes still have the effect of impeding women's rise to management positions.

These barriers occur in two stages. The first affects women's entry into the organization and access to the appropriate jobs. The second affects their upward mobility in the organization, a barrier often referred to as a "glass ceiling," an invisible but impenetrable barrier that denies access to the higher levels of the organization.

Access to the Organization

Public policy and contemporary values require that when a man and woman are equally qualified they should be given equal treatment in applying for work. Most personnel decision makers believe that they comply with that standard and select purely on the basis of relative merit. But a good deal of evidence indicates that the perception of merit is easily influenced by sex.

For example, letters of application were sent in answer to newspaper advertisements for accounting jobs at several levels of skill. The qualifications listed were identical except for the sex of the applicant. Efforts were counted as "successful" if the employer scheduled an interview or just sent back an application form to be completed. The male applicants had considerably more success than identically qualified females. Yet when, several months later, the same employers were asked to respond to a survey on their hiring practices, 85 percent said they treat male and female applicants equally. A majority of the respondents said there was no discrimination in the accounting field (Firth 1982).

In another example, male and female students made duplicate telephone inquires in response to 256 different classified job advertisements. Clear-cut discrimination was found in over one-third of the cases ("This job isn't suitable for a man/woman," or "I don't think a man/woman would like this job"). In another one-third, the answers were ambiguous ("Well, I guess you could come in and apply" or "Are you sure you're really qualified for this job?"). In only one-third of the cases was there no apparent discrimination (Levinson 1975).

These advertised jobs were mostly fairly low-level, low-skilled jobs, while the accounting jobs obviously required higher levels of education and training. Job recruiters at two university placement offices, presumably well versed in the relative competencies of male and female applicants for professional jobs, were asked to evaluate a hypothetical applicant—either male or female—for a male-oriented or female-oriented position. And once again significantly more females were recommended for the female-oriented position and males for the male-oriented one (Cohen and Bunker 1975).

These studies and many more demonstrate the existence of access discrimination, but it is simplistic to say that men are preferred over women for all jobs or even that women and men are preferred for sex-specific jobs. Other variables enter in, including the sex-role orientation of the interviewer, the difficulty of the job, the scholastic performance and educational background of the applicants, the gender of the manager's subordinates, the level of inference required in the decision, the age and the competence of the applicants, their attractiveness, and even their choice of perfume (Baron 1983).

The sex-role orientation of the applicant may be more important than sex itself in determining perceived suitability for a sex-typed job. Both androgynous and masculine applicants are considered suitable for masculine-typed jobs; both feminine and androgynous individuals are considered suitable for both feminine and sex-neutral jobs (Jackson 1983a). The sex-role orientation of the interviewer also affects the way s/he perceives an applicant's suitability for a sex-typed job. Interviewers who hold conventional sex-role stereotypes are more likely to discriminate in evaluating job applicants than those who do not, and they are more likely to discriminate against a woman applicant for a male-oriented job than the reverse (Sharp and Post 1980).

Women may unwittingly contribute to the problem, because they tend to behave in a stereotypically feminine way when they believe that the interviewer holds conventional stereotypes. In both verbal and nonverbal ways, and even in their dress, they present themselves to traditional males in a more typically "feminine" manner (von Baeyer, Sherk, and Zanna 1981). Obviously, if they are applying for female-oriented positions, that behavior might enhance their job prospects, but for a male-dominated occupation it would probably decrease their chances. These findings might be less alarming if it could be demonstrated that there is a decrease in sex-role stereotyping among decision makers, but that does not seem to be the case. Even among undergraduate business majors, substantial numbers of males, and more males than females, hold conventional sex-role stereotypes (Tomkiewicz and Brenner 1982).

The composition of the applicant pool is also significant, especially for masculine positions. When women are tokens—less than 25 percent of the applicants—their qualifications are rated lower and they are less likely to be recommended for hiring. As the number of women candidates rises, so too does their perceived suitability for the job (Heilman 1980).

When a managerial job is highly demanding, male applicants are seen as more suitable than equally qualified females. They are also seen as higher on potential for long service with the organization and on potential for fitting in well (Rosen and Jerdee 1974c). Females in this study were seen as more suitable for a routine managerial job than for a demanding one. The lowest acceptance rates and the poorest overall evaluations were given to women applying for the demanding and challenging positions. Men were also preferred when the job called for supervising men, and women were seen as more suitable for jobs requiring the supervision of women (Rose and Andiappan 1978).

A fascinating inversion of this phenomenon shows that when women and men are applying for the same position, the job itself may be perceived differently depending on the sex of the applicant. Job descriptions for a job described only as "white collar" were written so that either a male or a female might perform it. When the applicant was female, the evaluators perceived the job as primarily a clerical one, and characteristics they considered to be relevant were "personality/appearance" and "skills/education." When the applicant for the job was male, the job was perceived as more of an administrative management position, and the relevant characteristics were "motivation/ability" and "interpersonal relations" (Cecil, Paul, and Olins 1973).

Although this job description was perhaps artificially vague, managerial positions, as we noted above, are characterized by a good deal of ambiguity, requiring a fairly high level of inference, and therefore of risk, on the part of the decision maker. It has been argued that employment interviews are in reality "a search for negative information" (Shaw 1972). Since interviewers rarely are rewarded for hiring good people and often criticized for hiring misfits, they tend to become cautious and to develop a sensitivity for negative evidence. This sensitivity is especially acute when the evaluation is based on ambiguous information. Decisions on managerial occupations, which require a high level of inference, are therefore riskier than those on occupations that require specialized, advanced training, such as engineer or scientist. It follows that "negative traits" such as female gender or physical disability have a differential impact and are more central to some occupations than to others. Thus, when the job description is specific and the tasks are challenging and demanding, or when the job requires supervising other men, men are more likely to be seen as suitable for the job. When the job description is vague or ambiguous, the perceived difficulty, and therefore the perceived qualifications, vary depending on who is applying.

Obviously factors other than gender are involved. Grade point average, educational background, and competence are in some ways more important predictors of access than gender, but the gender factor always mediates the effect. Professional interviewers ranking bogus resumés rated scholastic standing as the most important criteria, but they showed a strong bias in favor of males over females having equal scholastic standings (Dipboye, Fromkin, and Wiback 1975). Corporate personnel directors responded more favorably to applicants with high grades than to those with average ones. But applicants who were identified only by first initial (hence whose gender was unspecified) fared better than those identified as female, regardless of their GPA. The highest response was to an applicant with high grades whose gender was unspecified. The smallest response (0 out of 15) came to the female applicant with only average grades (Zikmund, Hitt, and Pickens 1978). Employers in another study clearly preferred competent to barely competent employees. They made little distinction between barely competent males and barely competent females, but for individuals with high competence, males were preferred over females (Haefner 1977). What all of this seems to suggest is that the highly qualified female will have a difficult time competing with men of equal ability, and the average female will have little chance at all against the average male.

On the other hand, the applicant's undergraduate or graduate degree is an important factor in selecting managerial candidates, often overriding the effects of sex. Candidates with undergraduate degrees in business administration are regarded as most suitable for a managerial position, followed in order by industrial sociology, industrial engineering, history, and English literature (Renwick and Tosi 1978). So, although a woman with a business degree would be seen as less qualified than a man with the identical degree, she might be considered more qualified than a man with a degree in art history.

Attractiveness affects job access as well as job evaluation. Males are preferred for masculine jobs, females for feminine jobs; but within those roles, attractive applicants are preferred over less attractive ones. For nonsextyped jobs, attractive applicants are preferred (Cash, Gillen, and Burns 1977) and higher salaries are recommended (Jackson 1983a). Scholastic standing takes precedence over attractiveness, but among equally qualified applicants, interviewers will prefer males over females and attractive applicants over unattractive ones (Dipboye, Fromkin, and Wiback 1975). These results hold regardless of the sex or attractiveness of the interviewer (Dipboye, Arvey, and Terpstra 1977). The bias against women and against unattractive candidates is most pronounced when deciding which one of all the candidates should be ranked first or which one should actually be hired. Since in many cases there is, in fact, only one opening or one position, the impact of this bias is larger than at first appears.

Access discrimination, then, is still very much a part of the organizational world. Employers clearly believe that they evaluate candidates equally and equitably, considering only valid criteria such as scholastic standing, undergraduate or graduate education, or other specialized qualifications. Equally clearly, such invalid factors as the sex and the sex-role orientation of the applicant, the sex-typing of the job, the sex and sex-role orientation of the decision maker, plus the attractiveness of the applicant, all contribute to the decision process. The greatest problem seems to exist in access to occupations that are perceived as masculine, to jobs that are seen as difficult and challenging, and to positions where the job description is ambiguous or unclear and the requirements are subjective. In these cases, the decision maker must rely on less specific information, make greater inferences, and take greater risks in choosing one applicant over the others. And under those conditions, the decision maker is most likely to choose a well-qualified male over an equally qualified female, particularly if the male is physically attractive. Often the preference will be for an average male over a well-qualified female. Rarely will the preference go to the average female, even to an attractive one.

The Glass Ceiling

Once the selection decision has been made and the individual enters the organization, a new set of potentially discriminatory decision situations arises. These include the tasks or responsibilities that newcomers are assigned to, the career support they are given, and the rewards that they receive. There are two perceptions of treatment discrimination. One is that it is less problematic than access discrimination, since the experience of working with competent women tends to reduce the influence of stereotypes (Bartol and Butterfield 1976). The other is that observations of the success of one competent female do not generalize to all females. Each new woman in the organization is faced with overcoming for herself the effect of feminine stereotypes. Treatment discrimination is subtle, covert, pervasive, and real.

When individuals are hired by large organizations, they are typically not hired for a specific position. Rather, they are placed according to the organization's needs at the time they enter, and then rotated through a series of positions to develop their managerial skills and organizational expertise. The initial placement decision is important, since it is the newcomer's chance to demonstrate competence, to attract a mentor, and to prepare for further career development. It is also the place where the newcomer assesses his/her own competence and relative strengths in the organization, and begins to set performance and career goals. If women do not have the same access as men to challenging, demanding tasks, then they would be disadvantaged from the start, both in terms of their credibility in the organization and their own aspirations.

Both males and females, when asked to make initial placement decisions, are likely to see females as more suitably placed in unchallenging rather than challenging positions (Taylor and Ilgen 1981). However, when choosing a subordinate, the "similar to me" phenomenon may operate. In a study of placement decisions, men again demonstrated a preference for men for the challenging task, but women tended to choose other women.

Men and women chose same-sex others for the challenging job because they expected a more rewarding relationship with these individuals. Thus, the participants felt that there would be less conflict during the work with individuals of their own sex. In addition, men seemed to justify their prejudices on the basis of role stereotyping, that is, Paul is more competent for the challenging task, and Jane is more competent for the dull task and she would be more interested in getting the job done (Mai-Dalton and Sullivan 1981).

The preference for subordinates of the same sex has shown up in situations that involve sharing decision-making authority and encouraging others to assume leadership positions. When a group leader and a member make decisions together, the member is able to assume status as a *de facto* leader. Those with whom the leader becomes close are also those most likely to receive support in return. People tend to groom for leadership those with whom they share a close relationship; men tend to choose other men and women other women (Larwood and Blackmore 1978).

We could conclude that to the extent that women are in positions to support and encourage the career development of other women, treatment discrimination will be reduced. But, unfortunately, men still hold control over the majority of decisions, and they still prefer to invest organizational resources in men rather than women. For example, in an in-basket exercise often used in research projects and management training seminars, one incident asked participants to recommend an employee to attend a highly regarded supervisory training conference. Background information is provided for a candidate who is a business school graduate and who is described as "having demonstrated good potential for higher level supervisory positions." When this candidate is described as a male, about 60 percent of the workshop participants recommend sending him for training; but when the candidate is a female, only 35 percent recommend the training (Rosen and Jerdee 1977). Very similar results were found in many repetitions of the study, for example: in a survey of readers of *Harvard Business Review*, 95 percent of whom were male (Rosen and Jerdee 1974a); in a study of male bank supervisors (Rosen and Jerdee 1974b); and in a group of college seniors, of whom one-half were male and one-half female (Kovach 1981).

Other forms of treatment discrimination have been revealed by this research, some of it against men. Managers clearly expect male employees to give top priority to their jobs when career and family obligations conflict and expect women to sacrifice their careers for their families. A request for a month's leave of absence to resolve a child care problem is far more frequently judged as inappropriate for a male accountant than for a female accountant, and is much more likely to be denied to the male. If it is granted, the woman is more likely than the man to be paid.

However, the survey respondents show greater concern for the career success of male employees than female ones. Wives of young male executives are overwhelmingly expected to support their husbands' careers by participating in job-related social events, but young husbands are not expected to give reciprocal support to their wives' careers. Respondents indicate much more willingness to try to retain a valued male employee who is considering following his wife to a new location than they do for a similarly situated female employee; and they indicate a good deal less willingness to promote a woman than a man who shows a strong commitment to family responsibilities. In a disciplinary situation, more severe sanctions are recommended for a female who is habitually late than for a male offender; but in a more ambiguous situation where the employee's private, off-the-job behavior threatens to interfere with work, the executives are more willing to intercede with the male than with the female employee.

Sex-role orientation is more powerful than sex as a determinant. When personnel consultants were given information about an employee's gender traits, they tended to use that information, rather than sex, in making their decisions. But regardless of the sex-typing of the job, masculine employees still were preferred over feminine ones for the challenging job assignment while feminine employees were most likely to be assigned to the routine task. Also, regardless of the sex-typing of the job, androgynous persons were more likely than masculine or feminine persons to receive recommendations for a special training program (Jackson 1983b).

These results can be viewed positively or negatively. They suggest that knowledge of the gender traits of individuals overrides stereotypes in matching up actual traits with the situational requirements of the job. However, personnel decision makers must be able to distinguish individuals from categories. If they assume that traits are inextricably tied to gender, they will continue to make discriminatory decisions. As was noted above, personnel consultants, executives, and even the students who are managers of the future tend to hold very traditional stereotypes, and women tend to behave in more stereotypically feminine ways in the presence of someone they know to hold conventional sex-role attitudes. Women may actually be reinforcing stereotypes among the people whose beliefs they most need to change.

A final form of treatment discrimination comes in the form of rewards. Just as women's contributions are evaluated differently, so also are they rewarded differently. These differences can cut both ways. When a woman performs a masculine task in a masculine way, she tends to be more highly rewarded than a man who performs the same task in the same way. However, the reverse is not true for the male, that is, he does not get higher rewards for performing a feminine task in a feminine way. Further, when the woman performs a feminine task in a feminine way, her performance is rated more highly than when she uses a masculine mode, but her reward is not increased (Taynor and Deaux 1975). The important point here is not who gets paid more or less, or for what performance, but the fact that rewards are allocated differently depending on sex, sex-role, and sex-typing of the task.

Treatment discrimination has decreased as more women have entered traditionally masculine occupations. Males who have the experience of working with competent females learn to reduce their reliance on stereotypes. On the other hand, significant subtle, mostly unconscious, discrimination continues to exist, particularly in areas of ambiguity and uncertainty. Employers continue to expect men to sacrifice their families for their careers and women to sacrifice their careers for their families. They continue to offer more personal and career support and encouragement to males, to assign males to more challenging tasks or positions, to promote them to more responsible positions, and to reward them generously for their efforts. Much has changed in recent years, but much remains to be done.

SUMMARY

In this chapter we consider the actual and perceived differences in women's performance. We found that women are no less competent than men, although they do sometimes tend to be more conforming and persuasable, and hence less amenable to risk-taking. We found some differences in confidence, particularly in situations where women are in a minority and have lower status than men, tasks are sex-typed as masculine, and ambiguity is high and feedback low.

When it comes to performance evaluation, however, significant sex differences appear, mostly in the form of a pro-male bias. The factors that contribute to this bias were explored along with some situational variables. We found that the pro-male bias is exhibited by women as well as men, although to a somewhat lesser degree. And we learned that perceptions of competence can be manipulated by extremely subtle nonverbal behavior.

In the last section we addressed the question of the extent to which these differences in performance and performance evaluation have resulted in discriminatory actions. We found that, despite Civil Rights laws that prohibit it, women continue to suffer access discrimination. While qualifications such as grades, scholastic standing, or competence clearly override sex, they are also mitigated by sex. Given two equally highly qualified candidates, employers prefer a male over a female and an attractive candidate over an unattractive one. Employers clearly prefer a less qualified male to an equally less qualified female. The most discouraging finding is that some employers seem to prefer a less qualified male to a more qualified female.

Although some have argued that treatment discrimination is less of a problem than access discrimination, the evidence suggests that women still receive less challenging assignments and less career support than males, while males receive less support than females in family/career conflicts.

Nevertheless, it would be a mistake to end this chapter on such a discouraging note. While it is undeniable that a pro-male bias exists in organizations and results in discriminatory treatment for both women and men, it is also true that great strides have been made in recent years. Women still face access discrimination, but they have at last gained access to occupations which until recently were closed to them altogether. Women still face treatment discrimination, but they have gained the insight and the knowledge and the power to demand equal treatment. True equality may be a long way away, but, as they say in the ad, "You've come a long way, baby."

11

Career Choices and Career Development

The *theory of human capital* as an explanation for occupational segregation was discussed in Chapter 3. It refers to the "investment" that individuals and organizations make in education and training. This education and training bring increased productivity, which in turn is rewarded by higher income or status. A decision to invest in human capital is influenced by the individual's age and time in the labor force on a cost-benefit basis. The older one is, or the less time one is likely to remain in the labor force, the less time there is to recover the costs of investment and reap benefits. For men, age and time in the labor force are roughly equivalent. For women, the prospect of interruptions in employment will result in decisions to invest less in human capital, in less time to accumulate human capital in the labor market, and in depreciation of previously acquired human capital during breaks in employment. In general, women would be expected to have less effective human capital than men (Rosenfeld 1979).

The human capital theory often is used to explain differences between women's and men's labor force experiences. Women, the theory posits, fail to enter male-dominated occupations because, anticipating that their careers will be discontinuous, they decline to invest in the required schooling or experience (McLure and Piel 1978). Women enter female-dominated professions such as nursing, teaching, or social work, where the depreciation of human capital over breaks in employment is less (Polachek 1981). The theory has been used to explain the differences in male and female wages (Mincer and Polachek 1978), and to justify employers' reluctance to hire women in occupations that require extended training and development.

The human capital theory has an intuitive appeal, and in fact it can be used to explain part of the difference between male and female labor market experience. But it is at best only a partial explanation (Rosenfeld 1979).

Women do, in fact, invest in their human capital very much to the same extent that men do, although their investment strategies tend to vary. Men more frequently will use job training or job changes to increase their human capital, while women are more likely to invest in additional schooling (Gurin 1981). However, these differences in choice of strategies may be a function of differential access, specifically of women's opportunities to participate in career development and training programs. In other words, it may be the employer, rather than the employee, side of the equation that is deficient. It may be that many women who are willing and anxious to invest in their own human capital are denied equal access to the development opportunities that their employers offer to equally qualified males.

We turn now to a discussion of these two sides of the coin. To what extent do women, anticipating interruptions in their work lives, decide not to invest in their own human capital, and to what extent do organizations offer them the opportunity to do so?

INDIVIDUAL INVESTMENT IN HUMAN CAPITAL

Women and men have different decisions to make. Men must decide between a job and a career. But a woman starts with a more fundamental choice. She first must decide whether to join the paid labor force. (Every mother is a working mother, and women who do not work for wages outside the home frequently have full and productive lives in addition to homemaking.) If she chooses market work, she again has two choices. She must decide between a *career*—a sequential and occupationally related set of increasingly responsible or technical positions—or a *job*. If she chooses a career, she again has two choices. She must decide between a career in a traditionally female-dominated occupation or one in a traditionally male-dominated occupation. And if she chooses a career, she faces yet another choice, whether to—and how to—combine her career with marriage and children. The choice she makes at each decision point is at least partially a function of how she perceives her feminine role and how she values familial roles.

Career, Job, or Neither

Children begin to internalize sex-role stereotypes from a very early age. They understand that boys grow up to be men and that grown men work. Rarely do children see a man over school age and under retirement age who is not either working at a job or seeking work. By kindergarten age they have a fairly clear view of what adult males do. They may be less clear about what adult women do. Women do nurturing things in the home: they cook, clean, wash and iron clothes, and take care of children and other adults; they may also work for pay outside the home. By kindergarten age children already have pretty stereotypical ideas about what kinds of paid work women and men do and do not do. Rather surprisingly, they are more likely to exclude women from men's sex-typed jobs than men from women's sex-typed jobs. It is apparently not so much that they feel that "women's place is in the home" as that women's place is in female-dominated occupations (Schlossberg and Goodman 1972).

For a declining number of women, the career choice may be homemaking. A controversial *theory of marriage* by Nobel laureate political economist Gary Becker (1974) argues that a traditional division of labor within the marriage may be the most rational. In choosing a marriage partner, the optimal choice for most traits—ability, education, race, income, and height—is "a mating of likes." But for such traits as wage rates, the mating of "unlikes" is preferable. Becker argues that among the motivations for marriage is the efficiency associated with specialization of male and female time within marriage. If the woman's potential earnings are lower than the man's, but she is at least as productive as he within the household, then the marriage is most efficient if she uses her less expensive time doing homemaking tasks while he uses his more expensive time earning the family's living.

Critics of the theory, which also is known as the *New Home Economics*, argue that it is at best a description of the *status quo* and at worst a justification for the further exploitation of women. Further, since women are steadily increasing their human capital, both through education and time in the labor market, it may be a moot point.

Only a small proportion of high-school–aged women expect to be full-time homemakers at age 30. These women are likely to come from very traditional, white, rural, working-class families, and to have low scholastic achievement. Consistent with Becker's theory, they would presumably have low earnings potential in the market place and might realistically expect to contribute their time to the homemaking role while their husbands apply their more expensive time to the breadwinner role (Falkowski and Falk 1983).

Among college-aged women, the number who choose homemaking as a career has declined steadily in recent years (Betz 1984). Most college women plan to combine career—often in a male-dominated occupation—with motherhood, and they expect to have two or three children (Baber and Monaghan 1988). They expect to interrupt their careers for childrearing for anywhere between six months to five years. They also expect not only that their husbands will be the major earner, but that his income will be sufficient to support the family in a middle-class lifestyle. They assume that the marriage will survive throughout their lives, so they expect to work for reasons of self-fulfillment or independence, not primarily for money (Machung 1989). They do expect to earn as much as their male classmates at the beginning of their careers, but they do not expect to be promoted as fast nor to earn as much over time, whether or not they interrupt their careers for childrearing (Blau and Ferber 1990).

These expectations appear to be consistent with those of the men in their age cohort. Like women students, men favor a sequential pattern of work for married women: paid work, withdrawal from the labor market for childrearing, and eventual return to work (Komarovsky 1973). Even the most traditional men are willing to help out with household chores; even the most traditional of women expect them to do so. But "helping out" for them is a far cry from "sharing equally," and women seem to expect more equality than men do (Machung 1989).

Follow-up studies of college women show that those who expect to have careers and to combine career and family are probably fairly realistic. The number of women doing so has increased dramatically in recent years. Those who expect to be full-time homemakers may be less realistic; few families can survive without joint incomes. Those who expect extended interruptions for childrearing also may be unrealistic; a large and increasing number of women workers are continuously employed through their work lives. And many who expect to stay happily married will find themselves supporting themselves and their children for a substantial portion of their lives (Machung 1989).

Those who expect equality in their marriages are probably unrealistic about the demands of a two-career marriage. Even when both the wife and the husband espouse a belief in egalitarian marriage, if a decision has to be made that will adversely affect the career of one or the other and there is no option available that provides a compromise, feminism gives way to traditional values and the wife's career gets sacrificed to the husband's (Foster, Wallston, and Berger 1980).

However well expectations are met, the chances are that individuals will experience some stress and role conflict. Few young people are prepared for the stress created by the demands of pursuing a career while simultaneously raising a family. Noncareer employed women, that is, women who describe themselves as having a job, not a career, report more role conflict than career women, especially in the absence of support from the husband (Holahan and Gilbert 1979a). In dual-career families, women with high career aspirations experience more role conflict than those with lower ambition, while the opposite is true for men (Holahan and Gilbert 1979b).

For some women, one option is volunteer work as a primary career (Jenner 1981), a choice that allows participation in meaningful and satisfying work without defying social convention and without threatening the familial role. However, it is a choice not open to the majority of women whose life style depends upon their income and one not viable to many women who see it as exploitation of women and further reinforcement of sexual stereotypes.

Thus we see that, throughout the years in which career decisions are being formed, males and females are subject to different influences and different constraints. Social change has had its impact. The majority of girls from high-school age on plan on some sort of occupational role. But rather than abandoning the more traditional role of homemaker, they expect to integrate that role with their occupational role and give it priority, an expectation that is consistent with those of their male cohorts.

Even among those women who choose homemaking as their primary career, many will find themselves in the labor market, supporting themselves and their families. Among the majority of young people with ambitious plans for professional and technical careers, many will find these ambitions unrealized. Among the women and men who expect that women will interrupt their careers for childrearing, many will find this choice unrealistic and unaffordable. Among those women who combine paid work and homemaking, many will suffer role conflicts. Among men in dual-career families who lower their own career aspirations to share familial roles, many will also experience role conflicts. The choices are never easy, and many people, both women and men, find that their choices are limited by circumstances.

Traditional versus Nontraditional Careers

As increasing numbers of women enter formerly male-dominated fields, interest has focused on the influences that affect these choices. Why do some young talented women pursue careers in nursing, teaching, or social work? For that matter, why do some men seek careers in female-dominated fields such as nursing?

Gender Roles. One argument is that women who choose traditional roles differ from those who choose nontraditional ones in their perception of the feminine role. Women with traditional views are less likely to set high educational goals (Lipman-Blumen 1972), are more likely to choose traditional female professions, and are more conservative with respect to marital relationships (Crawford 1978). Women with high career aspirations tend to be nontraditional in their values and behaviors, confident of their career plans, and satisfied with their lives. They have as many romantic and friendship relationships with men as do more traditional women, and they often look to a boyfriend for role support (Tangri 1972), but they are willing to postpone marriage while they pursue career goals (Parsons, Frieze, and Ruble 1978). Women with traditional views prefer to seek satisfaction through supporting their husbands' or children's achievements, while contemporary women are more likely to prefer to accomplish their goals through their own efforts (Lipman-Blumen 1972).

External Influences. Of course, external influences contribute to the developments of one's ideology about sex roles, as well as directly affecting life choices. But the impact of these influences is far from clear. The most significant determinant of a nontraditional career choice appears to be parents who have a fairly egalitarian marriage. Other obvious socio-economic factors—religion, rural versus urban or suburban background, family disruption through divorce or death, the presence or absence of siblings of either gender, birth order, or whether or not the mother worked—all seem to have less influence than the relationship between the parents (Lipman-Blumen 1972).

Mothers probably serve as role models for their daughters, but the nature of their influence is complex. It is too simplistic to say that mothers who work outside the home produce nontraditional daughters. A more important predictor may be the mother's overall satisfaction with life. A mother who is dissatisfied with her role, whether that role is as homemaker or wage earner, is more likely to be dissatisfied with life in general, and she is more likely to have nontraditional daughters with high career aspirations (Parsons, Frieze, and Ruble 1978). It is also true that nontraditional careers are usually fostered by identification with and the emotional support of both the mother and the father, not the mother alone (Lunneborg 1982).

Other role models may have an effect, although the impact is often hard to measure. Those who choose nontraditional careers often credit someone of the same sex who demonstrated appropriate gender-role behaviors, gave them specific vocational information, and offered positive encouragement (Betz and O'Connell 1992).

Schools have come in for a great deal of criticism for the way in which they shape women's occupational roles. And indeed there is considerable evidence of sexism in the schools. Reading textbooks in the primary grades tend to show traditional roles—men as both fathers and jobholders but women as mothers. If women work, it is only out of necessity, and the work is in traditional female occupations. By junior high school boys are being counseled into math and science courses. The girls, on the other hand, are counseled into language and literature classes and permitted to drop out of math courses, effectively and severely limiting their later career choices (Wirtenberg and Nakamura 1976).

Counselors, both male and female, seem more responsive to girls with traditional career plans and to take the boys' career plans more seriously. The vocational tests (or vocational interest inventories) used for career counseling in high school also show considerable sex-typing. It's perhaps fortunate that these tests seem to have relatively little impact on career choice (Wirtenberg and Nakamura 1976). It should come as little surprise, then, that talented female high-school seniors express a lack of information about steps in preparing for a technical career and receive inadequate encouragement from teachers and counselors (McLure and Piel 1978).

On the other hand, adult women working successfully in nontraditional fields say they received strong support from their teachers (Lunneborg 1982). And women and men in nontraditional careers frequently have been influenced and supported by members of the dominant sex in their chosen profession, which suggests that it is the opportunities offered by an occupation, rather than its sex-appropriateness, that affect the decision (Betz and O'Connell 1992).

Occupational prestige obviously affects decisions. Traditional male occupations have always carried more status and prestige than those of females. As a job shifts from being male- to female-dominated, it tends to lose prestige. When students become convinced that a prestigious male-dominated occupation may soon be admitting increased numbers of women, they find it less desirable (Touhey 1974a). Conversely, if they believe increased numbers of men will be entering a female-dominated occupation, its prestige and desirability increase (Touhey 1974b).

The prestige of a job is even influenced by the gender of the person holding it. Women in craft jobs such as carpentry or auto mechanics receive less prestige than men in those jobs. On the other hand, men in any female occupation, professional or nonprofessional, receive less prestige than women, even though these jobs are already lower in status (Beyard-Tyler and Haring 1984).

What can be said, then, about the influences that affect the decision to enter a nontraditional career? Women who make these decisions do seem to have a different sex-role orientation from their more traditional sisters— stronger ambitions both for education and career, a stronger sense of their own competence, more confidence in their decisions and satisfaction with their lives, and preference for a direct mode of achievement. They have less conservative views about marriage and are willing to delay marriage for the sake of their careers. Yet they have as many and as important relationships with males. They are influenced a good deal by their families. They come from families where both parents were supportive and where the parents had a fairly egalitarian marriage. Yet they often have mothers who are dissatisfied with their own lives—either as homemakers or as jobholders. They are influenced by education—by textbooks, teachers and counselors, and, to a much lesser extent, by sex-based vocational tests—but these influences tend to push them toward traditional, rather than nontraditional, choices. They are influenced by organizational prestige, which varies across occupational categories according to the sex composition of the occupation as well as within occupations according to the gender of the jobholder. If there is a trend or a pattern here, it is hard to detect.

ORGANIZATIONAL INVESTMENT IN HUMAN CAPITAL

Organizations invest in the human capital of their employees in a number of ways: most obviously by providing opportunities for training and development, and less obviously by providing opportunities to gain marketable skills, knowledge, and ability through work experience. The issue of organizational placement of new hires was discussed in Chapter 3; we turn here to direct investments, through training and through the opportunity for mentoring.

Training

Training can take many forms in an organization, and the most effective training no doubt includes elements of several forms. The least formal training method is on-the-job, which can be nothing more than casual observation or can include an intense and protracted mentoring relationship. The most formal is highly structured classroom lectures, seminars, or workshops, either on-site or off-site. Other types of training include self-paced individual courses of study, tuition reimbursements for college and university credits, and attendance at conferences. In a perfect world, employers would offer the combination of training programs that would have optimal utility for the firm and the individual, and offer them without prejudice to all employees. This is not a perfect world.

There is substantial disagreement among trainers and also advocates for women as to the most desirable approach for training women for managerial careers. The questions involve whether women should be given segregated instruction, and, if so, which women should receive it and what should be the content of the course.

The arguments for women-only training speak to two issues: the problems of overcoming the socialization of women into feminine roles and behaviors, and the organizational skills that women lack. For example, it is argued that because of their feminine socialization:

- When men are present, women tend to revert to the comfortable, established pattern of deferring to men for advice and leadership (Larwood, Wood, and Inderlied 1978).

- When men are present, women may be assigned stereotypically feminine roles in group activities and simulations (for example, personnel or consumer functions) and not get the opportunity to practice and develop skills in the stereotypically male functions of finance or production (Hartnett and Novarra 1980).

- Women may be unable to speak as honestly as they would like in front of men (Larwood, Wood, and Inderlied 1978; Colwill and Vinnicombe 1991). (This argument could presumably be used in favor of excluding women from all-male classes.)

- In women-only courses, women experience the feeling of shared competence, enjoy the association of other competent women, and have the opportunity to establish a network of female peers.

- In women-only classes, women have the experience of women role models as teachers and can participate in stereotype-free career planning (Colwill and Vinnicombe 1991).

As a further argument in favor of women-only training, it often is pointed out that graduates of women's colleges tend to have a much higher record of career achievement than women graduates of co-educational institutions. The problem with that approach is that it ignores the fact that women's colleges tend to be private, expensive, and elite. The same argument can be made for male-only training, that is, that a disproportionate percentage of successful males are graduates of all-male or predominately male colleges, most of which are highly exclusive.

In addition to the arguments based on roles and stereotypes, there are also arguments that speak to the special training needs of women, for example:

- Women need to raise their self-esteem, to learn new behaviors for managing interpersonal conflict, and to develop leadership and team-building skills (Heinen et al. 1975).
- Women, more than men, need to juggle family and work roles, and need help with values clarification and career planning (Feldman 1989).
- Women need to learn the perceptions, strategies, and behavioral skills needed in the corporate arena (White, Crino, and DeSanctis 1981).
- Women need to become more politically sophisticated.
- Women, particularly those in middle management, tend to overemphasize the importance of education and hard work and to underestimate the importance of political awareness in moving up in the organization (Radin 1980).

All of these arguments speak to the need for special training programs for women, usually in addition to or as a preliminary to sex-integrated training programs.

Even so, there is strong opposition to any segregated instruction for women. Among the arguments against it are:

- Training resources are always scarce, and, regardless of the intent, women may get only the women's training (Colwill and Vinnicombe 1991),
- It is not clear that women have unique problems that cannot be resolved through traditional development programs (White, Crino, and DeSanctis 1981),
- It is not clear that women, but not men, need training to overcome the effects of role socialization, to be assertive, to plan careers, to make a commitment to work, and to learn to manage their time.
- If women have difficulty asserting themselves with men, they are not going to get over it in a segregated classroom. Sooner or later they are going to have to learn to deal with men (Larwood, Wood, and Inderlied 1978).
- The presence of such programs creates the appearance that the corporate environment either should not or cannot be changed, and the onus is on women to adapt to the organizational climate as it exists (White, Crino, and DeSanctis 1981).

- These programs are ineffective because it is the structure of the organization, not the behavior of individuals, that needs to be changed (Kanter 1977).

- The "separate but equal" doctrine does not work here any better than it does in public education. Regardless of the quality of the program, men will be perceived as having been trained while women will be perceived as having had remedial training.

- Most of the training is designed for a relatively homogeneous work force with similar skills, and women are not a particularly homogeneous class of workers. They tend to be at different stages in their training needs (Albrecht 1978).

- Many of the requisite managerial skills are now taught in schools of business and public administration, at both the graduate and undergraduate levels, which are now well attended by women. Those who need training are the women who have been out of school for ten or twenty years (Hammer 1983).

Some sex-segregated programs are very expensive and of questionable value. Typically, they cover a range of topics that includes intrapersonal, interpersonal, and technical areas. The content of the courses varies widely, but there are a number of common themes that reflect the assumptions mentioned above. Most programs include a segment on communication, which often includes some emphasis on assertiveness and confidence-building, or other approaches to overcome feminine passivity and dependence. Many also include substantive topics such as human resource management, financial management, problem analysis, planning and decision making, leadership skills, and team dynamics (Gomez-Mejia and Balkin 1980).

The disagreements stem in part from two issues: the lack of perspective on what type of training is needed and the absence of rigorous evaluation. A study that attempted to identify the training needs of women found that, even in the public sector, there is no clear model of a successful career pattern. Without a clear pattern it is difficult indeed to design training and development programs that will help women to move up.

Evaluation of training is even more problematic—and necessary. The evaluation of most training programs consists of a reaction sheet from the participants at the close of the program. What they measure is not learning but the sense of euphoria that can be created by an adept trainer. Even programs that make an effort to measure change more often than not measure attitude rather than behavioral change (Middlebrook and Rachel 1983). Unfortunately, few organizations are willing to undertake pretraining and posttraining studies, production records analysis, or other special longitudinal studies to validate the cost-effectiveness of their programs. Such studies would help to determine whether women are either benefited or harmed by women-only training.

If we assume for the moment that at least some women will benefit from special, remedial training, then the question becomes who should get it?

Some employers adopt a low-risk policy. One author, for instance, suggests that training efforts should be directed at:

those women who are perceived by others as having the characteristics that are considered most important for managers (and) have expertise in their field which is clearly superior to the great majority of those to be supervised (Brenner 1972).

He also recommends that the initial placement of women managers should be in positions where the majority of the subordinates are experienced, the superior is exceptionally supportive, and where expertise is a large and important component of authority, as in staff positions.

A woman staff manager with a high level of expertise, surrounded by experienced subordinates, and supervised by an exceptionally supportive manager would not appear at first glance to be in dire need of special training. However, she may be the very woman who is the most "trainable." An evaluation of an extensive, well-funded, and carefully designed training program for women managers showed that significant gains were made in both assertiveness and attitudes toward women (the two dimensions measured). But the greatest gains were made by women already in the professional and managerial classifications. In a group made up of secretarial supervisors who were older, less educated, lower in self-concept, and very traditional in their role attitudes, scores actually declined (Rader 1979). In other words, the training was successful for those women who needed it least and actually counterproductive for those who may have needed it the most.

We come, then, back to the questions that we raised at the beginning of this section. Should organizations sponsor or encourage special training programs for women only? If so, what should that training consist of? And who should be trained? The first answer has to be that the whole process of training needs to be studied. There is little agreement about what constitutes appropriate training for entry level and middle managers, male or female, and what form it should take. Until we understand better what the requirements are for management jobs, until we can set some clear and measurable objectives for training, until we agree to conscientiously assess the outcomes of training and development programs, each class or seminar constitutes little more than a shot in the dark.

It is also clear that in the absence of good information it is impossible to prescribe course work exclusively for women. It is no doubt true that women find it personally rewarding to work and study with a group of women peers and role models, away from competition with men. It is probably equally true that men enjoy the experience of training sessions away from the distractions of women. But it is exactly this situation that women have objected to for so long, for obvious reasons. The danger exists that when women have completed their women-only training, they may have completed *all* of their training. Even though few people argue that women-only training is a substitute for mixed-sex training, there is a real danger that it will, in fact, become so. In all organizations at all times, resources are scarce. When women's training resources have been spent on women-only training, there may be nothing left over for further offerings.

It is surely clear that not all women need remedial training, or that all men do not. Any sensible approach to training must start with a skills assessment and a carefully drawn, individual career plan. Training should be matched to the developmental needs of the individual and coordinated with the staffing needs of the organization. Training resources should be allotted to those who need them, not on the basis of gender.

So far in this discussion we have talked about a limited concept of training, the self-contained program or seminar. One of the major sources of executive development is learning from others, a less costly—for the organization—and highly effective method of executive learning often referred to as "mentoring" (Kram and Hall 1991).

MENTORS AND MENTORING

The issue of mentoring has created enormous interest and discussion in recent years. The exclusion of women from the protégé–sponsor system has been identified as a major deterrent to the career development of women (Epstein 1971). Successful male managers often benefit from "sponsored mobility," that is, their careers are enhanced by the support and encouragement of mentors (Kanter 1977). An ambitious and well-publicized research project at Yale that looked at the stages of adult development in men confirmed that mentoring was a crucial element in career development which often is unavailable to women (Levinson et al. 1978). However, as we shall see, it is also unavailable to the majority of men, and further, there may be alternatives that can accomplish the same objectives.

First, let us look at some aspects of the mentor/protégé relationship.

The Prevalence of Mentoring

Mentoring relationships are fairly extensive among the elite of the business world and have tended to become more common in recent years. Surveys of male managers find that roughly two-thirds of the respondents have had at least one mentor, who was nearly always a male (Roche 1979). Among top women executives in the United States, about two-thirds have had at least one mentor, and the majority have had two or more; most of their mentors have been men (Phillips 1977; Missarian 1982). Both men and women who have been mentored have received more promotions, have higher incomes, and are more satisfied with their pay and benefits than those with less extensive mentoring relationships (Dreher and Ash 1990; Whitely, Dougherty, and Dreher 1991).

The Role of the Mentor

The functions performed by a mentor seem to be a combination of purely career-related (utilitarian) roles and more personal (affective) ones.

Utilitarian roles include:

- *Teacher*—enhancing the young person's skills and intellectual development, giving feedback on performance, teaching "tricks of the trade," and socializing the protégé to the value differences within the organization (Kram and Hall 1991).
- *Sponsor*—using his/her influence to facilitate the younger person's entry and advancement, fighting for the protégé—standing up for her/him in meetings if controversy arises, promoting his/her candidacy for promising opportunities and challenging assignments, publicizing accomplishments, providing reflected power—putting the resources of the sponsor behind the protégé, and providing exposure and visibility as well as protection (Kram 1983).
- *Host and guide*—welcoming the initiate into a new occupational and social world and acquainting him/her with its values, customs, resources, and cast of characters, giving maximum responsibility and exposure to new functional areas, by-passing the hierarchy—getting inside information, shortcutting cumbersome procedures or red tape (Kanter 1977).

Affective roles include:

- *Role model*—through his/her own virtues, achievements, and way of living, being an exemplar that the protégé can admire and seek to emulate.
- *Counselor*—providing advice and moral support, providing help in problem solving and in defining and redefining goals, active listening—reflecting thoughts back, helping to identify options, providing suggestions and advice, and encouraging—showing unfailing confidence, and "bestowing his blessing" (Levinson et al. 1978; Phillips 1977).

This "bestowing of blessing" is the crucial element for male mentor/ protégé relationships, according to Levinson. Young men have "a Dream"—a vision or dream of their own future. The crucial function of the mentor is the "realization of the dream":

He fosters the young adult's development by believing in him, sharing the youthful Dream and giving it his blessing, helping to define the newly emerging self in its newly discovered world, and creating a space in which the young man can work on a reasonably satisfactory life structure that contains the Dream (Levinson et al. 1978).

The functions and activities that mentors perform for women differ very little from those performed for men, but the emphasis tends to be different.

At lower organizational levels, women may need more of the *affective* roles—providing encouragement, support, and advice. At this level, the mentor can use his/her status to give the protégé legitimacy and also ensure that she receives credit for her work so that she can build her own reputation. At higher levels, the mentors spend more time on the career functions, that is, "selling" their protégés (Fitt and Newton 1981).

Stages in the Mentor/Protégé Relationship

Mentor/protégé relationships go through a series of stages that seem to be pretty predictable. They are labeled in various ways by various researchers; for our purposes here we will use a four-stage model (Kram 1983):

• *Initiation*: This stage starts with a fantasy—the young manager admires and respects the senior person for his/her competence and capacity to provide advice and guidance. The senior person sees the junior as someone with potential, "coachable," and enjoyable to work with. S/he sees the possibility of contributing to the junior's growth and success. During the first year, fantasy becomes transformed into concrete positive expectations.

• *Cultivation*: This stage typically lasts two to five years but can range up to ten to twelve years. The career functions emerge first; in time, as the interpersonal bond grows, the affective functions emerge.

• *Separation*: This usually occurs "from six months to two years after a significant change in the role relationship and/or in the emotional experience of the relationship" (Hunt and Michael 1983). For example, the protégé is promoted to a new job or transferred to another location. Or, it may end gradually—part of the growing up process. Men rarely have mentors after age 40. Separation is always a period of adjustment for both mentor and protégé, and is often accompanied by anxiety, resentment, turmoil, and feelings of loss, especially if it occurs prematurely. In many respects, mentoring is like the intense relationship between parents and grown offspring, or between lovers or spouses. It is difficult to end it in a rational, civil way (Levinson et al. 1978).

• *Redefinition*: This stage sometimes leads to an uneasy truce, to peer status characterized by ambivalence and discomfort, hostility and resentment, and bitterness. But after a cooling-off period, it often resolves into a lasting friendship. After the separation, the personality of the protégé may be enriched further as s/he makes the valued qualities of the mentor more fully a part of him/herself. In some respects, the main value of the relationship is created after it ends, but only if there was something worthwhile there while it was happening (Levinson et al. 1978).

Mentoring and Power

Mentors are most likely to be individuals at mid-career or in their mid-40s in age (Kram and Hall 1991). They have, almost without exception, been protégés themselves. This means that they are old enough to be a big brother but too young to be a father. It also means that they are powerful enough to be able to provide concrete assistance. The issue of power is critical to the issue of mentoring, and, not unexpectedly, the stages of development of the mentor/protégé relationship can be equated to McClelland's stages of power development discussed in Chapter 6:

- In Stage 1 of power development, the individual's source of strength and power is others. In the initiation stage of the mentor/protégé relationship, the young person seeks out a more powerful senior person as mentor or, in the absence of such a person, seeks to build a peer network.

- In Stage 2 of power development, the individual learns self-control and begins to experience his/her own strengths. In the cultivation stage of the mentor/protégé relationship, the young person begins to take on added responsibility, to become more independent and autonomous.

- In Stage 3 of power development, the individual learns to control others, either by being exploitive and competitive or by being helpful. Following the separation and redefinition stages of the mentor relationship, the former protégé often experiences power by mentoring others (Hunt and Michael 1983).

The power implications of the mentor/protégé relationship cannot be overestimated. The person who can successfully identify and sponsor the future managers of an organization has both exercised and demonstrated power. The affective roles of a mentor can be, and often are, performed by powerless people, but the utilitarian roles can only be performed successfully by people who have both influence and control of concrete resources in the organization. One result of this reflected power is that the protégé who is able to move upward through "sponsored mobility," that is, with the help of a mentor, receives substantially more support and encouragement from others than the person who moves up through "contest," or open mobility. The former often finds the upward path smooth and easy, the latter finds it steep and rough. The former will most likely use his/her own power, when it is acquired, to sponsor others; the latter may insist that others climb the rocky path.

This power dimension helps to explain both why managers chose to be mentors and why some relationships end in bitterness. The mentor is rewarded with enhanced self-esteem—a positive view of self as an effective coach and developer of young talent (Kram 1988); also, the mentor's own career advancement may be enhanced by having a loyal following of subordinates. The mentor may get genuine pleasure from the ward's successes, but s/he is not unaware of the impact on his/her own power sources. If the protégé fails to meet expectations, the mentor's judgment may be questioned and valuable resources will have been squandered. On the other hand, if the mentor lacks the political power to intercede for the protégé, or declines to do so, the protégé may have decreased his/her credibility by being aligned with a loser. In either case, the careers of both have been damaged.

Mentoring and Organizations

It is generally agreed that organizations gain a good deal from mentoring. Employees who have been protégés are better educated, better paid, less mobile and more satisfied with their work and career progress than those who have not (Hunt and Michael 1983). They also earn more money at a younger age, are more likely to follow a career plan, and sponsor more protégés themselves (Roche 1979). For the organization, mentoring not only aids in the development of young talent but also provides an opportunity for greater use of older managerial talent. The mentor often experiences a sense of rejuvenation and achievement not offered by his/her formal organizational duties. Some organizations consider mentoring so important that they have institutionalized formal mentoring programs for all employees (Lunding, Clements, and Perkins 1978) or for women and minority employees (Cook 1979).

On the other hand, mentoring may be detrimental to the organization to the extent that it inhibits the process of changing the culture away from a male-dominated one to one that supports diversity. A system that permits or encourages senior managers to groom their successors may, at the same time, perpetuate the *status quo* (Harris 1993).

Not all organizations lend themselves to mentoring. An organization's reward system, culture, job design, and personnel practices either encourage or create obstacles to mentoring (Kram 1988). Paradoxically, mentor/protégé relationships are probably least vital in the organizations in which they are easiest to establish (Fitt and Newton 1981). Mentors are most important, especially for women, in large organizations with few women managers and in hierarchical organizations, where there are many levels of management and competition is intense for the ever diminishing number of positions at the top of the pyramid. Hierarchical organizations, however, tend to be highly bureaucratic, mechanistic, and conservative. Mentor/protégé relationships flourish in organic structures where there is enthusiasm for innovation, rather than severe resistance to change, and support for more equal treatment of women and minorities (Hunt and Michael 1983). Devices such as formalized career planning, special assignments spanning several management levels, job rotation, fast-track career development plans, and affirmative action plans encourage relationships by increasing exposure. Mentors can be more influential if promotion and assignment decisions are made by committees.

Mentors and Women

As we saw earlier, most successful managers of either sex have had mentors. For the most part, the mentors have been men, partially because there have been few powerful women to act as mentors. We need now to ask three questions: Can women mentor other women? Will men mentor women? Do women—or men—really need mentors?

Can (and will) women mentor other women? In the strictest sense of the word, the answers still may be "no" and "yes." Women are as likely and as willing as men to be mentors. But the number of women available to serve as mentors is still small, and the risks and the possible benefits associated with assuming a protégé are magnified for a woman (Ragins and Scandura 1994).

Mentoring is a power behavior, and while the number of women managers has risen in recent years, the number of women in positions of real power still remains small. Many women with management titles are in staff positions, where their organizational power is limited. Women who do possess sufficient influence can, and obviously do, act as mentors to both women and men juniors, but they must use their power carefully, particularly if they are in relatively isolated positions.

Will men mentor women? Of course, and many have done so and will continue to do so. But relationships that cross gender-group boundaries— or, for that matter, racial or ethnic boundaries—are more difficult to initiate and maintain than same-sex relationships. Women face a number of barriers in finding mentors that are nonexistent for men (Ragins and Cotton 1991).

One barrier is the fear that the relationship will develop into a sexual entanglement or that others will perceive it that way—causing destructive gossip and innuendo. Another arises from the traditional role expectation that men will take the aggressive role, and women the passive role, in initiating relationships. Women may be reluctant to initiate a mentor relationship with a man lest he construe it as a sexual advance; instead, they wait for him to make the first move (Ragins and Cotton 1991). These fears are not entirely unfounded. As was noted above, these often are very intense "love" relationships, and in our society love and sex are inexorably linked. Sex without love is accepted for men and to some extent is becoming so for women, but love without sex is considered suspect, particularly between a man and a woman (Missarian 1982). Individuals often cope by adopting family roles such as father/daughter or brother/sister, so that incest taboos reduce the sexual tensions. Others throw themselves into a flurry of work and maintain a professional behavior at all times. In either case, the strategy is to put physical and psychological distance between themselves and the other, and to learn to cope with the rumors that inevitably arise.

There are, of course, other drawbacks to male/female mentoring. Women sometimes complain that no matter how supportive their male mentors are, they can never fully understand or empathize with the situations and constraints facing a woman in a male-dominated environment. Nor can a man, however willing, serve as a fully adequate role model for a woman protégé.

Worse, a male mentor may encourage such stereotypical behaviors as feelings of dependency and incompetence (Kram 1983). The problem occurs this way:

This cross gender mentoring can be of great value. Its actual value is often limited by the tendency to make her less than she is: to regard her as attractive but not gifted, as a gifted woman whose sexual attractiveness interferes with work and friendship, as an intelligent but impersonal pseudo-male or as a charming little girl who cannot be taken seriously (Levinson et al. 1978).

These very difficulties, however, are what make these relationships so important, for they provide a much needed context for learning how to work effectively in a diverse work place. Participants learn to strip away dysfunctional stereotypes and to collaborate effectively with others who are different from themselves (Kram and Hall 1991).

Do women need mentors? Despite the conventional wisdom that a mentor is a vital ingredient to success, and that mentors are less available to women than to men, there are some contrary arguments and some alternative approaches.

Mentors may not be as important or as prevalent as might appear at first glance. The research suggests repeatedly that those managers who have had a mentor are younger, better educated, make more money, are more satisfied, and are less mobile. But there is no evidence that this is a cause and effect relationship. How can we be sure that these people would have been less successful without the attentions of a mentor? Presumably they were already "comers" or "water walkers," bright and able young people who were selected as protégés because of their obvious ability and promise. It is interesting to note that executives who have had mentors do not credit their mentors with their success. Rather, they ascribe their success to their own personal characteristics—ability to make decisions, motivation, ability to motivate others, ability to lead, energy level, ability to complete assignments, and willingness to work long hours. They even rank luck as more important than having a mentor for their own success (Roche 1979).

It is possible that the mentor/protégé relationship is simply an artifact of the patriarchal system that has characterized many large, hierarchical organizations. To be sure, this system has benefited the elite among young males and excluded all others. It has also clearly benefited those organizations by providing an informal and essentially cost-free management development program. However, it suffers from the same problems as formal training and development programs in that its objectives have never been clearly defined, its processes and mechanisms have never been fully understood, and its results have never been measured.

When it is neither possible nor necessary to find one person to play the classical or primary mentor role, it is quite possible, and perhaps preferable, to have a number of secondary mentors (Whitely, Dougherty, and Dreher 1991). The kind of primary mentoring relationship we have been describing here is both comprehensive and mutual; it is also "intense, exclusionary, and elitist" (Shapiro, Haseltine, and Rowe 1978). Mentorship is not democratic, and the reality is that many women and men will not find mentors. Some may even choose not to have a single mentor, because of the political and sexual hazards involved (Cook 1979). In fact, it may be unwise to rely on only one mentor, because so many sources of knowledge and information are available. The alternatives for secondary mentors range along a continuum from the very paternalistic relationship of mentor/protégé, to *sponsors, guides*, and, finally, at the other end, *peer pals* (Shapiro, Haseltine, and Rowe 1978).

Sponsors serve as strong patrons but are less powerful than mentors in promoting and shaping the careers of the protégés. These may be direct supervisors who are too close in age and experience to act as mentors but senior enough to provide significant assistance.

Guides are individuals who are less able than mentors or sponsors to fulfill the roles of benefactor, protector, or champion, but are invaluable in explaining the system. Secretaries and administrative assistants often enact these roles.

Peer pals are people helping each other to succeed and progress by reciprocally sharing information and strategies, and providing sounding boards and advice for one another.

Mentors and mentoring relationships seem to be an important part of the career development of successful men and women; they contribute something important to the organization's career development goals. Mentor/protégé relationships can be enormously gratifying for both individuals. Successful mentoring involves an overt use of power, and there are risks on both sides of the relationship. These risks are even greater in cross-sexed relationships. Since there are few women managers with the power to serve as successful mentors, and since mentoring women increases the risks for women and men, women have tended to have less access to mentoring than perhaps equally qualified men. One solution has been to try to institutionalize or formalize mentoring within the organization, although it seems unlikely that a true mentor relationship could be mandated.

Another approach is for the individual to develop a range of less intense relationships, sponsors, guides, or peer pals to serve in partial roles to fulfill the essential functions. We turn now to a broader discussion of these peer relationships.

NETWORKS AND NETWORKING

Women often express anger and frustration about their exclusion from the "old boys' network." These illusive, informal relationships seem to control the power and the resources of the organization, sharing vital information and reaching prior consensus on important decisions, all the while excluding not only women but most men from full participation in the organization. Women have responded by forming women's organizations, sometimes referred to as "new girls' networks." These take various forms, such as occupational groups, organizations groups, and regional groups. Their stated purposes usually have been to replicate the advantages that men enjoy from their wide range of contacts. These groups may not be very successful in achieving that purpose, but they are useful in teaching women the importance of building contacts and the fine art of doing so.

There is little question that successful managers do develop and use networks or "trade routes." These networks include people both higher and lower in the organizational hierarchy as well as people at the same level in other units or functions. They also include people outside of the organization. The lateral relationships are important, and they must be reciprocal—hence the name trade routes (Kaplan 1984).

Managers depend on these contacts and literally cannot get their jobs done without them. However, instead of trading goods, they trade services—accurate information, technical expertise, advice, political backing, and moral support. Reciprocation does not always occur instantly—a balance is struck over time. Network members are allowed to open "charge accounts" so long as the debt is later repaid in needed services. They exchange help for a promise of future help (Kaplan 1984).

This kind of network cannot be mandated by the organization. Managers must cultivate their own networks. Most managers do it more or less deliberately, but it also occurs naturally. It takes time and is a continuous process. Every promotion or change in position requires rebuilding the network, but even if a manager remains in the same job, the environment is dynamic. The network must be constantly tended.

Women's networks differ from these trade routes in that they are formally organized for the purpose of career enhancement. But they may be premature, since the number of women needing support is far greater than the number available to give it. The majority of participants are often women at the supervisory or middle-management level, often because there are no women at higher levels. In that case, participants can increase their contacts at their own level, but they will have few opportunities to find much-needed career links or role models among executive-level women (DeWine and Casbolt 1983).

Even when women have reached executive levels, they may have limited time or resources to share with others. While women at lower levels often say they receive little or no support from women above them in their organizations, the successful women in turn believe they give a good deal of support. In other words, executive women see themselves as giving more support to those below them than those women feel they are receiving

(Warihay 1980). Because of this scarcity of executive-level women, formally organized women-only networks may narrow, rather than widen, the opportunities for developmental activities.

Formal networks can serve a useful purpose by helping members to develop their networking skills. Some women seem to need help in understanding the importance of network building and in making maximum use of the opportunities available. However, many women who join these networks never attend meetings, nor do they arrange to meet with other members outside of their own organizations. Those who do, most often meet with people they already know—friends or internal business associates—rather than with new acquaintances. Further, they rarely make much use of their network contacts outside of the organized meetings; they use friends and business acquaintances as their primary contacts rather than initiating contacts with less familiar individuals (DeWine and Casbolt 1983).

So the formal network may not be the place to build trade routes. But it can be a place where women begin to develop the skills of initiating contacts, of seeking and giving information, and of building alliances, if members choose to use them that way. Some women, particularly those with a highly feminine role orientation, may find these skills difficult to learn. Sooner or later they are going to have to develop reciprocal network relationships with men as well as with women, and a formal network will probably never be able to replace an informal, carefully developed one. But it can provide a relatively safe place to practice.

SUMMARY

Successful careers require the acquisition of "human capital." Both individuals and organizations must decide to what extent they will invest in their own and their employees' human capital.

Men must choose an occupation or a career. Women, unlike men, must choose between work or nonwork, job or career, and traditional or nontraditional careers. Fewer and fewer women opt for full-time homemaking, and more and more aspire to careers in traditionally male-dominated professions. The vast majority of young people have unrealistically high career ambitions and very few aspire to management careers. However, the decision-making process that young people undergo in choosing these life roles shows no significant sex differences.

There are few differences in the investment that women and men make in their human capital, but they tend to invest in different strategies. Women invest more in education and training, men more in job changes. Women in the past have tended to choose careers in which interruptions in service would not decrease their capital investment, but as more and more women plan for uninterrupted careers, those differences diminish.

Organizations invest in the human capital of their employees by providing both appropriate work experience and opportunities for training and development. Unfortunately, the state of the training art has advanced little in the last two decades; there is little understanding of the essentials of career development, little knowledge of what kinds of training are needed, and little evaluation of the effectiveness of the training that is being given. Formal training classes and seminars are a *hodge podge* of skill training and attitude adjustment which often are unrelated to the needs of either the individual or the organization. Women-only training, as an adjunct of mixed training, is advocated by many; but while such training may provide a satisfying experience for women, its disadvantages outweigh its advantages. Training opportunities should be allocated on the basis of individual and organizational need, not of sex.

Mentoring provides training opportunities that are seen as essential to managerial careers and are largely unavailable to women. While these relationships are usually of value to all concerned, they also involve significant risks. They are by definition elitist and exclusionary, and they are not available to the majority of potential managers, female or male. In fact, they may tend to perpetuate the *status quo* by legitimizing the masculine values and culture of the organization. They also appear to be more important in hierarchical structures but more possible in organic ones.

Those who are denied the advantages of having a mentor can compensate by building a network of relationships with others in the organization— sponsors, guides, and peer pals—and in fact this network may be more beneficial and less risky than a mentor–protégé relationship.

Successful managers also build networks—trade routes—both horizontally and vertically, and both in and out of their organizations. These networks are informal and spontaneous, but they must be carefully nurtured. Attempts to replicate these informal networks with formally organized women's networks have not lived up to expectations, although they can provide an opportunity for women to enhance and practice their skills in making and maintaining contacts.

Organizations that are sincere about providing women and minorities with the opportunity to break through the glass ceiling must look well beyond simply providing remedial training or support networks. They must be willing to challenge all of the assumptions that underlie long-held policies and practices, and to change those policies and practices when they are shown to be outdated and inappropriate.

12

A Look at the Future

Throughout the preceding pages we have examined the perception and the reality of sex and gender differences—in the society at large, in the labor force, in the organization, within and among occupations, and in the family. We have found that in every arena, with the possible exception of the family, masculinity is valued over femininity, maleness over femaleness. Societal expectations of appropriate sex-role behavior have the potential to trap both women and men in a narrow and restrictive repertoire of behaviors and lifestyles. To a great extent, women fare much worse than men in terms of occupational opportunities and rewards. However, both women and men who try to combine career and family suffer from stress and role conflicts, and men find even less organizational support than do women (Higgins and Duxbury 1992).

Throughout the book we have tried to reach a clear understanding of "what is." We have done so, in part, by examining "what was," that is, by tracing the social changes associated with the development of technology, the evolution of the modern family and the division of labor within the family, the path of government and union attempts to reform the work place, and the persistence of moral and religious views about sex roles and sexuality.

We turn now to "what will be," or perhaps "what could be" or "what should be." Masculine values are deeply embedded in society, and that will not change easily or quickly. But clearly some change is occurring. If we as a society or a nation are to remain competitive in world markets, if we are to have a healthy and growing economy, we must make full use of all of our resources, human and otherwise. If we are to support and preserve our families, we must find a way to reduce the conflict between the demands of the work place and the demands of the family.

First, however, we will return to our point of departure from Chapter 1 to review to what extent we were successful in challenging the assumptions of extant organizational theory.

POINT OF DEPARTURE REVISITED

Chapter 1 promised that this book would differ from others by challenging three sets of assumptions: the masculine model of work, the breadwinner model, and the industrial model. By this we meant that masculine values are deeply embedded in work organizations; that organizational processes, power, and reward systems assume a worker to be a male breadwinner with a dependent family; and that organizational systems and structures are based on the technology of nineteenth-century manufacturing.

Our purpose was to examine to what extent these assumptions operate, to what extent they are supported, and to what extent change has made them obsolete.

Chapter 2 traced the progression of technology from manual or hand labor (in agriculture and in craft work), to machine labor (mass-production manufacturing), to electronic labor (electronic information processing). It also showed how family life and structure adapted to each stage of change. The traditional family, a man who works for wages in an office or factory and a wife who works without pay in the home, was a creature of the Industrial Revolution, and it was essential to its success. Now, the nature of work and of the family have both changed; that traditional model is represented by only a handful of contemporary families.

Chapter 3 searched for ways to explain the dual phenomena of sex-segregated labor markets and low pay in female-dominated occupations. A number of economic theories were explored to explain occupational segregation, the phenomenon that keeps women working in low-paying, female-dominated occupations. The process of job evaluation, by which organizations determine the relative worth of jobs, also was explored. Job evaluation methods, which were developed nearly a century ago for use in manufacturing jobs, systematically put higher value on those skills typically found in male-dominated occupations, providing at least a partial explanation for the wage disparity.

Chapter 4 found that union efforts intended to either improve working conditions or protect women and children workers actually had the effect of excluding women from higher paying occupations. Civil Rights legislation passed since the 1960s provides remedies for women who are victims of discrimination or harassment. It has improved working conditions for many women but has done little to end occupational segregation or to decrease the gap in earnings between female- and male-dominated occupations. It has had virtually no effect on changing the basic assumptions under which organizations operate.

Chapters 5, 6, and 7 demonstrated the extent to which sex-role stereotypes, which are pervasive throughout the society, are carried into the work place, affecting our behavior, our language, and our relationships both within and between the sexes. All other things being equal, masculine traits continue to be preferred over feminine ones, women continue to be valued for their appearance over their abilities, and men enjoy higher status and legitimacy.

Chapters 8 and 9 confirmed the existence of the masculine model of work. These two chapters reviewed the literature on motivation, leadership, and power. Much of the research has used only male subjects, or, if women were included, sex was not considered as a variable. Research on women workers tends to ask to what extent and in what way they differ from men. But the results show that what differences exist are more a function of other variables—age, occupation, hierarchical level, sex-role orientation, and subordinates—than of sex or gender.

Chapter 10 confirmed that women's performance varies very little from men's, but it also clearly demonstrates that women's qualifications and performances are evaluated very differently from men's. And in most cases, women's abilities are devalued relative to men's.

Finally, Chapter 11 looked at two aspects of the concept of investment in human capital. Women are no less likely than men to invest in their own human capital. They are becoming more and more likely to do so as they increasingly anticipate a lifetime of employment. However, they expect to benefit less from their investment, partly because they expect to put a higher priority on family responsibilities and they expect to interrupt their careers at least briefly for childbearing. Organizations, on the other hand, are less likely to invest in women than in men in terms of opportunities for work experience, access to training, and the availability of mentors.

Organizational literature does assume a masculine culture, a typical male breadwinner worker, and a structure unsuitable for modern technology. The implication of these assumptions is that women are denied equal access to opportunity and power, equal evaluation of their performance and ability, and equal rewards for their contribution. Further, while women may find great difficulty in balancing the demands of the organization and the family, they receive more support from the organization than do men in dual-career marriages.

WHERE DO WE GO FROM HERE?

Where do we want to go from here? How should we measure progress? Will it be enough when there is an equal number of women and men in management positions? When occupational segregation has been eliminated? When women's and men's earnings are equal? When power and status are based on competence, rather than on sex? These are the measures that often are used to track women's progress in the labor market, and while they are relatively easy to measure, they tell only part of the story.

In a utopian world, opportunities for achievement would be distributed equally without regard to sex or marital status; division of labor—in both the work place and the home—would be assigned on grounds of ability or fairness, not sex; and rewards would be allocated equitably on the basis of contribution. Both women and men would have the freedom to choose the lifestyle that best suited them. This is not a utopian world, and these outcomes would be difficult to measure, but they come closer to capturing the nature of a gender-neutral work place.

The dominance of masculine culture, the higher status and power of males, and the preference for men workers over women in most occupations are deeply ingrained values in our society. They will not be changed easily; even small gains by women are often countered with a vehement and destructive backlash. Nevertheless, women have moved forward during the current generation. We see more and more women in elected offices, in the professions, and even in the executive suites and the boardrooms, although most women have gotten there by adapting to the masculine culture. Some headway has been made in closing the gap between the average earnings of women and men, although part of the distance has been closed by men earning less, rather than women earning more.

For progress to continue, and perhaps even to be speeded up, change needs to be accomplished at every level of the society, from the broadest to the most individual. The greatest need, however, and the greatest opportunity, is at the organizational level.

Government

The Government could do a great deal more than it does to ease the burden of working parents. Despite a great deal of political rhetoric about "family values," and unlike every other developed western nation, the United States does not have a comprehensive policy of support for working parents. What we have instead is a patchwork of laws that do very little for the workers who need help the most.

- *Parental Leave*: The Family Medical Leave Act guarantees workers up to twelve weeks of leave for the birth or adoption of a child or to care for a seriously ill family member. However, the circumstances must be extraordinary, and since leave is unpaid, it offers little to employees who cannot afford to forego three months' pay.

- *Child Care*: Middle- and low-income parents are entitled to a tax credit for child care expenses, but poor parents, and especially single parents, cannot afford the child care in the first place, and their tax bill is relatively small. Even for those who can afford it, high-quality child care is very difficult to find at any price.

- *Health Insurance*: Much of the new job creation in recent years has been in small firms in the service sector. These jobs are often part-time and intermittent; the wages are low, and there are no benefits beyond those mandated by government. A worker cannot provide food, clothing, shelter, and transportation, much less child care and health care, on these wages. Even a family with two incomes will lack economic security if at least one person does not have medical insurance.

- *Education*: College tuition has risen exponentially in recent years, even as earnings have fallen. The American dream of sending children to college is out of the reach of increasing numbers of families, and scholarships or financial aid are harder and harder to come by. The expectation that a student will work to earn her/his own college expenses also becomes less realistic as costs rise and wages fall.

Lack of a comprehensive approach to parental leave, child care, and health care causes working families to struggle just to survive. Lack of access to higher education denies them the opportunity to obtain skills and knowledge that would enhance their—and their children's—earnings potential. Since the responsibility for the family falls more heavily on women workers than on men, they are the ones who tend to be the most disadvantaged. Lack of support in these areas keeps women in the position of marginal members of the work force, and in fact may keep them out of the market altogether. Some workers, or potential workers, may be better off receiving public assistance than trying to work and raise children without adequate income or support.

For better or for worse, however, the present mood in the Congress and in the country makes it unlikely that we will see any change in government support for working families in the foreseeable future.

Individual

The purpose of this book is not to provide strategies for women workers to become successful in a "man's world." Rather, it is to address the issue from the organizational standpoint. Nonetheless, individuals must assume their share of responsibility. While individual workers may be powerless to change society at large, or even the organization, they can have an impact on their own sphere of influence. Both women and men can set an agenda for change. Two strategies are available: one is to invest in one's own human capital, and the other is to try to change the immediate culture by refusing to engage in stereotypical behavior.

Investing in Human Capital. Education must include technical skills, language and quantitative ability, and computer literacy. Many otherwise well-educated women are relegated to staff or dead-end positions because they lack appropriate skills for line management positions. Parents, teachers, counselors, and others must encourage young women to become competent in these areas, whether they plan to enter a traditional or a nontraditional occupation. Without these skills, they severely limit their choices.

Successful workers must develop leadership skills, and the ability to lead is an important element of one's human capital. Women, whether they seek a career in management, in the professions, or in some other occupation, will do well to develop their own leadership ability. If the job does not offer the opportunity, then it can be found in other arenas—in volunteer work, in political organizations, in social, civic, or community activities. Wherever there is a group of people working together to achieve a common goal, there is a need for a leader. Accepting a leadership position in an all-female group may be a good starting place; accepting a leadership role in a mixed group, even a predominantly male group, will be invaluable.

Successful people develop political skills and become adept at understanding the power structure of their organizations. Those who aspire to higher level positions must learn what positions and activities are most visible, which are considered most critical, and which lead to recognition and promotion (Martin, Harrison, and Dinitto 1983). They must learn who the powerful individuals are. Whether or not they have access to a mentor, they must develop a wide-ranging network of individuals with whom they can exchange information, advice, support, and other resources.

Avoiding Stereotypical Behavior. Both women and men can take small (or not so small) steps to change their immediate environment. Women can learn to speak authoritatively, avoiding the hesitancy and deference that render them powerless; they can refuse to respond to comments or jokes based on sexual stereotypes; and they can refuse to accept the feminine jobs and tasks in the organization. Men can both talk to and listen to women as equals; they can avoid making stereotypical assumptions; and they can use nonsexist language, whether or not women are present.

Men can share both the routine tasks (coffee making, minute taking) and the more difficult, demanding, or risky tasks. They can recognize and acknowledge women's abilities and achievements.

Both women and men can bring pressure to bear on the organization to make significant changes in the policies and procedures of the organization. Men as well as women can seek organizational support for family responsibilities and work–family conflicts.

And, of course, men can assume an equal share of the household and child care responsibilities.

ORGANIZATIONS

Any sweeping change in Government policy is unlikely in the foreseeable future. If any change occurs, it will more likely be in the direction of reducing the Government's role in achieving equality of opportunity through regulation. Individual workers can make change, but it will be incremental at best. The real opportunity—and responsibility—for change lies in work organizations. Organizations must take steps to reduce the dominance of male culture not only because it is unfair to women, but because it hinders the organization in achieving its goal of maximum effectiveness. It hinders the productivity of both women and men.

The approach that most organizations have taken is related to regulation, that is, efforts to achieve equity through compliance with affirmative action and equal opportunity requirements. For the most part, these have had disappointing results. An extensive program conducted in Great Britain with a consortium of large employers gave some insight as to why.

This project—called Opportunity 2000—was developed by chairs, chief executives, and directors of major British companies representing public and private sector firms that employ approximately 20 percent of the work force (Hammond 1992). The major research question was the same one frequently asked in the United States—why has so little change taken place, given the time and effort that have gone into enforcing civil rights legislation? Since most personnel policies and procedures are now usually screened to ensure that they are not discriminatory, "most action by employers has been directed at the changing attitudes and behaviors of women with the aim of making them match the traditional models of management" (Hammond 1992). Nevertheless, after twenty years of effort, the labor force is still segregated by gender, and men continue to dominate management. Why?

Equal Employment Opportunity. The study identified many common characteristics of less-than-successful organizational efforts to implement equal employment opportunity laws:

- While managers and organizations are aware of the importance and potential advantages of a balanced work force, it is rarely viewed as essential.

- The motivation behind equal opportunity remains unclear. It is poorly thought out and rarely explicitly linked to business objectives.

- Equal opportunity is rarely driven from the top of the organization. The EEO manager exists in a managerial vacuum, unaided and neglected. Alternatively, it is just one of the responsibilities of the Human Resources department, and is not considered to be important enough to be a line management objective.

- Even when a separate EEO manager or officer is created, the program and the job remain confined to the lower ranks in terms of status. The manager, cut off from channels of communication and power, is rendered powerless. Lack of support for an EEO manager is an obvious sign of management apathy.

- In some companies, involvement in EEO has worked to the detriment of a person's career. It is rarely regarded as a fast track to success.

- There is no unifying vision drawing people together to achieve a more balanced work force. A policy document lays out what people can and should do, but it rarely indicates how this fits into corporate objectives or how it benefits the organization.

- The policy is patently unrelated to reality. Some organizations do not provide a consistent message. For example, if women are depicted in advertising in sexist or stereotypical ways, it is difficult to give credence to statements about the importance of equal opportunity. Similarly, when external publicity material describing equal opportunity changes does not match the experience of women staff, credibility suffers.

- Equal opportunity messages are communicated through written memos or personnel memos delivered selectively to personnel practitioners or others who might have an interest—not to all staff. If they are generally disseminated, their tone is often instructional, telling people how—rather than why—to interpret and practice equal opportunity.

- The lack of communication means that people do not necessarily feel part of the effort. This detachment is exacerbated if rewards are not linked to improvements.

- Change is focused on recruiting women from the outside for higher level positions, ignoring the development potential of women already in the organization.

The obvious conclusion is that bringing women fully into the mainstream of organizational life requires more than changes in policies and procedures, and more than training aimed at women themselves. What is needed is a massive cultural shift (Hammond 1992).

Work–Family Conflict. In addition to equal opportunity approaches, many organizations have attempted to reduce work–family stress. These responses fall into two categories. First are benefits—services or help in obtaining services—that allow employees with family responsibilities to meet the requirements of work as currently defined. Such responses are meant to help employees, regardless of their family form, to fit the procedures originally designed for a breadwinner model, where 100 percent commitment to work and organization was assumed. These services include such benefits as on-site or sick-child day care, elder care, or help in acquiring these services. Second are policies that create flexibility in location and time as well as varying arrangements for personal leave. The aim of these policies is to give employees enough control and discretion over the conditions of their work to be able to meet their family's needs on their own (Bailyn 1992). Each of these approaches has its own risks as well as its own advantages.

Services such as day care, whether actually provided on-site or supported through referral and subsidies, are offered for a variety of purposes. Sometimes their purpose is to attract or retrain qualified women workers in occupations or organizations where there are shortages (hospitals, for instance). More frequently, their purpose is to reduce absenteeism and turnover and to increase productivity by reducing the amount of time women workers spend arranging and providing adequate care and increasing the amount of time they spend on work. And clearly, such a purpose reflects the masculine culture of most organizations—the masculine model of work. In many American corporations, commitment to career and organization is demonstrated by long hours of work, and the message to women is "if you want to succeed, you must be willing to put your job first, to work the same long hours that men do. And we'll help you by taking over some of your child care responsibility." The average executive—male or female— works 56 hours a week, a number that has increased in the last decade; and most managers agree that, compared to male executives at the same level, women actually work more hours (Korn/Ferry International 1993).

The second approach seeks to change the balance of time and priorities. It offers programs like flextime, reduced work hours, job sharing, telecommuting, a variety of personal leaves, or combinations of these. These schedule options are entirely consistent with electronic technology, which has the potential to free workers from the rigid demands of time and space that earlier technologies imposed (Harriman 1982). They are consistent with the demands of organizations operating in a global economy. They have the potential to provide much-needed flexibility to the employer as well as to the employee, and in turn to enhance productivity. For maximum effectiveness, they require a reevaluation of the firm's value system, its structure and technology, and its compensation and reward system, putting the emphasis not on inputs (the number of hours worked) but on outputs.

The danger associated with these policies is that they will be pasted on to existing organizational culture, and used by some but not all women and not by men at all. When that happens, those women who choose to take advantage of them will become a new kind of marginal worker. A highly controversial article in the *Harvard Business Review* advocated that firms offer two career paths to women, a fast track for the career-first woman, and a slower, less pressured track for women, but not men, who sought a better balance between work and family (Schwartz 1989). Unfortunately, the alternative was immediately tagged as "the mommy track," and the idea failed to get the serious consideration it deserves. The problem was not that the proposal was a bad one, but that it did not go far enough in including men in the equation and in attempting to alter the basic value system of the organization.

Changing the Culture. The Opportunity 2000 project identified not only the characteristics of those organizations that had been less than successful at integrating women, but also at those that had succeeded. (See Figure 12.1.) Among organizations that had been successful in implementing equal opportunities, four factors consistently appeared, and these same characteristics were found among organizations that successfully achieved cultural change:

Figure 12.1

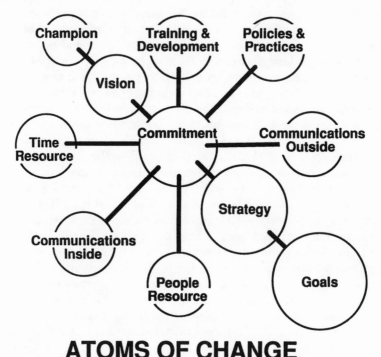

ATOMS OF CHANGE

Source: Val Hammond. Opportunity 2000: A cultural change approach to equal opportunity. Paper presented at the 2nd International Conference on Human Resources Management. July 2, 1992. Berkhamsted, Hertfordshire, U.K.

- *demonstrated commitment*—a strong, consistent vision from the very top of the organization;
- *changing behavior*—a strong vision, training, and measurement; change must challenge the fundamental structure of the organization;
- *building ownership*—change is the responsibility of everyone in an organization; ownership requires constant and effective communication;
- *making the investment*—adequate and realistic resources of time, people, and money must be allocated (Hammond and Holton 1991).

Successful change requires a systemic, organization-wide effort and the participation of all players and stakeholders, the same level of effort that is required to implement any cultural shift. (See Figures 12.2 and 12.3.)

- Commitment must be serious and continuous and must be conveyed to everyone in the organization. Change must be led with very clear, positive messages from top management, especially the CEO. Management must be actively involved.

Responsibility for implementing the program must go to a senior manager with genuine power and responsibility who reports directly to the chief executive.

- A clear and unequivocal reason for the program must be communicated. It must be seen as a strategic and important program, linked to the organization's future success, not just an isolated initiative.

- External consultants may be needed. Experts bring specialized knowledge that helps to develop an understanding of what is required. They can play an important role in the planning and implementation of programs.

- Positive actions are required; rhetoric is not enough.

- A pervasive, and persuasive, vision must drive change; it must include clear action points, plans, and measurement of progress. A clear and workable vision challenges and eventually changes the existing culture of the organization.

- Managers must be held accountable for clear and measurable goals.

- Training must be directed at all staff, including top management, so that new skills are learned and everyone becomes aware of the objectives and the issues involved.

- Ownership and shared awareness must be achieved through both internal and external communication. Active personal communications such as team and companywide meetings and participation in the development of action plans help to build ownership and motivate staff to absorb cultural change. By contrast, written formal communications delivered selectively to managers and supervisors, providing instructions on what to do, rather than why to do it, have little effect.

- Adequate resources—in terms of time, people, and money—must be invested. Change takes time, measured in years and not months.

Organizations committed to making maximum use of all of their employees will follow the model described above to bring about a redefinition of work. Rather than attempting to train women to be successful in male-dominated organizations, rather than attempting to ease the burden of family responsibilities to free women to work longer and harder, organizations will undertake transformations that challenge the basic assumptions of work and career, for all workers, men and women alike. It is never too soon to start.

Figure 12.2

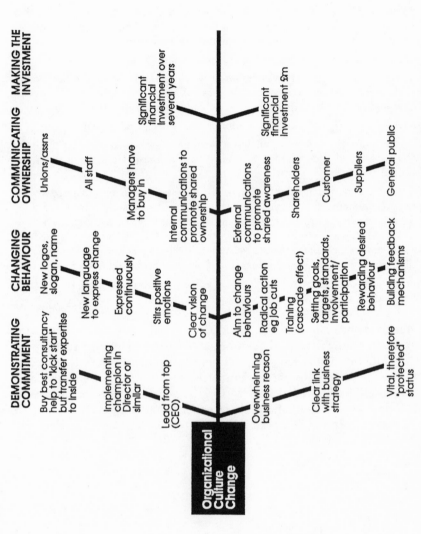

DEMONSTRATING COMMITMENT

Buy best consultancy help to "kick start" but transfer expertise to inside

Implementing champion in Director or similar

Lead from top (CEO)

Overwhelming business reason

Clear link with business strategy

Vital, therefore "protected" status

CHANGING BEHAVIOUR

New logos, slogan, name

New language to express change

Expressed continuously

Stirs positive emotions

Clear vision of change

Aim to change behaviours

Radical action eg job cuts

Training (cascade effect)

Setting goals, targets, standards, Involvement/ participation

Rewarding desired behaviour

Building feedback mechanisms

COMMUNICATING OWNERSHIP

Unions/assns

All staff

Managers have to buy in

Internal communications to promote shared ownership

External communications to promote shared awareness

Shareholders

Customer

Suppliers

General public

MAKING THE INVESTMENT

Significant financial investment over several years

Significant financial Investment £m

Organizational Culture Change

224

Source: Valerie Hammond and Viki Holton. *A Balanced Workforce? Achieving Cultural Change for Women: A Comparative Study.* Berkhamsted, Hertfordshire, U.K.: Ashridge Management Group, 1991.

Figure 12.3

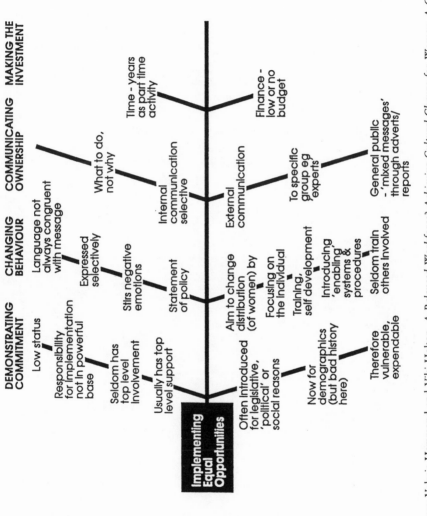

Source: Valerie Hammond and Viki Holton. *A Balanced Workforce? Achieving Cultural Change for Women: A Comparative Study.* Berkhamsted, Hertfordshire, U.K.: Ashridge Management Group. 1991.

225

References

Abbott, Aaron, and Richard Sebastian. 1981. Physical attractiveness and expectations of success. *Personality and Social Psychology Bulletin* 7:481–486.

Abramson, Joan. 1979. *Old Boys New Women: The Politics of Sex Discrimination.* New York: Praeger.

Abramson, Paul, Philip Goldberg, Judith Greenberg, and Linda Abramson. 1977. The talking platypus phenomenon: Competency ratings as a function of sex and professional status. *Psychology of Women Quarterly* 2:114–124.

Acker, Joan. 1978. Issues in the sociological study of women's work. In *Women Working*, edited by Ann H. Stromberg and Shirley Harkess, pp. 134–162. Palo Alto, CA: Mayfield.

———. 1990. Hierarchies, jobs, bodies: A theory of gendered organizations. *Gender and Society* 4(2):139–158.

Acker, Joan, and Donald Van Houten. 1974. Differential recruitment and control: The sex structuring of organization. *Administrative Science Quarterly* 19(June):152–163.

Adams, Kathrynn, and Audrey Landers. 1978. Sex differences in dominance behavior. *Sex Roles* 4:215–223.

Albrecht, Maryann. 1978. Women, resistance to promotion and self-directed growth. *Human Resource Management* 17:12–17.

Aldag, Ramon, and Arthur Brief. 1979. Some correlates of women's self-image and stereotypes of femininity. *Sex Roles* 5:319–327.

———. 1981. *Managing Organizational Behavior.* St. Paul, MN: West Publishing.

Amsden, Alice (Ed.). 1980. *The Economics of Women and Work.* New York: St. Martin's Press.

Anderson, Carolyn, and Philip Hunsaker. 1985. Why there's romancing at the office and why it's everybody's problem. *Personnel* Feb.:57–63.

Andrisani, Paul, and Mitchell Shapiro. 1978. Women's attitudes toward their jobs: Some longitudinal data on a national sample. *Personnel Psychology* 31:15–34.

Argyle, Michael, Veronica Salter, Hilary Nicholson, Marylin Williams, and Philip Burgess. 1970. The communication of inferior and superior attitudes by verbal and non-verbal signals. *Clinical Psychology* 9:222–231.

Argyris, Chris. 1957. *Personality and Organization*. New York: Harper.

Arrow, Kenneth. 1976. Economic dimensions of occupational segregation: Comment I. *Signs* 1:233–249.

Baber, Kristine, and Patricia Monaghan. 1988. College women's career and motherhood expectations: New options, old dilemmas. *Sex Roles* 19(3/4):189–203.

Baer, Judith. 1978. *The Chains of Protection: The Judicial Response to Women's Labor Legislation*. Westport, CT: Greenwood Press.

Bailyn, Lotte. 1992. Changing the conditions of work: Responding to increasing work force diversity and new family patterns. In *Transforming Organizations*, edited by Thomas Kochan and Michael Useem, pp. 188–202. New York: Oxford University Press.

Balswick, Jack, and Charles Peek. 1971. The inexpressive male: A tragedy of American society. *The Family Coordinator* 20:363–368.

Baron, Robert. 1983. "Sweet smell of success"? The impact of pleasant artificial scents on evaluation of job applicants. *Journal of Applied Psychology* 68:709–713.

Bar-Tal, Daniel, and Leonard Saxe. 1976. Physical attractiveness and its relationship to sex-role stereotyping. *Sex Roles* 2:123–132.

Bartol, Kathryn. 1978. The sex structuring of organizations: A search for possible causes. *Academy of Management Review* 3:805–815.

Bartol, Kathryn, and D. Anthony Butterfield. 1976. Sex effects in evaluating leaders. *Journal of Applied Psychology* 61:446–454.

Bartol, Kathryn, and Max Wortman. 1975. Male versus female leaders: Effects on perceived leader behavior and satisfaction in a hospital. *Personnel Psychology* 28:533–547.

Baxandall, Rosalyn, Linda Gordon, and Susan Reverby. 1976. *America's Working Women*. New York: Vintage Books.

Becker, Gary. 1965. A theory of the allocation of time. *The Economic Journal* 80:493–517.

———. 1971. *The Economics of Discrimination*, 2d ed. Chicago: The University of Chicago Press.

———. 1974. A theory of marriage: Part II. *Journal of Political Economy* 82(2):S11–S33.

Bem, Sandra. 1974. The measurement of psychological androgyny. *Journal of Consulting and Clinical Psychology* 42:155–162.

———. 1975. Sex role adaptability: One consequence of psychological androgyny. *Journal of Personality and Social Psychology* 31:634–643.

Bem, Sandra, and Ellen Lenney. 1976. Sex typing and the avoidance of cross-sex behavior. *Journal of Personality and Social Psychology* 33:48–54.

Bem, Sandra, Wendy Martyna, and Carol Watson. 1976. Sex typing and androgyny: Further explanations of the expressive domain. *Journal of Personality and Social Psychology* 34:1016–1023.

Bender, Marilyn. 1979. The changing rules of office romances. *Esquire* April 24:46–56.

Berch, Bettina. 1982. *The Endless Day: The Political Economy of Women and Work*. New York: Harcourt, Brace, Jovanovich.

Berg, J. 1976. *Managing Compensation*. New York: Amacon.

Bergmann, Barbara. 1974. Occupational segregation, wages and profits: When employers discriminate by race and sex. *Eastern Economic Journal* 1:103–110.

Betz, Ellen. 1984. A study of career patterns of women college graduates. *Journal of Vocational Behavior* 24:249–263.

Betz, Michael, and Lenehan O'Connell. 1992. The role of inside and same-sex influence in the choice of nontraditional occupations. *Sociological Inquiry* 62:98–106.

Beyard-Tyler, Karen, and Marilyn Haring. 1984. Gender-related aspects of occupational prestige. *Journal of Vocational Behavior* 24:194–203.

Bird, C. 1940. *Social Psychology*. New York: Appleton-Century.

Bird, Caroline. 1968. *Born Female*. New York: Doubleday.

Birdsall, Paige. 1980. A comparative analysis of male and female managerial communication style in two organizations. *Journal of Vocational Behavior* 16: 183–196.

Bischoping, Katherine. 1993. Gender differences in conversation topics, 1922–1990. *Sex Roles* 28(1/2):1–18.

Blau, Francine. 1978. The data on women workers, past, present, and future. In *Women Working*, edited by Ann H. Stromberg and Shirley Harkess, pp. 29–63. Palo Alto, CA: Mayfield.

Blau, Francine, and Carol Jusenius. 1976. Economists' approaches to sex segregation in the labor market: An appraisal. Part 2. *Signs* 1:181–199.

Blau, Francine, and Marianne Ferber. 1990. Career plans and expectations of young men and women: The earnings gap and labor force participation. *Journal of Human Resources* 26:581–607.

Blau, Peter, Cecilia Falbe, William McKinley, and Tracy Phelps. 1976. Technology and organization in manufacturing. *Administrative Science Quarterly* 21(3): 21–40.

Block, W. E., and M. A. Walker (Eds.). 1982. *Discrimination, Affirmative Action, and Equal Opportunity*. Vancouver B.C., Canada: The Fraser Institute.

Bly, Robert. 1990. *Iron John*. Reading, MA: Addison-Wesley.

Bradford, David, Alice Sargent, and Melinda Sprague. 1975. The executive man and woman: The issue of sexuality. In *Bringing Women into Management*, edited by Francine Gordon and Myra Strober, pp. 39–58. New York: McGraw-Hill.

Brenner, Marshall. 1972. Management development for women. *Personnel Journal* 51:165–169.

Brimelow, Peter, and Leslie Spencer. 1993. When quotas replace merit, everybody suffers. *Forbes* Feb. 15:80–102.

Broverman, I. K., S. R. Vogel, F. E. Clarkson, and P. S. Rosenkrantz. 1972. Sex-role stereotypes: A current appraisal. *Journal of Social Issues* 28(2): 59–78.

Broverman, I. K., D. M. Broverman, F. E. Clarkson, P. S. Rosenkrantz, and S. R. Vogel. 1970. Sex role stereotypes and clinical judgements of mental health. *Journal of Consulting and Clinical Psychology* 34:1–7.

Brown, Clifford, John Dovidio, and Steve Ellyson. 1990. Reducing sex differences in visual displays of dominance: Knowledge is power. *Personality and Social Psychology* 16(2):358–368.

Brown, Virginia, and Florence Geis. 1984. Turning lead into gold: Evaluations of women and men leaders and the alchemy of social consensus. *Journal of Personality and Social Psychology* 46:811–824.

Bureau of National Affairs. 1963. *Equal Pay for Equal Work: Summary, Analysis, Legislative History and Text of the Federal Equal Pay Act of 1963; with Summaries of Applicable State Laws*. Washington, DC: Bureau of National Affairs.

Burgoon, Judee. 1991. Relational message interpretations of touch, conversational distance, and posture. *Journal of Nonverbal Behavior*. 15(4):233–259.

Business Week. 1984. Romance in the workplace: Corporate rules for the game of love. June 18: 70–71.

Caldwell, Mayta, and Letitia Peplau. 1982. Sex differences in same-sex friendships. *Sex Roles* 8:721–732.

Caplan, Paula. 1981. *Barriers Between Women*. New York: SP Medical and Scientific Books.

Carbonell, Joyce. 1984. Sex roles and leadership revisited. *Journal of Applied Psychology* 69:44–49.

Carli, Linda. 1990. Gender, language, and influence. *Journal of Personality and Social Psychology* 59(5):941–951.

Cash, Thomas, Barry Gillen, and D. Steven Burns. 1977. Sexism and "beautyism" in personnel consultant decision making. *Journal of Applied Psychology* 62:301–310.

Cash, Thomas, and Claire Trimer. 1984. Sex and beautyism in women's evaluations of peer performance. *Sex Roles* 10:87–97.

Cecil, Earl, Robert Paul, and Robert Olins. 1973. Perceived importance of selected variables used to evaluate male and female job applicants. *Personnel Psychology* 26:397–404.

Chacko, Thomas. 1982. Women and equal employment opportunity: Some unintended consequences. *Journal of Applied Psychology* 67:119–123.

Chapman, J. Brad. 1975. Comparison of male and female leadership styles. *Academy of Management Journal* 18:645–650.

Chusmir, Leonard. 1982. Job commitment and the organizational woman. *Academy of Management Review* 7(4):595–602.

Chusmir, Leonard, and Barbara Parker. 1991. Gender and situational differences in managers' values: A look at work and home lives. *Journal of Business Research* 23:325–335.

Chusmir, L., C. Koberg, and M. Stecher. 1992. Self-confidence of managers in work and social situations: A look at gender differences. *Sex Roles* 26(1/12):497–512.

Clawson, James. 1980. Mentoring in managerial careers. In *Work, Family and the Career: New Frontiers in Theory and Research*, edited by C. Brooklyn Derr. New York: Praeger.

Clifton, A. Kay, Diane McGrath, and Bonnie Wick. 1976. Stereotypes of women: A single category? *Sex Roles* 2:135–149.

Cohen, Stephen, and Kerry Bunker. 1975. Subtle effects of sex role stereotypes on recruiters' hiring decisions. *Journal of Applied Psychology* 60:566–572.

Coleman, James. 1961. Athletics in high school. In *The Forty-nine Percent Majority: The Male Sex Role*, edited by Debra David and Robert Brannon, pp. 264–269. Reading, MA: Addison-Wesley.

Collins, Eliza. 1983. Managers and lovers. *Harvard Business Review* 61(5):142–153.

Collins, Eliza, and Timothy Blodgett. 1981. Sexual harassment: Some see it . . . some won't. *Harvard Business Review* 59(3):76–95.

Colwill, Nina, and Susan Vinnicombe. 1991. Women's training needs. In *Women at Work*, edited by Jenny Firth-Cozens and Michael West, Chap. 4. Bristol PA: Open University Press.

Cook, Mary. 1979. Is the mentor relationship primarily a male experience? *Personnel Administrator* 24(11):82–86.

Covin, Teresa, and Christina Brush. 1991. An examination of male and female attitudes toward career and family issues. *Sex Roles* 25(7/8):363–415.

Crawford, Jim. 1978. Career development and career choice in pioneer and traditional women. *Journal of Vocational Behavior* 12:129–139.

Crichton, Michael. 1992. *Rising Sun*. New York: Knopf.

Crino, Michael, Michael White, and Gerry DeSanctis. 1983. Female participation rates and occupational prestige: Are they inversely related? *Journal of Vocational Behavior* 22:243–255.

Davidson, Lynne. 1981. Pressures and pretense: Living with gender stereotypes. *Sex Roles* 7:331–347.

Deaux, Kay. 1979. Self-evaluations of male and female managers. *Sex Roles* 5:571–580.

Deaux, Kay, and Tim Emswiller. 1974. Evaluations of successful performance on sex linked tasks: What is skill for the male is luck for the female. *Journal of Personality and Social Psychology* 29:80–85.

DeCotiis, Thomas, and Timothy Summers. 1987. A path analysis of a model of antecedents and consequences of organizational commitment. *Human Relations* 40(7):445–470.

DeWine, Sue, and Diane Casbolt. 1983. Networking: External communication systems for female organizational members. *Journal of Business Communication* 20(2):57–67.

Dion, Karen, Ellen Berscheid, and Elaine Walster. 1972. What is beautiful is good. *Journal of Personality and Social Psychology* 24:285–290.

Dion, Kenneth, and Regina Schuller. 1990. Ms. and the manager: A tale of two stereotypes. *Sex Roles* 22(9/10):569–577.

Dipboye, Robert, Howard Fromkin, and Kent Wiback. 1975. Relative importance of applicant sex, attractiveness, and scholastic standing in evaluation of job applicant resumes. *Journal of Applied Psychology* 60:39–43.

Dipboye, Robert, Richard Arvey, and David Terpstra. 1977. Sex and physical attractiveness of raters and applicants as determinants of resume evaluations. *Journal of Applied Psychology* 62:288–294.

Dipboye, Robert, Walter Zultowski, Dudley Dewhirst, and Richard Arvey. 1979. Self esteem as a moderator of performance-satisfaction relationships. *Journal of Vocational Behavior* 15:193–206.

Dobbins, Gregory, William Long, Esther Dedrick, and Tayna Clemons. 1990. The role of self-monitoring and gender in leader emergence. A laboratory and field study. *Journal of Management* 16(1):609–618.

Doeringer, Peter. 1967. Determinants of the structure of industrial type labor. In *The Economics of Women and Work*, edited by Alice Amsden, pp. 211–232. New York: St. Martin's Press.

Doherty, Mary Helen, and Ann Harriman. 1981. Comparable worth: The equal employment issue of the 1980's. *Review of Public Personnel Administration* 1(3):11–32.

Donaghy, William. 1980. *Our Silent Language: An Introduction to Nonverbal Communication*. Dubuque, IA: Gorsuch Scarisbrick.

Donnell, Susan, and Jay Hall. 1980. Men and women as managers: A significant case of no significant differences. *Organizational Dynamics* 8:60–77.

Dovidio, John, Clifford Brown, Karen Heltman, Steve Ellyson, and Caroline Keating. 1988. Power displays between women and men in discussion of gender linked tasks: A multi-channel study. *Journal of Personality and Social Psychology* 55(4):580–587.

Dreher, George, and Ronald Ash. 1990. A comparative study of mentoring among men and women in managerial, professional and technical positions. *Journal of Applied Psychology* 75:539–546.

Driscoll, Jeanne, and Rosemary Bova. 1980. The sexual side of enterprise. *Management Review* 69:51–54.

Drory, Amos, and David Beaty. 1991. Gender differences in the perception of organizational influence tactics. *Journal of Organizational Behavior* 12:249–258.

Dubbert, Joe. 1979. *A Man's Place*. Englewood Cliffs, NJ: Prentice-Hall.

Duberman, Lucile. 1975. *Gender and Sex in Society*. New York: Praeger.

Dubin, Robert, and Daniel Goldman. 1972. Central life interests of American middle managers and specialists. *Journal of Vocational Behavior* 2:133–141.

Dundes, Alan. 1978. Into the endzone for a touchdown: A psychoanalytic consideration of American football. *Western Folklore* 37:75–88.

Eagly, Alice, and Blair Johnson. 1990. Gender and leadership style: A meta-analysis. *Psychological Bulletin* 108(2):233–256.

Eakins, Barbara, and R. Gene Eakins. 1978. *Sex Differences in Human Communication*. Boston: Houghton Mifflin.

EEOC. 1964. *Legislative History of Titles VII and IX of Civil Rights Act of 1964*. Washington, DC: U.S. Equal Opportunity Commission.

Elliot, A.G.P. 1981. Sex and decision making in the selection interview: A real-life study. *Journal of Occupational Psychology* 54:265–273.

Ellul, Jacques. 1964. *The Technological Society*. New York: Vintage Books.

Epstein, Cynthia. 1970. Encountering the male establishment: Sex-status limits on women's careers in the professions. *American Journal of Sociology* 75:965–983.

———. 1971. *Woman's Place*. Berkeley: University of California Press.

Etaugh, Claire, and Barry Brown. 1975. Perceiving the causes of success and failure in male and female performers. *Developmental Psychology* 11:103.

Ezell, Hazel, Charles Odewahn, and J. Daniel Sherman. 1981. The effects of having been supervised by a woman on perceptions of female managerial competence. *Personnel Psychology* 34:291–299.

Fagenson, Ellen. 1990. Perceived masculine and feminine attributes as a function of individual's sex and level in the organizational power hierarchy: A test of four theoretical perspectives. *Journal of Applied Psychology* 75(2):204–211.

Falbo, Toni, Michael Hazen, and Diane Linimon. 1982. The costs of selecting power bases or messages associated with the opposite sex. *Sex Roles* 8:147–157.

Falkowski, Carolyn, and William Falk. 1983. Homemaking as an occupational plan: Evidence from a national longitudinal study. *Journal of Vocational Behavior* 22:227–242.

Fasteau, Marc. 1974. *The Male Machine*. New York: McGraw-Hill.

Feagin, Joe, and Clairece Feagin. 1978. *Discrimination American style: Institutional Racism and Sexism*. Englewood Cliffs, NJ: Prentice-Hall.

Feather, N. T., and J. G. Simon. 1971. Causal attributions for success and failure in relation to expectations of success based upon selective or manipulative control. *Journal of Personality* 39:527–541.

Federal Register. 1980. Equal Employment Opportunity Commission: Discrimination because of sex under Title VII of the Civil Rights Act of 1964, as amended: adoption of final interpretive guidelines. *Rules and Regulations* 45(219):74676–74677.

Feirstein, Bruce. 1982. *Real Men Don't Eat Quiche*. New York: Pocket Books.

Feldberg, Roslyn, and Evelyn Glenn. 1979. Male and female: Job versus gender models in the sociology of work. *Social Problems* 26:524–538.

———. 1983. Technology and work degradation: Effects of office automation on women clerical workers. In *Machina ex Dea*, edited by Joan Rothschild, pp. 59–78. New York: Pergamon Press.

Feldman, Diane. 1989. Women of color build a rainbow of opportunity. *Management Review*. 78:18.

Ferree, Myra. 1976. Working-class jobs: Housework and paid work as sources of satisfaction. *Social Problems* 23:431–441.

Festinger, Leon. 1957. *A Theory of Cognitive Dissonance*. Evanston, IL: Row, Peterson.

Fidell, L. S. 1970. Empirical verification of sex discrimination in hiring practices in psychology. *Journal of Psychology* 25:1094–1098.

Fiedler, Fred. 1965. Engineering the job to fit the manager. *Harvard Business Review* 43(5):115–122.

Firestone, Shulamith. 1970. *The Dialectic of Sex*. New York: William Morrow.

Firth, Michael. 1982. Sex discrimination in job opportunities for women. *Sex Roles* 8:891–901.

Fitt, Lawton, and Derek Newton. 1981. When the mentor is a man and the protege is a woman. *Harvard Business Review* 59(2):56–60.

Forgionne, Guisseppi, and Celestine Nwacukwu. 1977. Acceptance of authority in female managed organizational positions. *University of Michigan Business Review* 29:23–28.

Foster, Martha, Barbara Wallston, and Michael Berger. 1980. Feminist orientation and job-seeking behavior among dual-career couples. *Sex Roles* 6(1):59–65.

Frances, Susan. 1979. Sex differences in nonverbal behavior. *Sex Roles* 5:519–535.

French, J.R.P., and Bertram Raven. 1959. The bases of social power. In *Studies in*

Social Power, edited by D. Cartwright, pp. 150–167. Ann Arbor: University of Michigan Press.

Friedman, Joel, Marcia Mobilia Boumil, and Barbara Ewert Taylor. 1992. *Sexual Harassment*. Deerfield Beach, FL: Health Communications, Inc.

Frieze, Irene. 1975. Women's expectations for and causal attributions of success and failure. In *Women and Achievement*, edited by Martha Mednick, Sandra Tangri, and Lois Hoffman. Washington, DC: Hemisphere.

Frieze, Irene, and Sheila Ramsey. 1976. Nonverbal maintenance of traditional sex roles. *Journal of Social Issues* 32:133–141.

Frieze, Irene, Bernard Whitley, Barbara Hanusa, and Maureen McHugh. 1982. Assessing the theoretical models for sex differences in causal attributions for success and failure. *Sex Roles* 8:333–342.

Frieze, Irene, Jacqueline Parsons, Paula Johnson, Diane Ruble, and Gail Zellman. 1978. *Women and Sex Roles*. New York: W. W. Norton.

Gagnon, John. 1976. Physical strength, once of significance. In *The Forty-nine Percent Majority*, edited by Debra David and Robert Brannon, pp. 169–178. Reading, MA: Addison-Wesley.

Galper, Ruth Ellen, and Dana Luck. 1980. Gender, evaluation, and causal attribution: The double standard is alive and well. *Sex Roles* 6:273–282.

Garland, Howard, and Kenneth Price. 1977. Attitudes toward women in management and attributions for their success and failure in a managerial position. *Journal of Applied Psychology* 62:29–33.

Ghiselli, Edwin. 1971. *Explorations in Managerial Talent*. Santa Monica, CA: Goodyear.

Gilbreath, Jerri. 1977. Sex discrimination and Title VII of the Civil Rights Act. *Personnel Journal* 56:23–26.

Gillen, Barry. 1981. Physical attractiveness: A determinant of two types of goodness. *Personality and Social Psychology Bulletin* 7:277–281.

Ginzberg, Eli. 1982. The mechanization of work. *Scientific American* 247(3):66–75.

Giuliano, Vincent. 1982. The mechanization of office work. *Scientific American* 247(3):148–165.

Glazer, Nathan. 1975. *Affirmative Discrimination: Ethnic Inequality and Public Policy*. New York: Basic Books.

Goktepe, Janet, and Craig Schneier. 1989. Roles of sex, gender roles, and attraction in predicting emergent leaders. *Journal of Applied Psychology* 74(1):165–167.

Goldberg, Herb. 1976. *The Hazards of Being Male*. New York: Nash.

Goldberg, Philip. 1968. Are women prejudiced against women? *Transaction* 5:28–30.

Golembiewski, Robert. 1977. Testing some stereotypes about the sexes in organizations: Differential centrality of work? *Human Resource Management* 16(4):21–24.

Gomez-Mejia, Luis. 1983. Sex differences during occupational socialization. *Academy of Management Journal* 26:492–499.

Gomez-Mejia, Luis, and David Balkin. 1980. Can internal management training programs narrow the male-female gap in managerial skills? *Personnel Administrator* 25(5):77–83.

Goode, William J. 1971. World revolution and family patterns. *The Journal of Marriage and the Family* 33:624–635.

Goodman, William, Stephen Antczak, and Laura Freeman. 1993. Women and jobs in recessions: 1969–92. *Monthly Labor Review* 116(7):26–34.

Gordon, Francine, and Myra Strober. 1975. *Bringing Women Into Management.* New York: McGraw-Hill.

Gould, Robert. 1976. Measuring masculinity by the size of the paycheck. In *The Forty-nine Percent Majority*, edited by Debra David and Robert Brannon, pp. 113–117. Reading, MA: Addison-Wesley.

Gould, Sam, and James Werbel. 1983. Work involvement: A comparison of dual wage earner and single wage earner families. *Journal of Applied Psychology* 68:313–319.

Greenlaw, Paul, and John Kohl. 1982. The EEOC's new Equal Pay Act guidelines. *Personnel Journal* 61:517–521.

Gross, Alan. 1978. The male role and heterosexual behavior. *Journal of Social Issues* 34:87–107.

Gurin, Patricia. 1981. Labor market experiences and expectancies. *Sex Roles* 7: 1079–1092.

Gutek, Barbara, and Denise Stevens. 1979. Effects of sex of subjects, sex of stimulus cue, and androgyny level on evaluations in work situations which evoke sex role stereotypes. *Journal of Vocational Behavior* 14:23–32.

Gutek, Barbara, and Laurie Larwood (Eds.). 1987. *Women's Career Development.* Newbury Park, CA: Sage.

Gutek, Barbara, Bruce Morasch, and Aaron Cohen. 1981. Interpreting social-sexual behavior in a work setting. *Journal of Vocational Behavior* 22: 30–48.

Hacker, Helen. 1975. Class and race differences in gender roles. In *Gender and Sex in Society*, edited by Lucille Duberman, pp. 134–184. New York: Praeger.

Hacker, Sally, 1983. The mathematization of engineering: Limits on women and the field. In *Machina ex Dea*, edited by Joan Rothschild, pp. 38–58. New York: Pergamon Press.

———. 1979. Sex stratification, technology and organizational change: A longitudinal case study of A.T.&T. *Social Problems* 26:539–557.

Haefner, James. 1977. Race, age, sex, and competence as factors in employer selection of the disadvantaged. *Journal of Applied Psychology* 62:199–202.

Hagen, Randi, and Arnold Kahn. 1975. Discrimination against competent women. *Journal of Applied Social Psychology* 5:362–376.

Hallblade, Shirley, and Walter Mathews. 1980. Computers and society: Today and tomorrow. In *Monster or Messiah? The Computer's Impact on Society*, edited by Walter Mathews, pp. 25–36. Jackson: University Press of Mississippi.

Hammer, Nancy. 1983. Companies must communicate their commitment to promoting women. *Personnel Administrator* 28(6):95–98.

Hammond, Val. 1992. Opportunity 2000: A cultural change approach to equal opportunity. Paper presented at the 2nd International Conference on Human Resources Management, July 2–4. Berkhamsted, Hertfordshire, U.K.

Hammond, Valerie, and Viki Holton. 1991. *A Balanced Workforce? Achieving Cultural Change for Women: A Comparative Study.* Berkhamsted, Hertfordshire U.K.: Ashridge Management Research Group.

Hansson, Robert, Madalyne Allen, and Warren Jones. 1980. Sex differences in conformity: Instrumental or communal response. *Sex Roles* 6:207–212.

Hantover, Jeffrey. 1978. The Boy Scouts and the validation of masculinity. *Journal of Social Issues* 34:184–195.

Harragan, Betty. 1978. *Games Mother Never Taught You: Corporate Gamesmanship for Women.* New York: Warner Books.

Harriman, Ann. 1982. *The Work/Leisure Trade-off: Reduced Work Time for Managers and Professionals.* New York: Praeger.

———. 1983. The summer of '81: Comparable worth in San Jose. Paper presented at the American Society for Public Administration, Annual Conference, New York, New York.

Harriman, Ann, and June Horrigan. 1984. Rip Van Winkle was a woman: The awakening of the comparable worth issue. Paper presented at the Western Political Science Association Annual Meeting, Sacramento, CA.

Harris, Roma. 1993. The mentoring trap. *Library Journal* 118(7):37.

Hartmann, Heidi. 1976. Capitalism, patriarchy, and job segregation. Part 2. *Signs* 1:137–169.

Hartmann, Heidi, and Donald Treiman. 1983. Notes on the NAS study of equal pay for jobs of equal value. *Public Personnel Management* 12:404–417.

Hartnett, Oonagh, and Virginia Novarro. 1980. Single sex management training and a woman's touch. *Personnel Management* 12(3):33–35.

Heilman, Madeline. 1980. The impact of situational factors on personnel decisions concerning women: Varying the sex composition of the applicant pool. *Organizational Behavior and Human Performance* 26:386–395.

Heilman, Madeline, and Lois Saruwatari. 1979. When beauty is beastly: The effects of appearance and sex on evaluations of job applicants for managerial and nonmanagerial jobs. *Organizational Behavior and Human Performance* 23: 360–372.

Heinen, Stephen, Dorothy McGlauchin, Constance Legeros, and Jean Freeman. 1975. Developing the woman manager. *Personnel Journal* 54:282–287.

Henley, Nancy. 1973–74. Power, sex and nonverbal communication. *Berkeley Journal of Sociology* 8:1–26.

———. 1976. Non-verbal communication and the social control of women. *Science for the People* 8(4):16–19.

———. 1977. *Body Politics: Power, Sex and Nonverbal Communication.* Englewood Cliffs, NJ: Prentice-Hall.

Hennig, Margaret, and Anne Jardim. 1977. *The Managerial Woman.* New York: Anchor Books/Doubleday.

Herzberg, Frederick. 1966. *Work and the Nature of Man.* New York: World.

Hickson, Janet, C. R. Hinings, C. A. Lee, R. E. Schneck, and J. M. Pennings. 1971. A 'Strategic Contingencies' theory of intra-organizational power. *Administrative Science Quarterly* 16:216–229.

Higgins, Christopher, and Linda Duxbury. 1992. Work-family conflict: A comparison of dual-career and traditional-career men. *Journal of Organizational Behavior* 13:389–411.

Hively, Janet, and William Howell. 1980. The male-female management team: A dance of death? *Management Review* 69:44–50.

Hochschild, Arlie. 1989. *The Second Shift: Working Parents and the Revolution at Home.* New York: Viking.

Hoffman, Donnie, and Linda Fidell. 1979. Characteristics of androgynous, undifferentiated, masculine, and feminine middle-class women. *Sex Roles* 5:765–781.

Hoffman, Lois. 1972. Early childhood experiences and women's achievement motives. *Journal of Social Issues* 28:129–155.

Holahan, Carole, and Stephan Cooke. 1981. When beauty isn't talent: The influence of physical attractiveness, attitudes toward women, and competence on impression formation. *Sex Roles* 7:867–876.

Holahan, Carole, and Lucia Gilbert. 1979a. Interrole conflict for working women: Careers versus jobs. *Journal of Applied Psychology* 64:86–90.

———. 1979b. Conflict between major life roles: Women and men in dual career couples. *Human Relations* 32:451–467.

Horner, Matina. 1972. Toward an understanding of achievement-related conflicts in women. *Journal of Social Issues* 28:157–175.

Horrigan, Michael, and James Markey. 1990. Recent gains in women's earnings: Better pay or longer hours? *Monthly Labor Review* 113(7):11–17.

Hoyenga, K. B., and K. T. Hoyenga. 1979. *The Question of Sex Differences.* Boston: Little, Brown.

Huckle, Patricia. 1981. The womb factor: Pregnancy policies and employment of women. *Western Political Quarterly* 34:114–126.

Hunt, David, and Carol Michael. 1983. Mentorship: A career training and development tool. *Academy of Management Review* 8:474–485.

Hunt, John, and Peter Saul. 1975. The relationship of age, tenure and job satisfaction in males and females. *Academy of Management Journal* 18:690–702.

Hunter, Jean E. 1976. Images of women. *Journal of Social Issues* 32:7–15.

Hyde, Janet, and Marcia Linn. 1988. Gender differences in verbal ability: A meta-analysis. *Psychological Bulletin* 104(1):53–69.

Hyland, Michael. 1989. There is no motive to avoid success: The compromise explanation for success-avoiding behavior. *Journal of Personality* 57(3):665–693.

Iacono, Suzanne. 1989. Occupational differences in computerized workplaces: The perpetuation of knights and ladies. In *Women at Work,* edited by Rosalind Schwartz and Judith Rich-Klonsky. Los Angeles: Institute of Industrial Relations Publication Center, UCLA.

Ireson, Carol. 1978. Girls' socialization for work. In *Women Working,* edited by Ann Stromberg and Shirley Harkess, pp. 176–200. Palo Alto, CA: Mayfield.

Jackson, Linda. 1983a. The influence of sex, physical attractiveness, sex role, and occupational sex-linkage on perceptions of occupational suitability. *Journal of Applied Social Psychology* 13:31–44.

———. 1983b. Gender, physical attractiveness, and sex role in occupational treatment discrimination: The influence of trait and role assumptions. *Journal of Applied Social Psychology* 13:443–458.

Jackson, Linda, Philip Gardner, and Linda Sullivan. 1992. Explaining gender differences in self-pay expectations: Social comparison standards and perceptions of fair pay. *Journal of Applied Psychology* 77(5):651–663.

Jacobson, Marsha, Judith Antonelli, Patricia Winning, and Dennis Opeil. 1977. Women as authority figures: The use and nonuse of authority. *Sex Roles* 3: 365–375.

Jacobson, Marsha, and Walter Koch. 1977. Women as leaders: Performance evaluation as a function of method of leader selection. *Organizational Behavior and Human Performance* 20:149–157.

Jamison, Kaleel. 1983. Managing sexual attraction in the work place. *The Personnel Administrator* 28:8.

Jenkins, Clive, and Barrie Sherman. 1979. *The Collapse of Work.* London: Eyre Methuen.

Jenner, Jessica. 1981. Volunteerism as an aspect of women's work lives. *Journal of Vocational Behavior* 19:302–314.

Jensen, Thomas, Donald White, and Raghavendra Singh. 1990. Impact of gender, hierarchical position, and leadership styles on work-related values. *Journal of Business Research* 20:145–152.

Johnson, Paula. 1976. Women and power: Toward a theory of effectiveness. *Journal of Social Issues* 32:99–109.

Josefowitz, Natasha. 1982. Sexual relationships at work: Attraction, transference, coercion or strategy. *The Personnel Administrator* 27(3):91–96.

Jourard, Sidney. 1974. Some lethal aspects of the male role. In *Men and Masculinity*, edited by Joseph Pleck and Jack Sawyer, pp. 21–29. Englewood Cliffs, NJ: Prentice-Hall.

Kanter, Rosabeth Moss. 1976. The impact of hierarchial structures on the work behavior of women and men. *Social Problems* 23:415–430.

———. 1977. *Men and Women of the Corporation.* New York: Basic Books.

———. 1979. Power failure in management circuits. *Harvard Business Review* 57(4):65–75.

Kaplan, Robert. 1978. Is beauty talent? Sex interaction in the attractiveness halo effect. *Sex Roles* 4:195–203.

———. 1984. Trade routes: The manager's network of relationships. *Organizational Dynamics* 12(4):37–52.

Kavanagh, Michael, and Michael Halpern. 1977. The impact of job level and sex differences on the relationship between life and job satisfaction. *Academy of Management Journal* 20:66–73.

Kemper, Susan. 1984. When to speak like a lady. *Sex Roles* 10:435–443.

Key, Mary Ritchie. 1975. *Male/Female Language.* Metuchen, NJ: Scarecrow Press.

Klein, Deborah. 1983. Trends in employment and unemployment in families. *Monthly Labor Review* 106(12):21–25.

Komarovsky, Mirra. 1973. Cultural contradictions and sex roles: The masculine case. *American Journal of Sociology* 78:873–885.

———. 1976. *Dilemmas of Masculinity: A Study of College Youth.* New York: W. W. Norton.

Korn/Ferry International. 1993. *Decade of the Executive Woman.* A joint study of Korn/Ferry International and UCLA Anderson Graduate School of Management.

Kortenhaus, Carole, and Jack Demarest. 1993. Gender role stereotyping in children's literature: An update. *Sex Roles* 28(3/4):219–232.

Kotler, Philip. 1980. *Marketing Management.* Englewood Cliffs, NJ: Prentice-Hall.

Kotter, John. 1977. Power, dependence, and effective management. *Harvard Business Review* 55(4):125–136.

Kovach, Kenneth. 1981. Implicit stereotyping in personnel decisions. *Personnel Journal* 60:716–722.

Kram, Kathy. 1983. Phrases of the mentor relationship. *Academy of Management Journal* 26:608–625.

———. 1988. *Mentoring at Work: Developmental Relationships in Organizational Life.* Lanham, MD: University Press of America.

Kram, Kathy, and Douglas Hall. 1991. Mentoring as an antidote to stress during corporate trauma. *Human Resource Management* 28:493–510.

Lacy, William, Janet Bokmeier, and Jon Shepard. 1983. Job attribute preferences and work commitment of men and women in the United States. *Personnel Psychology* 36:313–329.

Lakoff, Robin. 1975. *Language and Woman's Place.* New York: Harper and Row.

Lakoff, Robin Tolmach. 1990. *Talking Power: The Politics of Language.* New York: Basic Books.

Landrine, Hope. 1985. Race X class stereotypes of women. *Sex Roles* 13(1/2):65–75.

Landy, David, and Harold Sigall. 1974. Beauty is talent: Task evaluation as a function of the performer's physical attractiveness. *Journal of Personality and Social Psychology* 29:299–304.

Larwood, Laurie, and John Blackmore. 1978. Sex discrimination in managerial selection: Testing predictions of the vertical dyad linkage model. *Sex Roles* 4:359–367.

Larwood, Laurie, Marion Wood, and Sheila Inderlied. 1978. Training women for management: New problems, new solutions. *Academy of Management Review* 2:584–592.

Lasch, Christopher. 1980. "Endangered species" or "here to stay": The current debate about the family. In *Family in Transition*, 3rd. ed., edited by Arlene Skolnick and Jerome Skolnick, pp. 80–91. Boston: Little, Brown.

Lehne, Gregory. 1976. Homophobia among men. In *The Forty-nine Percent Majority*, edited by Debra David and Robert Brannon, pp. 66–88. Reading, MA: Addison-Wesley.

Lemkau, Jeanne. 1979. Personality and background characteristics of women in male-dominated occupations: A review. *Psychology of Women Quarterly* 4:221–240.

———. 1983. Women in male-dominated professions: Distinguishing personality and background characteristics. *Psychology of Women Quarterly* 8:144–165.

———. 1984. Men in female-dominated professions: Distinguishing personality and background features. *Journal of Vocational Behavior* 24:110–122.

Lenney, Ellen. 1977. Women's self confidence in achievement settings. *Psychological Bulletin* 84:1–13.

———. 1981. What's fine for the gander isn't always good for the goose: Sex differences in self-confidence as a function of ability area and comparison with others. *Sex Roles* 7:905–924.

Leontief, Vassily. 1982. The distribution of work and income. *Scientific American* 247(3):188–204.

Levenson, Hanna, Brent Burford, Bobbie Bonno, and Loren Davis. 1975. Are women still prejudiced against women? A replication and extension of Goldberg's study. *Journal of Psychology* 80:67–71.

Levin, Michael. 1990. Implications of race and sex differences of compensatory affirmative action and the concept of discrimination. *The Journal of Social, Political and Economic Studies* 15:2 175–212.

Levine, Robert, Michal-Judith Gillman, and Harry Reis. 1982. Individual differences or sex differences in achievement attributions? *Sex Roles* 455–464.

Levinson, Daniel, Charlotte Darrow, Edward Klein, Maria Levinson, and Braxton McKee. 1978. *Seasons of a Man's Life.* New York: Alfred Knopf.

———. 1976. Periods in the adult development of men: Ages 18 to 45. *The Counseling Psychologist* 6:21–25.

Levinson, Richard. 1975. Sex discrimination and employment practices: An experiment with unconventional job inquiries. *Social Problems* 22:533–547.

Levitan, Sar, and John Belous. 1981. *What's Happening to the American Family?* Baltimore, MD: The Johns Hopkins University Press.

Levitan, Sar, and Frank Gallo. 1990. Work and family: The impact of legislation. *Monthly Labor Review* 113(3):34–40.

Levitin, Teresa, Robert Quinn, and Graham Staines. 1971. Sex discrimination against American working women. *American Behavioral Science* 15:237–254.

Lewin, Ellen, and Virginia Olesen. 1980. Lateralness in women's work: New views of success. *Sex Roles* 6:619–629.

Lewis, Sinclair. 1922. *Babbitt.* New York: Harcourt Brace.

Lipman-Blumen, Jean. 1972. How ideology shapes women's lives. *Scientific American* 226(1):34–42.

———. 1975. Toward a homosocial theory of sex roles: An explanation of the sex segregation of social institutions. *Signs* 2:15–31.

Lockheed, Marlaine, and Katherine Hall. 1976. Conceptualizing sex as a status characteristic: Applications to leadership training strategies. *Journal of Social Issues* 32:111–123.

Lord, Robert, James Phillips, and Michael Rush. 1980. Effects of sex and personality on perceptions of emergent leadership, influence and social power. *Journal of Applied Psychology* 65:176–182.

Lunding, F. L., G. L. Clements, and D. S. Perkins. 1978. Everyone who makes it has a mentor. *Harvard Business Review* 56(4):89–101.

Lunneborg, Patricia. 1982. Role model influencers on nontraditional professional women. *Journal of Vocational Behavior* 20:276–281.

Lyman, Peter. 1987. The fraternal bond as a joking relationship: Case study of the role of sexist jokes in male group bonding. In *Changing Men: New Directions in Research on Men and Masculinity,* edited by Michael S. Kimmel. Newbury Park, CA: Sage.

Maccoby, Eleanor, and Carol Jacklin. 1974. *The Psychology of Sex Differences.* Stanford, CA: Stanford University Press.

Maccoby, Michael. 1976. *The Gamesman.* New York: Bantam Books.

Machung, Anna. 1989. Talking career, thinking job: Gender differences in career and family expectations of Berkeley seniors. *Feminist Studies* 15(1):35–57.

Mai-Dalton, Renate, and Jeremiah Sullivan. 1981. The effects of manager's sex on the assignment to a challenging or a dull task and reasons for the choice. *Academy of Management Journal* 24:603–612.

Mainiero, Lisa. 1986. A review and analysis of power dynamics in organizational romances. *Academy of Management Review* 11(4):750–762.

————. 1994. Getting anointed for advancement: The case of executive women. *Academy of Management Review* 8(2):53–67.

Major, Brenda, and Ellen Konar. 1984. An investigation of sex differences in pay expectations and their possible causes. *Academy of Management Journal* 27: 777–793.

Major, Brenda, Anne Marie Schmidlin, and Lynne Williams. 1990. Gender patterns in social touch: The impact of setting and age. *Journal of Personality and Social Psychology* 58(4):634–643.

Marshall, Jonathan. 1993. Women weathered the recession better than men, data show. *San Francisco Chronicle* Aug. 20:A4.

Martin, Patricia, Dianne Harrison, and Diana Dinitto. 1983. Advancement for women in hierarchical organizations: A multilevel analysis of problems and prospects. *Journal of Applied Behavioral Science* 19(1):19–33.

Maslow, Abraham. 1943. A theory of human motivation. *Psychological Review* 50:370–396.

Massengill, Douglas, and Nicholas DiMarco. 1979. Sex-role stereotypes and requisite management characteristics: A current replication. *Sex Roles* 5:561–570.

McClelland, David. 1965. Toward a Theory of Motive Acquisition. *American Psychologist* 20:321–333.

————. 1975. *Power: The Inner Experience*. New York: Irvington.

McClelland, David, and Richard Boyatzis. 1982. Leadership motive patterns and long term management success. *Journal of Applied Psychology* 67:737–743.

McClelland, David, and David Burnham. 1976. Power is the great motivator. *Harvard Business Review* 54:100–110.

McGregor, Douglas. 1960. *The Human Side of Enterprise*. New York: McGraw-Hill.

McHugh, Maureen, Irene Frieze, and Barbara Hanusa. 1982. Attributions and sex differences in achievement: Problems and new perspectives. *Sex Roles* 8:467–487.

McLure, Gail, and Ellen Piel. 1978. College-bound girls and science careers: Perceptions of barriers and facilitating factors. *Journal of Vocational Behavior* 12:172–183.

McMillan, Julie, Clifton A. Kay, Diane McGrath, and Sandra Gale. 1977. Women's language: Uncertainty or interpersonal sensitivity and emotionality. *Sex Roles* 3:545–559.

McMullen, Linda, and Deborah Pasloski. 1992. Effects of communication apprehension, familiarity of partner, and topic on selected "women's language" features. *Journal of Psycholinguistic Research* 21(1):17–30.

Meeker, B. F., and P. A. Weitzel-O'Neill. 1977. Sex roles and interpersonal behavior in task-oriented groups. *American Sociological Review* 42:91–105.

Megargee, Edwin. 1969. Influence of sex roles on the manifestations of leadership. *Journal of Applied Psychology* 53:377–382.

Messner, Michael. 1987. The life of a man's seasons: Male identity in the life course of the jock. In *Changing Men: New Directions in Research on Men and Masculinity*, edited by Michael S. Kimmel. Newbury Park, CA: Sage.

Meyers, Miriam. 1989. Adult writers' generic pronoun choices. In *Beyond Boundaries*, edited by Cynthia M. Cont and Sheryl Friedley. Fairfax, VA: George Mason University Press.

Middlebrook, Bill, and Frank Rachel. 1983. A survey of middle management training and development programs. *Personnel Administrator* 28(11):27–31.

Miller, Casey, and Kate Swift. 1976. *Words and Women: New Language in New Times*. New York: Anchor Press/Doubleday.

Miller, Jane, and Kenneth Wheeler. 1992. Unraveling the mysteries of gender differences in intentions to leave the organization. *Journal of Organizational Behavior* 13:465–478.

Mincer, Jacob, and Solomon Polachek. 1974. Family investments in human capital: Earnings of women. *Journal of Political Economy* 82:S76–S110.

———. 1978. Women's earnings reexamined. *The Journal of Human Resources* 13:118–134.

Miner, John. 1980. *Theories of Organizational Behavior*. Hinsdale, IL: The Dryden Press.

Mischel, Harriet. 1974. Sex bias in the evaluation of professional achievements. *Journal of Educational Psychology* 66:157–166.

Missarian, Agnes. 1982. *The Corporate Connection: Why Executive Women Need Mentors to Reach the Top*. Englewood Cliffs, NJ: Spectrum.

Mollison, Andrew. 1993. Women at work. *The Sacramento Bee* June 9:S1,3.

Moore, Dorothy. 1984. Evaluating in-role and out-of-role performers. *Academy of Management Journal* 27:603–618.

Moore, Loretta, and Annette Rickel. 1980. Characteristics of women in traditional and non-traditional managerial roles. *Personnel Psychology* 33:317–333.

Narus, Leonard, and Judith Fischer. 1982. Strong but not silent: A reexamination of the expressivity in the relationships of men. *Sex Roles* 8:159–168.

Newman, Winn. 1976. The Policy Issues: Presentation III. *Signs* 1(3-part 2):265–272.

———. 1983. Statement to the Equal Pay Joint Committee, Des Moines, Iowa. *Public Personnel Journal* 12:382–389.

Nielsen, Joyce. 1978. *Sex in Society*. Belmont, CA: Wadsworth.

Nieva, Veronica, and Barbara Gutek. 1980. Sex effects on evaluation. *Academy of Management Review* 5:267–276.

Nord, Stephen. 1969. The relationships among labor-force participation, service sector employment, and underemployment. *Journal of Regional Science* 29(3):407–421.

O'Leary, Virginia, and James Donaghue. 1978. Latitudes of masculinity: Reactions to sex role deviance in men. *Journal of Social Issues* 34:17–28.

O'Neill, June. 1991. The wage gap between men and women in the United States. *International Review of Comparative Public Policy* 3:353–369.

Orlofsky, Jacob. 1981. A comparison of projective and objective fear-of-success and sex-role orientation measures as predictors of women's performance on masculine and feminine tasks. *Sex Roles* 7:999–1018.

Osborn, Richard, and William Vicars. 1976. Sex stereotypes: An artifact in leader behavior and subordinate satisfaction analysis? *Academy of Management Journal* 19:439–449.

Parsons, Jacquelynne, Irene Frieze, and Diane Ruble. 1978. Intrapsychic factors influencing career aspirations in college women. *Sex Roles* 4:337–347.

Peck, Teresa. 1978. When women evaluate women, nothing succeeds like success: The differential effects of status upon evaluations of male and female professional ability. *Sex Roles* 4:205–213.

Pemberton, John (Ed.). 1975. *Equal Employment Opportunity Responsibilities, Rights, and Remedies*. New York: The Practicing Law Institute.

Persing, Bobbye. 1977. Sticks and stones and words: Women in the language. *Journal of Business Communication* 14:11–19.

Petty, M. M., and Nealia Bruning. 1980. A comparison of the relationships between subordinates' perceptions of supervisory behavior and measures of subordinates' job satisfaction for male and female leaders. *Academy of Management Journal* 23:717–725.

Petty, M. M., Gail McGee, and Jerry Cavender. 1984. A meta-analysis of the relationship between individual job satisfaction and individual performance. *Academy of Management Review* 9:712–721.

Pfeffer, Jeffrey. 1981. *Power in Organizations*. Mansfield, MA: Pitman Publishing.

———. 1992. Power: The not so dirty secret to success in organizations. *Stanford Business School Magazine* 60(3):10–18.

Phelps, Edmund. 1980. The statistical theory of racism and sexism. In *The Economics of Women and Work,* edited by Alice Amsden, pp. 206–210. New York: St. Martin's Press.

Pheterson, Gail, Sara Kiesler, and Philip Goldberg. 1971. Evaluation of the performance of women as a function of their sex, achievement and personal history. *Journal of Personality and Social Psychology* 19:114–118.

Phillips, Linda. 1977. Mentors and protégés: A study of the career development of women managers and executives in business and industry. Ph.D. diss., University of California, Los Angeles.

Piedmont, Ralph. 1988. An interactional model of achievement motivation and fear of success. *Sex Roles* 19(7/8):467–490.

Pleck, Joseph. 1976. The male sex role: Definitions, problems, and sources of change. *Journal of Social Issues* 32:155–164.

———. 1977. The work-family role system. *Social Problems* 24:417–427.

Polachek, Solomon. 1981. Occupational self-selection: A human capital approach to sex differences in occupational structure. *The Review of Economics and Statistics* 58:60–69.

Powell, Gary. 1990. One more time: Do female and male managers differ? *Academy of Management Executive* 4(3):68–75.

Powell, Gary, and D. Anthony Butterfield. 1979. The "good managers": Masculine or androgynous? *Academy of Management Journal* 22:395–403.

———. 1984. If "good managers" are masculine, what are "bad managers"? *Sex Roles* 10:477–484.

Pulakos, Elaine, and Kenneth Wexley. 1983. The relationship among perceptual similarity, sex, and performance ratings in manager-subordinate dyads. *Academy of Management Journal* 26:129–139.

Quinn, Robert. 1977. Coping with cupid: The formation, impact, and management of romantic relationships in organizations. *Administrative Science Quarterly* 22:30–45.

Quinn, Robert, and Patricia Lees. 1984. Attraction and harassment: Dynamics of sexual politics in the workplace. *Organizational Dynamics* 12(2):35–46.

Rader, Martha. 1979. Evaluating a management development program for women. *Public Personnel Journal* 8:139–145.

Radin, Beryl. 1980. Leadership training for women in state and local government. *Public Personnel Management* 9:52–61.

Ragins, Belle Rose. 1989. Power and gender congruency effects in evaluations of male and female managers. *Journal of Management* 15(1):65–76.

Ragins, Belle Rose, and John Cotton. 1991. Easier said than done: Gender differences in perceived barriers to gaining a mentor. *Academy of Management Journal* 34:939–951.

Ragins, Belle Rose, and Terri Scandura. 1994. Gender differences in expected outcomes of mentoring relationships. *Academy of Management Journal* 37:957–971.

Ragins, Belle Rose, and Eric Sundstrom. 1989. Gender and power in organizations: A longitudinal perspective. *Psychological Bulletin* 105(1):51–88.

———. 1990. Gender and perceived power in manager-subordinate relations. *Journal of Occupational Psychology* 63:273–287.

Rand, Thomas, and Kenneth Wexley. 1975. Demonstration of the effect, "similar to me," in simulated employment interviews. *Psychological Reports* 36:535–544.

Ratner, Ronnie. 1980. The paradox of protection: Maximum hours legislation in the United States. *International Labour Review* 119:185–197.

Raven, Bertram, and A. Kruglanski. 1970. Conflict and power. In *The Structure of Conflict*, edited by P. Swingle. New York: Academic Press.

Reid, Pamela, and Lillian Comas-Diaz. 1990. Gender and ethnicity: Perspectives on dual status. *Sex Roles* 22(7/8):397–408.

Remick, Helen. 1983. An update on Washington State. *Public Personnel Journal* 12:390–394.

Renwick, Patricia, and Henry Tosi. 1978. The effects of sex, marital status, and educational background on selection decisions. *Academy of Management Journal* 21:93–103.

Rhue, Judith, Steven Lynn, and John Garske. 1984. The effects of competent behavior on interpersonal attraction and task leadership. *Sex Roles* 10:925–937.

Roche, Gerard. 1979. Much ado about mentors. *Harvard Business Review* 57(1): 14–16, 20, 24.

Rose, Gerald, and P. Andiappan. 1978. Sex effects on managerial hiring decisions. *Academy of Management Journal* 21:104–112.

Rosen, Benson, and Thomas Jerdee. 1974a. Sex stereotyping in the executive suite. *Harvard Business Review* 52(2):45–58.

———. 1974b. Influence of sex role stereotypes on personnel decisions. *Journal of Applied Psychology* 59:9–14.

———. 1974c. Effects of applicant's sex and difficulty of the job on evaluations of candidates for managerial positions. *Journal of Applied Psychology* 59:511–512.

———. 1977. On-the-job sex bias: Increasing managerial awareness. *The Personnel Administrator* 22(1):12–18.

———. 1978. Perceived sex differences in managerially relevant characteristics. *Sex Roles* 4:837–843.

Rosener, Judy. 1990. Ways women lead. *Harvard Business Review* 68(6):119–145.

Rosenfeld, Carl, and Scott Brown. 1979. The labor force status of older workers. *Monthly Labor Review* 102(11):12–18.

Rosenfeld, Rachel. 1979. Women's occupational careers: Individual and structural explanations. *Sociology of Work and Occupations* 6:283–311.

Rosenthal, Doreen, and Diane Chapman. 1982. The lady spaceman: Children's perceptions of sex-stereotyped occupations. *Sex Roles* 8:959–965.

Rothschild, Joan (Ed.). 1983. *Machina ex Dea*. New York: Pergamon.

Rubery, Jill. 1978. Structured labor markets, worker organization and low pay. In *The Economics of Women and Work*, edited by Alice Amsden, pp. 242–270. New York: St. Martin's Press.

Rubin, Lillian. 1985. *Just Friends: The Role of Friendship in Our Lives*. New York: Harper and Row.

Safilios-Rothschild, Constantina. 1977. *Love, Sex and Sex Roles*. Englewood Cliffs, NJ: Prentice-Hall.

Sagrestano, Lynda. 1992. Power strategies in interpersonal relationships. *Psychology of Women Quarterly* 16:481–495.

Salancik, Gerald, and Jeffrey Pfeffer. 1983. Who gets power—and how they hold on to it: A strategic-contingency model of power. In *Organizational Influence Processes*, edited by Robert Allen and Lyman Porter, pp. 52–71. Glenview, IL: Scott, Foresman.

Sandell, Steven, and David Shapiro. 1978. An exchange: The theory of human capital and the earnings of women. A re-examination of the evidence. *Journal of Human Resources* 13:103–117.

San Francisco Chronicle. 1993a. Large increase in births out of wedlock. July 14: 1, 15.

San Francisco Chronicle. 1993b. Grandmas striking a walnut plant begin a fast. July 22:A21.

Sashkin, Marshall, and Norman Maier. 1971. Sex effects in delegation. *Personnel Psychology* 24:471–476.

Sattel, Jack. 1976. The inexpressive male: Tragedy or sexual politics? *Social Problems* 23:469–477.

Sawyer, Sandra, and Arthur Whatley. 1980. Sexual harassment: A form of sex discrimination. *The Personnel Administrator* 25(1):36–44.

Scanzoni, Letha, and John Scanzoni. 1981. *Men, Women and Change*. New York: McGraw-Hill.

Scarr, Sandra. 1988. Race and gender as psychological variables: Social and ethical issues. *American Psychologist* 43(1):56–59.

Schein, Virginia. 1973. The relationship between sex role stereotypes and requisite management characteristics. *Journal of Applied Psychology* 57:95–100.

———. 1975. The relationship between sex role stereotypes and requisite management characteristics among female managers. *Journal of Applied Psychology* 60:340–344.

———. 1978. Sex role stereotyping, ability and performance: Prior research and new directions. *Personnel Psychology* 31:259–268.

Schlossberg, Nancy, and Jane Goodman. 1972. A woman's place: Children's sex stereotyping of occupations. *The Vocational Guidance Quarterly* 20:266–270.

Schor, Judith. 1991. *The Overworked American: The Unexpected Decline of Leisure*. New York: Basic Books.

Schroeder, Karen, Linda Blood, and Diane Maluso. 1992. An inter-generational analysis of expectations for women's career and family roles. *Sex Roles* 26(7/8):273–291.

Schwartz, Felice. 1989. Management women and the new facts of live. *Harvard Business Review* 67(1):65–76.

Scott, Joan. 1982. The mechanization of women's work. *Scientific American* 247(3): 166–187.

Sekaran, Uma. 1982. An investigation of the career salience of men and women in dual career families. *Journal of Vocational Behavior* 20:111–119.

———. 1983. How husbands and wives in dual-career families perceive their family and work worlds. *Journal of Vocational Behavior* 22:288–302.

Senger, John. 1971. Managers' perceptions of subordinates' competence as a function of personal value orientation. *Academy of Management Journal* 14:415–423.

Seymour, William. 1979. Sexual harassment: Finding a cause of action under Title VII. *Labor Law Journal* 30:139–156.

Shapiro, Eileen, Florence Haseltine, and Mary Rowe. 1978. Moving up: Role models, mentors, and the "patron system." *Sloan Management Review* 19:51–58.

Sharp, Cheryl, and Robin Post. 1980. Evaluation of male and female applicants for sex-congruent and sex-incongruent jobs. *Sex Roles* 6:391–401.

Shaw, Edward. 1972. Differential impact of negative stereotyping in employee selection. *Personnel Psychology* 25:333–338.

Silvern, Louise, and Victor Ryan. 1979. Self-rated adjustment and sex typing on the Bem Sex-Role Inventory. Is masculinity the primary predictor of adjustment? *Sex Roles* 5:739–763.

Sistrunk, Frank. 1972. Masculinity-femininity and conformity. *The Journal of Social Psychology* 87:161–162.

Sistrunk, Frank, and John McDavid. 1971. Sex variables in conforming behavior. *Journal of Personality and Social Psychology* 17:200–207.

Smith, Althea, and Abigail Steward. 1983. Approaches to studying racism and sexism in black women's lives. *Journal of Social Issues* 39(3): 1–15.

Smythe, Mary Jeanette, and David Schlueter. 1989. Can we talk? A meta-analytic review of the sex differences in language literature. In *Beyond Boundaries*, edited by Cynthia M. Cont and Sheryl Friedley. Fairfax, VA: George Mason University Press.

Snyder, Robert, and Nealia Bruning. 1979. Sex differences in perceived competence: An across organizations study. *Administration in Social Work* 3:349–359.

Sowell, Thomas. 1982. Weber and Bakke, and the presuppositions of "Affirmative Action." In *Discrimination, Affirmative Action, and Equal Opportunity*, edited by W. E. Block and M. A. Walker. Vancouver, British Columbia: The Fraser Institute.

Spence, Janet, and Robert Helmreich. 1972. Who likes competent women: Competence, sex-role congruence of interests, and subjects' attitudes toward women as determinants of interpersonal attraction. *Journal of Applied Social Psychology* 2:197–213.

Spence, Janet, Robert Helmreich, and J. Stapp. 1974. The Personal Attributes Questionnaire: A measure of sex-role stereotypes and masculinity-femininity. *JSAS Catalog of Selected Documents in Psychology* 4:43 (Ms. No. 617).

Staines, Graham, Carol Tavris, and Toby Jayaratne. 1974. The Queen Bee Syndrome. *Psychology Today* 7:55–60.

Stein, Aletha, and Margaret Bailey. 1975. The socialization of achievement motivation in females. In *Women and Achievement: Social and Motivational Analyses*, edited by Martha Mednick, Sandra Tangri, and Lois Hoffman, pp. 151–157. Washington, DC: Hemisphere.

Stein, Peter, and Steven Hoffman. 1978. Sports and male role strain. *Journal of Social Issues* 34:136–150.

Steinberg, Ronnie. 1990. Social construction of skill. *Work and Occupations* 17(4): 449–482.

Stockdale, Janet. 1991. Sexual harassment at work. In *Women at Work: Psychological and Organizational Prospects*, edited by Jenny Firth-Cozen and Michael West, pp. 54–65. Bristol: Open University Press.

Stogdill, R. M. 1948. Personal factors associated with leadership: A survey of the literature. *Journal of Psychology* 25: 35–71.

———. 1974. *Handbook of Leadership: A Survey of Theory and Research.* New York: Free Press.

Stokes, Joseph, and Judith Peyton. 1986. Attitudinal differences between full-time homemakers and women who work outside the home. *Sex Roles* 15(5/6): 299–310.

Stouffer, Samuel. 1949. Masculinity and the role of the combat soldier. In *The Forty-nine Percent Majority*, edited by Debra David and Robert Brannon, pp. 179–182. Reading, MA: Addison-Wesley.

Summerhayes, Diana, and Robert Suchner. 1978. Power implications of touch in male-female relationships. *Sex Roles* 4:103–110.

Summers, Timothy, Kevin Sightler, and Michael Stahl. 1992. Gender differences in preference for over-reward and tolerance for under-reward. *Journal of Social Behavior and Personality* 7(1):177–188.

Swim, J., E. Borgida, G. Maruyama, and D. Myers. 1989. Joan McKay versus John McKay: Do gender stereotypes bias evaluations? *Psychological Bulletin* 105: 409–429.

Tangri, Sandra. 1972. Determinants of occupational role innovation among college women. *Journal of Social Issues* 28:177–199.

Tannahill, Reay. 1980. *Sex in History.* New York: Stein and Day.

Tavris, Carol, and Carole Offir. 1977. *The Longest War: Sex Differences in Perspective.* New York: Harcourt, Brace, Jovanovich.

Taylor, Fredrick. 1947. *Scientific Management.* New York: Harper and Row.

Taylor, Susan, and Daniel Ilgen. 1981. Sex discrimination against women in initial placement decisions: A laboratory investigation. *Academy of Management Journal* 24:859–865.

Taynor, Janet, and Kay Deaux. 1973. When women are more deserving than men: Equity, attributions, and perceived sex differences. *Journal of Personality and Social Psychology* 28:360–367.

———. 1975. Equity and perceived sex differences: Role behavior as defined by the task, the mode, and the actor. *Journal of Personality and Social Psychology* 32:381–390.

Teich, Albert (Ed.). 1981. *Technology and Man's Future.* New York: St. Martin's Press.

Tiger, Lionel. 1969. *Men in Groups.* New York: Random House.

Tilly, Chris. 1991. Continuing growth of part-time employment. *Monthly Labor Review* 114(3):10–18.

Tilly, Louise A., and Joan W. Scott. 1978. *Women, Work and Family.* New York: Holt, Rinehart and Winston.

Time. 1980. The robot revolution. Dec. 8:72–83.

Toffler, Alvin. 1980. *The Third Wave*. New York: William Morrow.

Tomkiewicz, Joseph, and O. C. Brenner. 1982. Organizational dilemma: Sex differences in attitudes toward women held by future managers. *The Personnel Administrator* 27(7):62–65.

Touhey, John. 1974a. Effects of additional women professionals on ratings of occupational prestige and desirability. *Journal of Personality and Social Psychology* 29:86–89.

———. 1974b. Effects of additional men on prestige and desirability of occupations typically performed by women. *Journal of Applied Social Psychology* 4:330–335.

Trescott, Martha. 1983. Lillian Moller Gilbreth and the founding of modern industrial engineering. In *Machine ex Dea*, edited by Joan Rothschild, pp. 23–27. New York: Pergamon Press.

Tresemer, David. 1976. Trends in research on "fear of success." *Sex Roles* 2:211–216.

Trotter, Richard, Susan Zacur, and Wallace Gatewood. 1982a. The Pregnancy Disability Amendment: What the law provides, part I. *The Personnel Administrator* 27(2):47–54.

———. 1982b. The Pregnancy Disability Amendment: What the law provides, part II. *The Personnel Administrator* 27(3):55–58.

U.S. Department of Labor. 1990a. 20 Facts on Women Workers. *Facts on Working Women*. Women's Bureau, No. 90–2, September.

———. 1990b. Earnings Differences Between Women and Men. *Facts on Working Women*. Women's Bureau, No. 90–3, October.

———. 1992. Women Workers: Outlook to 2005. *Facts on Working Women*. Women's Bureau, No. 92, January.

Vanek, Joann. 1978. Housewives as workers. In *Women Working: Theories and Facts in Perspective*, edited by Ann Stromberg and Shirley Harkess, pp. 392–414. Palo Alto, CA: Mayfield.

Van Wagner, Karen, and Cheryl Swanson. 1979. From Machiavelli to Ms: Differences in male-female power styles. *Public Administration Review* 39:66–72.

von Baeyer, Carl, Debbie Sherk, and Mark Zanna. 1981. Impression management in the interview: When the female applicant meets the male (chauvinist) interviewer. *Personality and Social Psychology Bulletin* 7:45–51.

Wagner, Ellen. 1992. *Sexual Harassment in the Workplace*. New York: Amacom.

Waldman, Elizabeth. 1983. Labor force statistics from a family perspective. *Monthly Labor Review* 106(12):16–20.

Warihay, Philomena. 1980. The climb to the top: Is the network the route for women? *Personnel Administrator* 25:55–60.

Weaver, Charles. 1978. Sex differences in the determinants of job satisfaction. *Academy of Management Journal* 21:265–274.

Webber, Ross. 1976. Perceptions and behaviors in mixed sex work teams. *Industrial Relations* 15:121–129.

Weber, Max. 1930. *The Protestent Ethic and the Spirit of Capitalism*. London: Geo. Allen and Unwin.

Weiler, Paul. 1991. Comparable worth in United States' anti-discrimination law. *International Review of Comparative Public Policy* 3:333–351.

Weiner, B., I. Frieze, A. Kukla, S. Best, and R. M. Rosenbaum. 1971. *Perceiving the Causes of Success and Failure.* New York: General Learning Press.

Wentling, Rose Mary. 1992. Women in middle management: Their career development and aspirations. *Business Horizons* 34:47–54.

Wetzel, James. 1990. American families: 75 years of change. *Monthly Labor Review* 113(3):4–8.

Wexley, Kenneth, and Elaine Pulakos. 1982. Sex effects on performance ratings in manager-subordinate dyads: A field study. *Journal of Applied Psychology* 67:433–439.

Wheale, Peter. 1984. Scientific management at work. In *People, Science and Technology,* edited by Charles Boyle, Peter Wheale, and Brian Sturgess, pp. 195–211. Totowa, NJ: Barnes and Noble Books.

White, Michael, Michael Crino, and Gerry DeSanctis. 1981. A critical review of female performance, performance training and organizational initiatives designed to aid women in the work role environment. *Personnel Psychology* 34:227–248.

Whitely, William, Thomas Dougherty and George Dreher. 1991. Relationship of career mentoring and socioeconomic origin to managers' and professionals' early career progress. *Academy of Management Journal* 34:331–351.

Whyte, William. 1956. *The Organization Man.* New York: Simon & Schuster.

Wiersma, Uco. 1990. Gender differences in job attribute preferences: Work-home role conflict and job level mediating variables. *Journal of Occupational Psychology* 63:231–243.

Wiley, Mary, and Arlene Eskilson. 1982. The interaction of sex and power base on perceptions of managerial effectiveness. *Academy of Management Journal* 25:671–677.

———. 1988. Gender and family/career conflict: Reactions of bosses. *Sex Roles* 19(7/8):445–466.

Wirtenberg, T. Jeana, and Charles Nakamura. 1976. Education: Barrier or boon to occupational roles of women? *Journal of Social Issues* 32:165–179.

Wong, Maria Mei-ha, and Mihaly Csikszentmihalyi. 1991. Affiliation motivation and daily experience: Some issues on gender differences. *Journal of Personality and Social Psychology* 60(1):154–164.

Woolf, Virginia. 1932. *A Room of One's Own.* Toronto: McClelland and Stewart.

Wright, Paul. 1982. Men's friendships, women's friendships and the alleged inferiority of the latter. *Sex Roles* 8:1–20.

Yankelovich, Daniel. 1981. *The New Rules.* New York: Random House.

Yorburg, Betty. 1974. *Sexual Identity: Sex Roles and Social Change.* New York: John Wiley.

Young, Michael, and Peter Willmott. 1973. *The Symmetrical Family.* New York: Pantheon.

Yukl, Gary. 1981. *Leadership in Organizations.* Englewood Cliffs, NJ: Prentice-Hall.

Zikmund, William, Michael Hitt, and Beverly Pickens. 1978. Influence of sex and scholastic performance on reactions to job applicant resumes. *Journal of Applied Psychology* 63:252–254.

Author Index

Abbott, Aaron, 179
Abramson, Joan, 58
Abramson, Paul, 176
Acker, Joan, 2–4
Adams, Kathrynn, 172
Albrecht, Maryann, 200
Aldag, Ramon, 142, 154
Amsden, Alice, 34, 36–37
Anderson, Carolyn, 99
Andrisani, Paul, 149
Argyle, Michael, 126
Argyris, Chris, 143
Arrow, Kenneth, 39

Baber, Kristine, 193
Baer, Judith, 46–48, 54, 56–57
Bailyn, Lotte, 220
Baron, Robert, 182
Bar-Tal, Daniel, 178
Bartol, Kathryn, 158, 178, 185
Baxandall, Rosalyn, 14, 46
Becker, Gary, 193
Bem, Sandra, 90–91
Bender, Marilyn, 100, 103
Berch, Bettina, 48
Berg, J., 41
Bergmann, Barbara, 36
Betz, Ellen, 193
Betz, Michael, 196–97
Beyard-Tyler, Karen, 197

Bird, Caroline, 150, 154
Birdsall, Paige, 158
Bischoping, Katherine, 104
Blau, Francine, 10, 14, 36–37, 39, 194
Blau, Peter, 24
Block, W. E., 53–54
Bly, Robert, 79–80
Bradford, David, 94
Brenner, Marshall, 201
Brimelow, Peter, 53
Broverman, I. K., 72–73, 78
Brown, Virginia, 177
Burgoon, Judee, 132

Caldwell, Mayta, 104
Caplan, Paula, 105–6
Carbonell, Joyce, 156
Carli, Linda, 121
Cash, Thomas, 178, 184
Cecil, Earl, 183
Chacko, Thomas, 140
Chapman, J. Brad, 158
Chusmir, Leonard, 138–39, 173
Clifton, A. Kay, 77–78
Cohen, Stephen, 182
Coleman, James, 82
Collins, Eliza, 101–2
Colwill, Nina, 198–99
Cook, Mary, 206, 209
Covin, Teresa, 138

Crawford, Jim, 195
Crichton, Michael, 84

Davidson, Lynne, 85
Deaux, Kay, 150
DeCotiis, Thomas, 137
DeWine, Sue, 210–11
Dion, Karen, 178
Dion, Kenneth, 155
Dipboye, Robert, 184
Dobbins, Gregory, 156
Doeringer, Peyer, 37
Doherty, Mary Helen, 41, 50, 52
Donaghy, William, 126, 130
Donnell, Susan, 155
Dreher, George, 203
Driscoll, Jeanne, 102
Dubbert, Joe, 79–81
Duberman, Lucile, 70–71
Dubin, Robert, 4
Dundes, Alan, 83

Eagly, Alice, 159
Eakins, Barbara, 117, 119–22,
   124–25, 129–31, 133
Ellul, Jacques, 9
Epstein, Cynthia, 174, 202
Ezell, Hazel, 180

Fagenson, Ellen, 155
Falkowski, Carolyn, 193
Fasteau, Marc, 82, 111
Feagin, Joe, 54
Feather, N. T., 150
Feirstein, Bruce, 84
Feldberg, Roslyn, 24–25
Feldman, Diane, 199
Ferree, Myra, 141
Festinger, Leon, 71
Fidell, L. S., 176
Fiedler, Fred, 158
Firestone, Shulamith, 129
Firth, Michael, 181
Fitt, Lawton, 204, 206
Forgionne, Guisseppi, 167
Foster, Martha, 194
Frances, Susan, 130
French, J.R.P., 169

Friedman, Joel, 62
Frieze, Irene, 129, 133, 149, 151,
   160–61, 163

Gagnon, John, 81
Galper, Ruth Ellen, 150
Garland, Howard, 151
Ghiselli, Edwin, 155
Gilbreath, Jerri, 55
Gillen, Barry, 178
Ginzberg, Eli, 23
Giuliano, Vincent, 12
Glazer, Nathan, 54
Goktepe, Janet, 156
Goldberg, Herb, 86, 112
Goldberg, Philip, 179
Golembiewski, Robert, 140
Gomez-Mejia, Luis, 140, 200
Goode, William, 12, 17
Goodman, William, 32
Gould, Robert, 83
Gould, Sam, 139
Greenlaw, Paul, 49
Gross, Alan, 59
Gurin, Patricia, 192
Gulek, Barbara, 99, 180

Hacker, Helen, 75
Hacker, Sally, 24
Haefner, James, 184
Hagen, Randi, 177
Hallblade, Shirley, 17
Hammer, Nancy, 200
Hammond, Valerie, 219–20, 222,
   224–25
Hansson, Robert, 173
Hantover, Jeffrey, 80
Harragan, Betty, 82
Harriman, Ann, 65–67, 221
Harris, Roma, 206
Hartman, Heidi, 42
Hartnett, Oonagh, 198
Heilman, Madeline, 179, 183
Heinen, Stephen, 199
Henley, Nancy, 126–27
Hennig, Margaret, 156
Herzberg, Frederick, 143
Hickson, Janet, 165

Higgins, Christopher, 213
Hively, Janet, 97
Hochschild, Arlie, 20
Hoffman, Donnie, 91
Hoffman, Lois, 144
Holahan, Carole, 178, 194
Horner, Matina, 145
Horrigan, Michael, 34
Hoyenga, K. B., 144
Huckle, Patricia, 58
Hunt, David, 204–6
Hunt, John, 141
Hunter, Jean 76–77
Hyde, Janet, 69
Hyland, Michael, 146

Iacono, Suzanne, 25
Ireson, Carol, 2

Jackson, Linda, 141, 182, 184, 187
Jacobson, Marsha, 177
Jamison, Kaleel, 103
Jenkins, Clive, 15–16, 23
Jenner, Jessica, 194
Jensen, Thomas, 158
Johnson, Paula, 162
Josefowitz, Natasha, 100
Jourad, Sidney, 85

Kanter, Rosabeth Moss, 94–96, 107,
    112, 139, 165–67, 179, 200, 202–3
Kaplan, Robert, 178, 210
Kavanagh, Michael, 140
Kemper, Susan, 119
Key, Mary Ritchie, 118–19, 130
Klein, Deborah, 32
Komarovsky, Mirra, 86, 111, 194
Korn/Ferry, 221
Kortenhaus, Carole, 72
Kotler, Philip, 115
Kovach, Kenneth, 187
Kram, Kathy, 202–6, 208

Lacy, William, 138
Lakoff, Robin, 116–19, 124
Landrine, Hope, 74
Landy, David, 178
Larwood, Laurie, 186, 198–99

Lasch, Christopher, 17, 19
Lehne, Gregory, 87–88
Lenney, Ellen, 173–74
Leontief, Vassily, 15, 23
Levenson, Hanna 179, 202–4
Levinson, Daniel, 208
Levinson, Richard, 182
Levitan, Sar, 18, 31
Levitin, Teresa, 141
Lewin, Ellen, 141
Lewis, Sinclair, 84
Lipman-Blumen, Jean, 111, 195–96
Lockheed, Marlaine, 172, 174
Lord, Robert, 180
Lunding, F. L., 206
Lunneborg, Patricia, 196
Lyman, Peter, 111

Maccoby, Eleanor, 70, 104
Maccoby, Michael, 110
Machung, Anna, 193–94
Mai-Dalton, Renate, 186
Mainiero, Lisa, 98
Major, Brenda, 131, 141
Marshall, Jonathan, 34
Martin, Patricia, 218
Maslow, Abraham, 142
Massengill, Douglas, 155
McClelland, David, 143, 146–48
McGregor, Douglas, 143
McLure, Gail, 191, 196
McMillan, Julie, 118
McMullen, Linda, 121
Meeker, B. F., 174
Megargee, Edwin, 156
Messner, Michael, 82
Meyers, Miriam, 125
Middlebrook, Bill, 200
Miller, Casey, 123, 125
Miller, Jane, 139
Mincer, Jacob, 35–36, 191
Miner, John, 143, 145
Mischel, Harriet, 176
Missarian, Agnes, 202, 207
Mollison, Andrew, 33
Moore, Loretta, 157

Narus, Leonard, 89
Newman, Winn, 65

Nielsen, Joyce, 1
Nieva, Veronica, 176–77, 180
Nord, Stephen, 31, 172

O'Leary, Virginia, 89
O'Neill, June, 32–33
Orlofsky, Jacob, 150
Osborn, Richard, 158

Parsons, Jacquelynne, 195–96
Peck, Teresa, 179
Pemberton, John, 52
Persing, Bobbye, 125
Petty, M. M., 140, 158
Pfeffer, Jeffrey, 159, 164
Phelps, Edmund, 37
Pheterson, Gail, 176, 179
Phillips, Linda, 202–3
Pleck, Joseph, 78
Polachek, Solomon 35, 181
Powell, Gary, 155
Pulakos, Elaine, 179

Quinn, Robert, 99–101

Rader, Martha, 201
Radin, Beryl, 199
Ragins, Belle Rose, 161, 163, 167,
    169, 207
Rand, Thomas, 179
Ratner, Ronnie, 47–48, 57
Raven, Bertram, 161
Reid, Pamela, 72
Remick, Helen, 66
Renwick, Patricia, 184
Rhue, Judith, 178
Roche, Gerard, 202
Rose, Gerald, 183
Rosen, Benson, 154, 183, 186–87
Rosener, Judy, 159
Rosenfeld, Carl, 31–32
Rosenfeld, Rachel, 36–37, 191
Rosenthal, Doreen, 125
Rothschild, Joan, 13
Rubery, Jill, 37
Rubin, Lillian, 112

Safilios-Rothschild, Constantina, 76,
    97
Sandell, Steven, 36
Sashkin, Marshall, 172
Sattel, Jack, 89
Sawyer, Sandra, 61
Scanzoni, Letha, 19–21
Scarr, Sandra, 72
Schein, Virginia, 154
Schlossberg, Nancy, 193
Schor, Judith, 20, 30–31
Schwartz, Felice, 221
Scott, Joan, 11–14
Sekaran, Uma, 139
Senger, John, 179
Seymour, William, 61
Shapiro, Eileen, 209
Sharp, Cheryl, 182
Shaw, Edward, 183
Silvern, Louise, 91
Sistrunk, Frank, 123, 172
Smith, Althea, 74
Smythe, Mary Jeanette, 121
Snyder, Robert, 173
Sowell, Thomas, 54
Spence, Janet, 177
Staines, Graham, 109
Steinberg, Ronnie, 42
Stogdill, R. M., 154
Stokes, Joseph, 142
Stouffer, Samuel, 82
Summerhayes, Diana, 131
Swim, J., 179

Tangri, Sandra, 195
Tannahill, Reay, 21, 77, 87
Tavris, Carol, 111
Taylor, Fredrick, 4, 40
Taynor, Janet, 176, 188
Taylor, Susan, 186
Tiger, Lionel, 111
Tilly, Chris, 30–31
Tilly, Louise, 10–12
Toffler, Alvin, 10, 15
Tomkiewicz, Joseph, 183
Touhey, John, 197
Trescott, Martha, 13

Tresemer, David, 145
Trotter, Richard, 59

Vanek, Joann, 13
Van Wagner, Karen, 148
von Baeyer, Carl, 182

Wagner, Ellen, 62, 64
Waldman, Elizabeth, 32
Warihay, Philomena, 211
Weaver, Charles, 140
Webber, Ross, 172
Weber, Max, 84, 153
Weiler, Paul, 67
Weiner, B., 150
Wetzel, James, 18–19

Wexley, Kenneth, 180
Wheale, Peter, 23
White, Michael, 199
Whitely, Thomas, 203, 209
Whyte, William, 84
Wiley, Mary, 151
Wirtenberg, T. Jeana, 196
Wong, Maria Mei-ha, 144
Woolf, Virginia, 133
Wright, Paul, 194, 112

Yankelovich, Daniel, 143
Yorburg, Betty, 76
Young, Michael, 10
Yukl, Gary, 154, 157

Zikmund, William, 184

Subject Index

AT&T, 23
absenteeism, 140
achievement motivation (n-Ach), 142–44, 152–53, 159
affiliation motivation (n-Aff), 144, 152
affirmative action, 23, 29, 52–54 206; and quotas, 53
American Federation of State, County and Municipal Employees (AFSCME), 66, 67
American Home Economics Association, 13
athletics, 58, 72, 76, 79–84, 89, 104–12, 121
Attorney General, and Title VII, 54
attribution/aspiration theory, 149–52
automation, 9, 22, 24

beauty, 98, 100, 105, 127, 132, 156, 175, 177–79, 180, 184
Bem Sex Role Inventory (BSRI), 90, 150
benefits, 37, 79, 142, 203; and child care, 22; and health insurance, 16, 26, 57–59; and parental leave, 22
birth rates, 17, 18–21, 26
Bohemian Grove, and male/male relationships, 110
Bona Fide Occupational Qualification (BFOQ), 55–57
Boy Scouts of America, 79, 80, 82, 110

breadwinner model, 2, 16–17, 25–26, 75
Bush, President George, 53, 82

Calvin, John, 84
Carnegie, Andrew, 84
Carter, President Jimmy, 54
Cellar, Congressman Emanuel, 57
Chartists, 15
childbearing, 39
child care, 26, 40
childrearing, 13, 19, 20, 26, 35, 39, 141, 193–94
Chisholm, Congresswoman Shirley, 169
City of Los Angeles v. Manhart, 58
civil rights, 44, 49, 88
Civil Rights Act of 1964, 47, 50–52, 60, 64, 68; and "ladies day," 50; and Title VII, 50–52, 54–67; and Title VII 1972 amendments, 54–60
Civil Rights Act of 1991, 53, 60, 64
Clinton, President Bill, 86
cognitive dissonance, 71
comparable worth, 29, 41–43, 45, 64–67
conformity, 6, 90, 171–73, 179, 188
Come v. Bausch and Lomb, 60
County of Washington v. Gunther, 66

Desert Storm, 82
Dias v. Pan American World Airways,
   55
Dictionary of Occupational Titles
   (DOT), 40
diffuse status characteristics and
   expectations states theory, 174
discrimination. *See* glass ceiling
discrimination, access, 182, 185, 188–
   89
division of labor, 9, 14–15, 25, 35–36,
   115, 165, 193
divorce, 17–18, 26, 77
domestic science movement, 13

Edison, Thomas A., 84
equal employment opportunity, 29
Equal Employment Opportunity
   Commission (EEOC), 42, 49
Equal Pay Act of 1963, 33–34, 49, 51,
   64–65, 68; and affirmative defenses,
   48–49, 66
Equal Rights Amendment, 21
euphemisms, 122
exclusionary language, 124–26, 134
Executive Orders, issuance of, 52–55,
   64

Fair Labor Standards Act of 1938, 48–
   49
Family Medical Leave Act, 216
family, two career, 194
family, two paycheck, 27
family values, 216
family wage economy, 11, 13
feminism, 21, 91, 118, 132, 194
football, and ritualized behavior, 82–
   83
Ford, Henry, 84

Gates, Bill, 84
Geguldig v. Aiello, 58
gender model, 4
General Electric Company v. Gilbert,
   58
glass ceiling, 171, 181, 185–89
Griffiths, Congresswoman Martha, 51
Griggs v. Duke Power, 55

Harris v. Forklift Systems, Inc., 63
Hill, Anita, Thomas-Hill hearings, 60.
   See also sexual harassment
homemaker, 2, 18, 26, 75, 141–42,
   193–95, 197
homemaking, 91, 141, 192–93, 195,
   211
homosexuality, 80, 82, 87, 106, 113;
   and homophobia, 87–89; and
   homosexism, 88; and homosocial
   behavior, 111
hours of work, 20, 22–24, 33, 46–48,
   67, 100, 138
human capital, 7, 40, 43, 191–93,
   197, 211–12; theory of, 29, 35–37,
   42–43
human sexuality, 3

industrial model, 2, 7
Industrial Revolution, 3–5, 9, 17, 22,
   25, 45, 67
institutional theories, 29, 37–39
internal labor market theory, 37, 39,
   43

job commitment, 6, 35, 129, 137–38,
   140, 152, 199
job evaluation, 38, 40–42, 65
job model, 4
job satisfaction, 4, 6, 137, 140–42,
   158
Justice, Department of, 49

*Kaiser Aluminum and Chemical
   Company v. Brian Weber,* 53–54
Kennedy, President John, 49–50, 65
Kinesics. *See* nonverbal communication

labor force participation, 30–32
labor movement, 16, 26, 45–48, 65,
   67
Labor, Department of, 30, 33, 40, 49;
   Women's Bureau, 51
leaders, emergent, 158
leadership, 6
leadership, motive pattern, 148–49
leadership style, 6, 153, 157–59, 166–
   68

Lud, Ned, 15
Luddites, 15–23
Luther, Martin, 84

male bonding, 111–12
male verbal dueling, 83, 113
managerial effectiveness, 158
man's world, 156, 217
marital status, 4, 14, 72, 104, 152
marriage, theory of, 193
masculine model of work, 2
men's hut, 80, 110, 114
mento/protégé relationships, 96, 203, 208, 212
mentoring, 7, 198, 202–9, 212; cross gender, 208
mentors, 98, 156, 185, 202–9; women, 206–9
Meritor Savings Bank v. Vinson, 62, 102
mommy track, 221
motivation, 137, 142–52, 154, 180; motive to avoid failure (MAF), 144–46; motive to avoid success (MAS), 144–46

National Organization for Women (NOW), 58
Nashville Gas v. Satty, 52
needs theory, 143–49
neoclassical theory, 29, 34–37, 39
networking, 7, 174, 209–12; peer pals, 209; trade routes, 210
new home economics. *See* marriage, theory of
nonverbal communication: appearance, 127; body movement, 130–31; eye movements, 129–30; facial expression, 128–29; posture, 127–28; space, 132–34

occupational segregation, 5, 14, 25, 29, 32–33, 38–39, 42–43, 64, 191
Office of Federal Contract Compliance (OFCCP), 52
Opportunity 2000, 219, 221–22
organizational culture, 5
overcrowding theory, 29, 35–36

part-time employment, 30, 33
pay, 4–5, 33, 36–40, 43, 79, 141–42, 202
performance evaluation, 178, 180, 185
Perot, H. Ross, 84
Personality Attributes Questionnaire (PAQ), 90
Phyllis Schlafly, 59
power, 6, 84, 87, 89, 96, 98–99, 101, 108, 113, 117, 139, 146, 171, 180, 204–6; interpersonal, 160–64, 167; interpersonal bases of, 160–61; typology of, 147–48
power, structural, 164–68; and politics, 164
powerlessness, 134, 166–67
power motivation (n-Pow), 143, 146, 152–53
pregnancy, 57–59; parental leave, 57–59; Pregnancy Discrimination Act, 57–59, 68; reproductive hazards, 59
primary labor market, 37
protective legislation, 5, 45, 47–49, 54, 68
protégé, and mentor relationships, 209
Protestant Work Ethic, 79, 84
Proxemics. *See* nonverbal communication (space)
psychological androgyny, 6, 85–91, 150, 155, 180, 182

rewards, 6, 99, 101, 107, 137, 140, 142, 152, 188
role models, 196, 198, 201, 210
Roosevelt, President Theodore, 19, 79–81
Rosenfeld v. Southern Pacific Company, 57

Scientific Management, 4, 13, 40
secondary labor market, 37, 39
segmented labor market theory. *See* institutional theories
self confidence, 6, 161–63, 171–75
Senate Judiciary Committee, 60
sex role, 3–5, 12, 14, 19–21, 29, 59, 70–72, 76, 92, 94, 116, 143, 172–79, 195; and orientation, 182–87;

and socialization, 70–71, 92, 146,
    175, 198–99; and status, 1–2
sex role stereotypes, 5–6, 12, 70–72,
    77, 125, 134, 137, 143, 164, 176–
    77, 180, 182, 185, 188, 192;
    expressive role, 84–89; feminine, 77–
    78, 95, 103, 106, 198; instrumental
    role, 79–84; masculine, 78–89, 95,
    106, 128
sex typing, 172, 175, 185, 187–88,
    196
sexual attraction, 3, 94, 98, 100, 103
sexual harassment, 3, 45, 59–64, 68,
    95, 98–99, 102; EEOC Guidelines,
    61–62; hostile environment, 62–63;
    quid pro quo, 62
sexual revolution, 17, 20–21
similar to me phenomenon, 179–81,
    186
single parent households, 30
single parents, 18
Smith, Congressman Howard, 50
social change, 2, 17, 74
social class, 72–76, 78, 95
Social Security, 31–32
spinsters, 10
sponsored mobility, 202
St. George, Congresswoman Katherine,
    51
steam engine, 5, 14, 16–17, 25
stereotypes, managerial, 158–59

technology, 2–4, 9–17, 22–25; and
    change, 5, 12, 23, 25, 31; and
    displacement of workers, 23–24
thematic apperception test (TAT), 143–
    45
Thomas, Clarence, Thomas-Hill
    hearings, 60. See also sexual
    harassment
Title VII, 45, 64–67
Tomkins v. Public Service Electric and
    Gas Co., 61

training, 7, 23, 35–36, 53, 187, 192,
    198–202, 212; evaluation of, 200;
    remedial, 200, 202, 212; women-
    only, 199–201
trait theory, 154
Triangle Shirtwaist Company fire, 46
Truman, President Harry S., 82
Trump, Donald, 84
turnover, 11, 37, 102, 139–40

U.S. Congress, 48–49, 60
U.S. Supreme Court, 19, 47, 53, 62–
    64, 102
UAW et al. v. Johnson Controls, Inc., 59
unemployment, 16, 23–24, 31–33
unions, 5, 15, 42, 47–48, 52, 65, 67;
    collective bargaining, 45–46, 68
University of California, Davis, v.
    Allan Bakke, 53
unmarried women, 138

Vietnam War, 21, 52, 82

war, 79, 81–83, 112
War Manpower Commission, 48
Weeks v. Southern Bell, 57
women's language, 116–26; disclaimer,
    119; expletives, 118; intensive
    adverbs, 118; minimal response,
    120; modal constructions, 119;
    qualifiers and fillers, 119; tag
    questions, 118
women leaders, 158
women managers, 6, 93, 139, 150,
    154, 156–58, 163, 167, 201, 207,
    209
work-family conflict, 138–39, 142,
    187, 189, 194, 199, 213, 218, 220
World War I, 21, 81
World War II, 17, 48, 65, 157

Young Men's Christian Association
    (YMCA), 79–80, 110

About the Author

ANN HARRIMAN is Professor Emeritus of Human Resources Management at California State University, Sacramento, and serves as affirmative action officer of the CSUS Foundation, an auxiliary organization to the University. She has written extensively in the area of gender and organizational behavior and is the author of *The Work/Leisure Trade-Off* (Praeger, 1982) and the first edition of *Women/Men/Management* (Praeger, 1985).

ISBN 0-275-94684-3

90000>

HARDCOVER BAR CODE